Network+
Fast Pass

Bill Ferguson

Wiley Publishing, Inc.

Publisher: Neil Edde
Acquisitions Editor: Jeff Kellum
Developmental Editor: Jeff Kellum
Production Editor: Rachel Gunn
Technical Editor: Patrick Bass
Copyeditor: Liz Welch
Compositor: Kate Kaminski, Happenstance Type-O-Rama
Graphic Illustrator: Jeffrey Wilson
CD Coordinator: Dan Mummert
CD Technician: Kevin Ly
Proofreaders: Jim Brook, Nancy Riddiough, Jennifer Larsen
Indexer: Nancy Guenther
Book Designers: Judy Fung, Bill Gibson
Cover Designer: Richard Miller, Calyx Design
Cover Illustrator/Photographer: Richard Miller, Calyx Design

Copyright © 2005 by Wiley Publishing, Inc., Indianapolis, Indiana

Library of Congress Card Number: 2005920767

ISBN-13: 978-07821-4407-9
ISBN-10: 0-7821-4407-1

No part of this publication may be reproduced, stored in a retrieval system or transmitted in any form or by any means, electronic, mechanical, photocopying, recording, scanning or otherwise, except as permitted under Sections 107 or 108 of the 1976 United States Copyright Act, without either the prior written permission of the Publisher, or authorization through payment of the appropriate per-copy fee to the Copyright Clearance Center, 222 Rosewood Drive, Danvers, MA 01923, (978) 750-8400, fax (978) 646-8600. Requests to the Publisher for permission should be addressed to the Legal Department, Wiley Publishing, Inc., 10475 Crosspoint Blvd., Indianapolis, IN 46256, (317) 572-3447, fax (317) 572-4355, or online at `http://www.wiley.com/go/permissions`.

TRADEMARKS: Wiley, the Wiley logo, and the Sybex logo are trademarks or registered trademarks of John Wiley & Sons, Inc. and/or its affiliates, in the United States and other countries, and may not be used without written permission. All other trademarks are the property of their respective owners. Wiley Publishing, Inc., is not associated with any product or vendor mentioned in this book.

Screen reproductions produced with FullShot 99. FullShot 99 © 1991-1999 Inbit Incorporated. All rights reserved.
FullShot is a trademark of Inbit Incorporated.

The CD interface was created using Macromedia Director, COPYRIGHT 1994, 1997-1999 Macromedia Inc. For more information on Macromedia and Macromedia Director, visit http://www.macromedia.com.

Sybex is an independent entity from CompTIA and is not affiliated with CompTIA in any manner. Neither CompTIA nor Sybex warrants that use of this publication will ensure passing the relevant exam. Network+ is either a registered trademark or trademark of CompTIA in the United States and/or other countries.

The author and publisher have made their best efforts to prepare this book, and the content is based upon final release software whenever possible. Portions of the manuscript may be based upon pre-release versions supplied by software manufacturer(s). The author and the publisher make no representation or warranties of any kind with regard to the completeness or accuracy of the contents herein and accept no liability of any kind including but not limited to performance, merchantability, fitness for any particular purpose, or any losses or damages of any kind caused or alleged to be caused directly or indirectly from this book.

Manufactured in the United States of America

10 9 8 7 6 5 4 3 2

Wiley Publishing, Inc.
End-User License Agreement

READ THIS. You should carefully read these terms and conditions before opening the software packet(s) included with this book "Book". This is a license agreement "Agreement" between you and Wiley Publishing, Inc. "WPI". By opening the accompanying software packet(s), you acknowledge that you have read and accept the following terms and conditions. If you do not agree and do not want to be bound by such terms and conditions, promptly return the Book and the unopened software packet(s) to the place you obtained them for a full refund.

1. License Grant. WPI grants to you (either an individual or entity) a nonexclusive license to use one copy of the enclosed software program(s) (collectively, the "Software," solely for your own personal or business purposes on a single computer (whether a standard computer or a workstation component of a multi-user network). The Software is in use on a computer when it is loaded into temporary memory (RAM) or installed into permanent memory (hard disk, CD-ROM, or other storage device). WPI reserves all rights not expressly granted herein.

2. Ownership. WPI is the owner of all right, title, and interest, including copyright, in and to the compilation of the Software recorded on the physical packet included with this Book "Software Media". Copyright to the individual programs recorded on the Software Media is owned by the author or other authorized copyright owner of each program. Ownership of the Software and all proprietary rights relating thereto remain with WPI and its licensors.

3. Restrictions On Use and Transfer.
(a) You may only (i) make one copy of the Software for backup or archival purposes, or (ii) transfer the Software to a single hard disk, provided that you keep the original for backup or archival purposes. You may not (i) rent or lease the Software, (ii) copy or reproduce the Software through a LAN or other network system or through any computer subscriber system or bulletin-board system, or (iii) modify, adapt, or create derivative works based on the Software.
(b) You may not reverse engineer, decompile, or disassemble the Software. You may transfer the Software and user documentation on a permanent basis, provided that the transferee agrees to accept the terms and conditions of this Agreement and you retain no copies. If the Software is an update or has been updated, any transfer must include the most recent update and all prior versions.

4. Restrictions on Use of Individual Programs. You must follow the individual requirements and restrictions detailed for each individual program in the About the CD-ROM appendix of this Book or on the Software Media. These limitations are also contained in the individual license agreements recorded on the Software Media. These limitations may include a requirement that after using the program for a specified period of time, the user must pay a registration fee or discontinue use. By opening the Software packet(s), you will be agreeing to abide by the licenses and restrictions for these individual programs that are detailed in the About the CD-ROM appendix and/or on the Software Media. None of the material on this Software Media or listed in this Book may ever be redistributed, in original or modified form, for commercial purposes.

5. Limited Warranty.
(a) WPI warrants that the Software and Software Media are free from defects in materials and workmanship under normal use for a period of sixty (60) days from the date of purchase of this Book. If WPI receives notification within the warranty period of defects in materials or workmanship, WPI will replace the defective Software Media.
(b) WPI AND THE AUTHOR(S) OF THE BOOK DISCLAIM ALL OTHER WARRANTIES, EXPRESS OR IMPLIED, INCLUDING WITHOUT LIMITATION IMPLIED WARRANTIES OF MERCHANTABILITY AND FITNESS FOR A PARTICULAR PURPOSE, WITH RESPECT TO THE SOFTWARE, THE PROGRAMS, THE SOURCE CODE CONTAINED THEREIN, AND/OR THE TECHNIQUES DESCRIBED IN THIS BOOK. WPI DOES NOT WARRANT THAT THE FUNCTIONS CONTAINED IN THE SOFTWARE WILL MEET YOUR REQUIREMENTS OR THAT THE OPERATION OF THE SOFTWARE WILL BE ERROR FREE.
(c) This limited warranty gives you specific legal rights, and you may have other rights that vary from jurisdiction to jurisdiction.

6. Remedies.
(a) WPI's entire liability and your exclusive remedy for defects in materials and workmanship shall be limited to replacement of the Software Media, which may be returned to WPI with a copy of your receipt at the following address: Software Media Fulfillment Department, Attn.: *Network+ Fast Pass*, Wiley Publishing, Inc., 10475 Crosspoint Blvd., Indianapolis, IN 46256, or call 1-800-762-2974. Please allow four to six weeks for delivery. This Limited Warranty is void if failure of the Software Media has resulted from accident, abuse, or misapplication. Any replacement Software Media will be warranted for the remainder of the original warranty period or thirty (30) days, whichever is longer.
(b) In no event shall WPI or the author be liable for any damages whatsoever (including without limitation damages for loss of business profits, business interruption, loss of business information, or any other pecuniary loss) arising from the use of or inability to use the Book or the Software, even if WPI has been advised of the possibility of such damages.
(c) Because some jurisdictions do not allow the exclusion or limitation of liability for consequential or incidental damages, the above limitation or exclusion may not apply to you.

7. U.S. Government Restricted Rights. Use, duplication, or disclosure of the Software for or on behalf of the United States of America, its agencies and/or instrumentalities "U.S. Government" is subject to restrictions as stated in paragraph (c)(1)(ii) of the Rights in Technical Data and Computer Software clause of DFARS 252.227-7013, or subparagraphs (c) (1) and (2) of the Commercial Computer Software - Restricted Rights clause at FAR 52.227-19, and in similar clauses in the NASA FAR supplement, as applicable.

8. General. This Agreement constitutes the entire understanding of the parties and revokes and supersedes all prior agreements, oral or written, between them and may not be modified or amended except in a writing signed by both parties hereto that specifically refers to this Agreement. This Agreement shall take precedence over any other documents that may be in conflict herewith. If any one or more provisions contained in this Agreement are held by any court or tribunal to be invalid, illegal, or otherwise unenforceable, each and every other provision shall remain in full force and effect.

To my father, who (in the 1980s) told me to learn as much about computers as I could and to buy and hold Microsoft stock; unfortunately I only took part of his good advice. Seriously, his purchase of an IBM PC XT computer in 1983 has made all the difference in my life and in my IT career. Thanks, Dad!

Acknowledgments

Several people have assisted me in many ways, so I'd like to acknowledge their contributions and offer my sincere appreciation. First, I'd like to thank Jeff Kellum for giving me the opportunity to write this important book.

My thanks to Maureen Adams, who set me up with the right resources to get the book off to a strong start. Many thanks to Rachel Gunn, who assisted me when necessary to keep the project on schedule. Special appreciation to my technical editors whose attention to even the finest detail is absolutely amazing. To all of the copyeditors, compositors, and proofreaders...thank you for a job well done!

Finally I'd like to acknowledge the encouragement and prayers of my family and friends and the students in my technical classes and Sunday school classes. In Him, all things are possible!

Contents at a Glance

Introduction *xiii*

Chapter 1 Domain 1 Media and Topologies 1
Chapter 2 Domain 2 Protocols and Standards 41
Chapter 3 Domain 3 Network Implementation 111
Chapter 4 Domain 4 Network Support 155

Index *205*

Contents

Introduction   *xiii*

Chapter 1   **Domain 1 Media and Topologies**   1

    1.1 Recognizing Logical and Physical Network Topologies   4
        Critical Information   5
        Exam Essentials   8
    1.2 Specifying the Main Features of Networking Technologies   8
        Critical Information   9
        Exam Essentials   12
    1.3 Specifying the Characteristics of Cable Standards   13
        Critical Information   13
        Exam Essentials   15
    1.4 Recognizing Media Connectors   16
        Critical Information   16
        Exam Essentials   20
    1.5 Recognizing Media Types   21
        Critical Information   21
        Exam Essentials   24
    1.6 Identifying Network Components   25
        Critical Information   25
        Hubs   26
        Switches   26
        Bridges   26
        Routers   27
        Gateways   27
        CSU/DSU   27
        NICs   27
        ISDN Adapters   28
        Wireless Access Point   28
        Modems   28
        Transceivers   28
        Firewalls   29
        Exam Essentials   29
    1.7 Specifying the Characteristics of Wireless Technologies   31
        Critical Information   31
        Infrared   31
        Bluetooth   32
        Exam Essentials   32

		1.8 Identifying Wireless Service Performance Factors	33
		Critical Information	33
		Exam Essentials	34
		Review Questions	35
		Answers to Review Questions	38
Chapter	**2**	**Domain 2 Protocols and Standards**	**41**
		2.1 Identifying a MAC Address and Its Parts	45
		Critical Information	46
		Exam Essentials	47
		2.2 Identifying the Seven Layers of the OSI Model and Their Functions	47
		Critical Information	48
		Exam Essentials	49
		2.3 Identifying the OSI Layers at Which Various Components Operate	50
		Critical Information	50
		Exam Essentials	52
		2.4 Differentiating Between Network Protocols	52
		Critical Information	52
		Exam Essentials	56
		2.5 Identifying the Components and Structure of IP Addresses	57
		Critical Information	57
		Exam Essentials	59
		2.6 Identifying Classful IP Ranges and Their Subnet Masks	59
		Critical Information	59
		Exam Essentials	60
		2.7 Identifying the Purpose of Subnetting	61
		Critical Information	61
		Exam Essentials	62
		2.8 Identifying the Differences Between Public and Private Addressing Schemes	62
		Critical Information	63
		Exam Essentials	64
		2.9 Identifying and Differentiating Between Addressing Methods	65
		Critical information	65
		Exam Essentials	69
		2.10 Using Protocols in the TCP/IP Suite	69
		Critical Information	69
		Exam Essentials	81
		2.11 Defining the Function of TCP/UDP Ports	81
		Critical Information	81
		Exam Essentials	82

2.12 Identifying Well-Known Ports Associated with Services and Protocols		82
Critical Information		83
Exam Essentials		84
2.13 Identifying the Purpose of Network Services and Protocols		84
Critical Information		84
Exam Essentials		86
2.14 Identifying the Basic Characteristics of Various WAN Technologies		87
Critical Information		87
Exam Essentials		89
2.15 Identifying the Basic Characteristics of Various Internet Technologies		90
Critical Information		90
Exam Essentials		91
2.16 Defining the Function of Remote Access Protocols and Services		92
Critical Information		92
Exam Essentials		96
2.17 Identifying the Purpose and Function of Various Security Protocols		96
Critical Information		97
Exam Essentials		99
2.18 Identifying Authentication Protocols		100
Critical Information		100
Exam Essentials		102
Review Questions		104
Answers to Review Questions		108
Chapter 3	**Domain 3 Network Implementation**	**111**
3.1 Identifying Server Operating System Access to Network Resources		113
Critical Information		113
Exam Essentials		117
3.2 Identifying Capabilities Clients Need to Use Network Resources		118
Critical Information		118
Exam Essentials		119
3.3 Identifying Tools Used for Wiring		120
Critical Information		120
Exam Essentials		124

3.4 Configuring a Remote Connection		125
Critical Information		125
Exam Essentials		127
3.5 Identifying the Purpose, Benefits, and Characteristics of Firewalls		128
Critical Information		128
Exam Essentials		130
3.6 Identifying the Purpose, Benefits, and Characteristics of Using a Proxy Service		130
Critical Information		131
Exam Essentials		132
3.7 Determining the Impact of Network Configurations		133
Critical Information		133
Exam Essentials		134
3.8 Identifying the Main Characteristics of VLANs		135
Critical Information		135
Exam Essentials		136
3.9 Identifying Characteristics and Purposes of Extranets and Intranets		137
Critical Information		137
Exam Essentials		138
3.10 Using Antivirus Software		139
Critical Information		139
Exam Essentials		140
3.11 Identifying the Purpose and Characteristics of Fault Tolerance		141
Critical Information		141
Exam Essentials		143
3.12 Identifying the Purpose and Characteristics of Disaster Recovery		144
Critical Information		145
Review Questions		149
Answers to Review Questions		152
Chapter 4	**Domain 4 Network Support**	**155**
4.1 Troubleshooting Using the Appropriate Network Utility		157
Critical Information		157
Exam Essentials		169
4.2 Identifying Network Utilities and Their Output		170
Critical Information		170
Exam Essentials		174

4.3 Interpreting Visual Indicators in a Network	176
Critical Information	176
Exam Essentials	177
4.4 Troubleshooting Client Access to Remote Services in a Network	178
Critical Information	178
Exam Essentials	183
4.5 Identifying Common Network Problems	184
Critical Information	184
Exam Essentials	189
4.6 Determining the Impact of Modifying, Adding, or Removing Network Services	190
Critical Information	190
Windows Internet Name Services (WINS)	191
Exam Essentials	192
4.7 Troubleshooting Various Network Topologies	193
Critical Information	193
Exam Essentials	194
4.8 Troubleshooting Various Network Infrastructures	195
Critical Information	195
Exam Essentials	196
4.9 A Troubleshooting Strategy for Network Problems	197
Critical Information	197
Exam Essentials	198
Review Questions	199
Answers to Review Questions	202
Index	*205*

Introduction

The Network+ certification was developed by the Computer Technology Industry Association (CompTIA) to provide an industry-wide means of certifying the competency of computer service technicians in basics of computer networking. The Network+ certification is granted to those who have attained the level of knowledge and networking skills that show a basic competency with networking needs of both personal and corporate computing environments.

CompTIA's exam objectives are periodically updated to keep their exams applicable to the most recent developments. However, this is not a regular occurrence since the foundational elements remain constant even as the higher-end technology advances. The Network+ objectives have recently been changed to a small degree to reflect the very latest changes in technology. This book is current for the 2005 objectives as stated by CompTIA (www.comptia.org).

What Is Network+ Certification?

The Network+ certification was created to offer an introductory step into the complex world of IT networking. You need to pass only a single exam to become Network+ certified. But obtaining this certification does not mean you can provide realistic networking services to a company. In fact, this is just the first step toward true networking knowledge and experience. By obtaining Network+ certification, you will be able to obtain more networking experience and gain an interest in networks in order to pursue more complex and in-depth network knowledge and certifications.

For the latest pricing on the exam and updates to the registration procedures, call Prometric at (866) 776-6387 or (800) 776-4276. You can also go to either www.2test.com or www.prometric.com for additional information or to register online. If you have further questions about the scope of the exams or related CompTIA programs, refer to the CompTIA website at www.comptia.org.

Is This Book for You?

Network+ Fast Pass is designed to be a succinct, portable exam review guide that can be used either in conjunction with a more complete study program (Sybex's *Network+ Study Guide, Fourth Edition*, computer-based training courseware, classroom/lab environment) or as an exam review for those who don't feel the need for more extensive test preparation. It isn't our goal to give the answers away, but rather to identify those topics on which you can expect to be tested and to provide sufficient coverage of these topics.

Perhaps you've been working with information technologies for years now. The thought of paying lots of money for a specialized IT exam-preparation course probably doesn't sound too appealing. What can they teach you that you don't already know, right? Be careful, though. Many experienced network administrators have walked confidently into the test center only to walk sheepishly out of it after failing an IT exam. After you've finished reading this book, you should have a clear idea of how your understanding of the technologies involved matches up with the expectations of the Network+ test makers.

Or perhaps you're relatively new to the world of IT, drawn to it by the promise of challenging work and higher salaries. You've just waded through an 800-page study guide or taken a class at a local training center. Lots of information to keep track of, isn't it? Well, by organizing the *Fast Pass* book according to CompTIA's exam objectives, and by breaking up the information into concise, manageable pieces, we've created what we think is the handiest exam review guide available. Throw it in your briefcase and carry it to work with you. As you read the book, you'll be able to quickly identify those areas you know best and those that require a more in-depth review.

The goal of the *Fast Pass* series is to help Network+ candidates brush up on the subjects on which they can expect to be tested in the Network+ exam. For complete in-depth coverage of the technologies and topics involved, we recommend the *Network+ Study Guide, Fourth Edition* from Sybex.

How Is This Book Organized?

This book is organized according to the official objectives list prepared by CompTIA for the Network+ exam. The chapters correspond to the four major domains of objective and topic groupings. In fact, the exam itself is weighted across these four domains as follows:

- Domain 1.0 – Media and Topologies (20%)
- Domain 2.0 – Protocols and Standards (20%)
- Domain 3.0 – Network Implementation (25%)
- Domain 4.0 – Network Support (35%)

Within each chapter, the top-level exam objective from each domain is addressed in turn. Each objective's section is further divided into two sections:

Critical Information The Critical Information section presents the greatest level of detail on information that is relevant to the objective. This is the place to start if you're unfamiliar with or uncertain about the technical issues related to the objective.

Exam Essentials Here you are given a short list of topics that you should explore fully before taking the test. Included in the Exam Essentials areas are notations of the key information you should have taken out of the *Network+ Study Guide, Fourth Edition* or the Critical Information section.

At the end of each chapter are Review Questions. These questions are designed to help you gauge your mastery of the chapter.

The Exam Objectives

The following are the areas (referred to as domains, according to CompTIA) in which you must be proficient in order to pass the Network+ exam:

Domain 1: Media and Topologies   This content area deals with basics of the logical and physical shape of various networks and how the topology of the network affects the technologies used in the network. We will also discuss common network devices and the connectors that you can use to form various types of networks.

Domain 2: Protocols and Standards   This content area deals with the OSI model of communication and how all of the network devices and network protocols are organized based on the model. We will focus on the TCP/IP suite of protocols and differentiate between all of the protocols in the suite.

Domain 3: Network Implementation   This content area deals with connecting the various components of a network together to create a functioning network. We will also discuss firewalls, VLANs, fault tolerance, and disaster recovery.

Domain 4: Network Support   This content area deals with troubleshooting a network. We will discuss the tools and utilities that you can use to troubleshoot a network as well as a troubleshooting methodology that has been proven effective.

How to Contact the Publisher

Sybex welcomes feedback on all of its titles. Visit the Sybex website at www.sybex.com for book updates and additional certification information. You'll also find forms you can use to submit comments or suggestions regarding this or any other Sybex title.

The Network+ Exam Objectives

At the beginning of each chapter in this book, we have included the complete listing of the Network+ objectives as they appear on CompTIA's website. These are provided for easy reference and to assure you that you are on track with the objectives.

Exam objectives are subject to change at any time without prior notice and at CompTIA's sole discretion. Please visit the Network+ Certification page of CompTIA's website (http://www.comptia.org/certification/network/default.aspx) for the most current listing of exam objectives.

Domain 1.0 Media and Topologies

1.1 Recognize the following logical or physical network topologies given a diagram, schematic or description:

- Star
- Bus
- Mesh
- Ring

1.2 Specify the main features of 802.2 (Logical Link Control), 802.3 (Ethernet), 802.5 (token ring), 802.11(wireless), and FDDI (Fiber Distributed Data Interface) networking technologies, including:

- Speed
- Access method (CSMA / CA (Carrier Sense Multiple Access/Collision Avoidance) and CSMA / CD (Carrier Sense Multiple Access / Collision Detection))
- Topology
- Media

1.3 Specify the characteristics (For example: speed, length, topology, and cable type) of the following cable standards:

- 10BASE-T and 10BASE-FL
- 100BASE-TX and 100BASE-FX
- 1000BASE-TX, 1000BASE-CX, 1000BASE-SX and 1000BASE-LX
- 10GBASE-SR, 10GBASE-LR and 10GBASE-ER

1.4 Recognize the following media connectors and describe their uses:

- RJ-11 (Registered Jack)
- RJ-45 (Registered Jack)
- F-Type
- ST (Straight Tip)
- SC (Standard Connector)
- IEEE1394 (FireWire)
- LC (Local Connector)
- MTRJ (Mechanical Transfer Registered Jack)

1.5 Recognize the following media types and describe their uses:

- Category 3, 5, 5e, and 6
- UTP (Unshielded Twisted Pair)
- STP (Shielded Twisted Pair)
- Coaxial cable

- SMF (Single Mode Fiber) optic cable
- MMF (Multimode Fiber) optic cable

1.6 Identify the purposes, features and functions of the following network components:

- Hubs
- Switches
- Bridges
- Routers
- Gateways
- CSU / DSU (Channel Service Unit / Data Service Unit)
- NICs (Network Interface Card)
- ISDN (Integrated Services Digital Network) adapters
- WAPs (Wireless Access Point)
- Modems
- Transceivers (media converters)
- Firewalls

1.7 Specify the general characteristics (For example: carrier speed, frequency, transmission type and topology) of the following wireless technologies:

- 802.11 (Frequency hopping spread spectrum) 802.11*x* (Direct sequence spread spectrum)
- Infrared
- Bluetooth

1.8 Identify factors which affect the range and speed of wireless service (For example: interference, antenna type and environmental factors).

Domain 2.0 Protocols and Standards

2.1 Identify a MAC (Media Access Control) address and its parts.

2.2 Identify the seven layers of the OSI (Open Systems Interconnect) model and their functions.

2.3 Identify the OSI (Open Systems Interconnect) layers at which the following network components operate:

- Hubs
- Switches
- Bridges
- Routers
- NICs (Network Interface Card)
- WAPs (Wireless Access Point)

2.4 Differentiate between the following network protocols in terms of routing, addressing schemes, interoperability and naming conventions:
- IPX / SPX (Internetwork Packet Exchange / Sequence Packet Exchange)
- NetBEUI (Network Basic Input / Output System Extended User Interface)
- AppleTalk / AppleTalk over IP (Internet Protocol)
- TCP / IP (Transmission Control Protocol / Internet Protocol)

2.5 Identify the components and structure of IP (Internet Protocol) addresses (IPv4, IPv6) and the required setting for connections across the Internet.

2.6 Identify classful IP (Internet Protocol) ranges and their subnet masks (For example: Class A, B and C).

2.7 Identify the purpose of subnetting.

2.8 Identify the differences between private and public network addressing schemes.

2.9 Identify and differentiate between the following IP (Internet Protocol) addressing methods:
- Static
- Dynamic
- Self-assigned (APIPA (Automatic Private Internet Protocol Addressing))

2.10 Define the purpose, function and use of the following protocols used in the TCP / IP (Transmission Control Protocol / Internet Protocol) suite:
- TCP (Transmission Control Protocol)
- UDP (User Datagram Protocol)
- FTP (File Transfer Protocol)
- SFTP (Secure File Transfer Protocol)
- TFTP (Trivial File Transfer Protocol)
- SMTP (Simple Mail Transfer Protocol)
- HTTP (Hypertext Transfer Protocol)
- HTTPS (Hypertext Transfer Protocol Secure)
- POP3 / IMAP4 (Post Office Protocol version 3 / Internet Message Access Protocol version 4)
- Telnet
- SSH (Secure Shell)
- ICMP (Internet Control Message Protocol)
- ARP / RARP (Address Resolution Protocol / Reverse Address Resolution Protocol)
- NTP (Network Time Protocol)
- NNTP (Network News Transport Protocol)
- SCP (Secure Copy Protocol)
- LDAP (Lightweight Directory Access Protocol)
- IGMP (Internet Group Multicast Protocol)
- LPR (Line Printer Remote)

2.11 Define the function of TCP / UDP (Transmission Control Protocol / User Datagram Protocol) ports.

2.12 Identify the well-known ports associated with the following commonly used services and protocols:

- 20 FTP (File Transfer Protocol)
- 21 FTP (File Transfer Protocol)
- 22 SSH (Secure Shell)
- 23 Telnet
- 25 SMTP (Simple Mail Transfer Protocol)
- 53 DNS (Domain Name Server)
- 69 TFTP (Trivial File Transfer Protocol)
- 80 HTTP (Hypertext Transfer Protocol)
- 110 POP3 (Post Office Protocol version 3)
- 119 NNTP (Network News Transport Protocol)
- 123 NTP (Network Time Protocol)
- 143 IMAP4 (Internet Message Access Protocol version 4)
- 443 HTTPS (Hypertext Transfer Protocol Secure)

2.13 Identify the purpose of network services and protocols (For example: DNS (Domain Name Service), NAT (Network Address Translation), ICS (Internet Connection Sharing), WINS (Windows Internet Name Service), SNMP (Simple Network Management Protocol), NFS (Network File System), Zeroconf (Zero configuration), SMB (Server Message Block), AFP (Apple File Protocol) and LPD (Line Printer Daemon)).

2.14 Identify the basic characteristics (For example: speed, capacity and media) of the following WAN (Wide Area Networks) technologies:

- Packet switching
- Circuit switching
- ISDN (Integrated Services Digital Network)
- FDDI (Fiber Distributed Data Interface)
- T1 (T Carrier level 1) / E1 / J1
- T3 (T Carrier level 3) / E3 / J3
- OCx (Optical Carrier)
- X.25

2.15 Identify the basic characteristics of the following internet access technologies:

- xDSL (Digital Subscriber Line)
- Broadband Cable (Cable modem)
- POTS / PSTN (Plain Old Telephone Service / Public Switched Telephone Network)
- Satellite
- Wireless

2.16 Define the function of the following remote access protocols and services:
- RAS (Remote Access Service)
- PPP (Point-to-Point Protocol)
- SLIP (Serial Line Internet Protocol)
- PPPoE (Point-to-Point Protocol over Ethernet)
- PPTP (Point-to-Point Tunneling Protocol)
- VPN (Virtual Private Network)
- RDP (Remote Desktop Protocol)

2.17 Identify the following security protocols and describe their purpose and function:
- IPSec (Internet Protocol Security)
- L2TP (Layer 2 Tunneling Protocol)
- SSL (Secure Sockets Layer)
- WEP (Wired Equivalent Privacy)
- WPA (Wi-Fi Protected Access)
- 802.1x

2.18 Identify authentication protocols (For example: CHAP (Challenge Handshake Authentication Protocol), MS-CHAP (Microsoft Challenge Handshake Authentication Protocol), PAP (Password Authentication Protocol), RADIUS (Remote Authentication Dial-In User Service), Kerberos and EAP (Extensible Authentication Protocol)).

Domain 3.0 Network Implementation

3.1 Identify the basic capabilities (For example: client support, interoperability, authentication, file and print services, application support and security) of the following server operating systems to access network resources:
- UNIX / Linux / Mac OS X Server
- NetWare
- Windows
- Appleshare IP (Internet Protocol)

3.2 Identify the basic capabilities needed for client workstations to connect to and use network resources (For example: media, network protocols and peer and server services).

3.3 Identify the appropriate tool for a given wiring task (For example: wire crimper, media tester/certifier, punch down tool or tone generator).

3.4 Given a remote connectivity scenario comprised of a protocol, an authentication scheme, and physical connectivity, configure the connection. Includes connection to the following servers:
- UNIX / Linux / MAC OS X Server
- NetWare
- Windows
- Appleshare IP (Internet Protocol)

3.5 Identify the purpose, benefits and characteristics of using a firewall.

3.6 Identify the purpose, benefits and characteristics of using a proxy service.

3.7 Given a connectivity scenario, determine the impact on network functionality of a particular security implementation (For example: port blocking / filtering, authentication and encryption).

3.8 Identify the main characteristics of VLANs (Virtual Local Area Networks).

3.9 Identify the main characteristics and purpose of extranets and intranets.

3.10 Identify the purpose, benefits and characteristics of using antivirus software.

3.11 Identify the purpose and characteristics of fault tolerance:

- Power
- Link redundancy
- Storage
- Services
- 3.12 Identify the purpose and characteristics of disaster recovery:

Backup / restore
Offsite storage
Hot and cold spares
Hot, warm and cold sites

Domain 4.0 Network Support

4.1 Given a troubleshooting scenario, select the appropriate network utility from the following:

- Tracert / traceroute
- ping
- arp
- netstat
- nbtstat
- ipconfig / ifconfig
- winipcfg
- nslookup / dig

4.2 Given output from a network diagnostic utility (For example: those utilities listed in objective 4.1), identify the utility and interpret the output.

4.3 Given a network scenario, interpret visual indicators (For example: link LEDs (Light Emitting Diode) and collision LEDs (Light Emitting Diode)) to determine the nature of a stated problem.

4.4 Given a troubleshooting scenario involving a client accessing remote network services, identify the cause of the problem (For example: file services, print services, authentication failure, protocol configuration, physical connectivity and SOHO (Small Office / Home Office) router).

4.5 Given a troubleshooting scenario between a client and the following server environments, identify the cause of a stated problem:

- UNIX / Linux / Mac OS X Server
- NetWare
- Windows
- Appleshare IP (Internet Protocol)

4.6 Given a scenario, determine the impact of modifying, adding or removing network services (For example: DHCP (Dynamic Host Configuration Protocol), DNS (Domain Name Service) and WINS (Windows Internet Name Server)) for network resources and users.

4.7 Given a troubleshooting scenario involving a network with a particular physical topology (For example: bus, star, mesh or ring) and including a network diagram, identify the network area affected and the cause of the stated failure.

4.8 Given a network troubleshooting scenario involving an infrastructure (For example: wired or wireless) problem, identify the cause of a stated problem (For example: bad media, interference, network hardware or environment).

4.9 Given a network problem scenario, select an appropriate course of action based on a logical troubleshooting strategy. This strategy can include the following steps:

1. Identify the symptoms and potential causes
2. Identify the affected area
3. Establish what has changed
4. Select the most probable cause
5. Implement an action plan and solution including potential effects
6. Test the result
7. Identify the results and effects of the solution
8. Document the solution and process

Chapter 1

Domain 1 Media and Topologies

COMPTIA NETWORK+ EXAM OBJECTIVES COVERED IN THIS CHAPTER:

✓ **1.1 Recognize the following logical or physical network topologies given a diagram, schematic or description:**
  - Star
  - Bus
  - Mesh
  - Ring

✓ **1.2 Specify the main features of 802.2 (Logical Link Control), 802.3 (Ethernet), 802.5 (token ring), 802.11 (wireless), and FDDI (Fiber Distributed Data Interface) networking technologies, including:**
  - Speed
  - Access method (CSMA / CA (Carrier Sense Multiple Access/Collision Avoidance) and CSMA / CD (Carrier Sense Multiple Access / Collision Detection))
  - Topology
  - Media

✓ **1.3 Specify the characteristics (For example: speed, length, topology, and cable type) of the following cable standards:**
  - 10BASE-T and 10BASE-FL
  - 100BASE-TX and 100BASE-FX
  - 1000BASE-TX, 1000BASE-CX, 1000BASE-SX and 1000BASE-LX
  - 10GBASE-SR, 10GBASE-LR and 10GBASE-ER

✓ **1.4 Recognize the following media connectors and describe their uses:**
- RJ-11 (Registered Jack)
- RJ-45 (Registered Jack)
- F-Type
- ST (Straight Tip)
- SC (Standard Connector)1
- IEEE1394 (FireWire)1
- LC (Local Connector)1
- MTRJ (Mechanical Transfer Registered Jack)1

✓ **1.5 Recognize the following media types and describe their uses:**
- Category 3, 5, 5e, and 6
- UTP (Unshielded Twisted Pair)
- STP (Shielded Twisted Pair)
- Coaxial cable
- SMF (Single Mode Fiber) optic cable
- MMF (Multimode Fiber) optic cable

✓ **1.6 Identify the purposes, features and functions of the following network components:**
- Hubs
- Switches
- Bridges
- Routers
- Gateways
- CSU / DSU (Channel Service Unit / Data Service Unit)
- NICs (Network Interface Card)
- ISDN (Integrated Services Digital Network) adapters
- WAPs (Wireless Access Point)
- Modems
- Transceivers (media converters)
- Firewalls

- ✓ **1.7 Specify the general characteristics (For example: carrier speed, frequency, transmission type and topology) of the following wireless technologies:**
  - 802.11 (Frequency hopping spread spectrum) 802.11*x* (Direct sequence spread spectrum)
  - Infrared
  - Bluetooth
- ✓ **1.8 Identify factors which affect the range and speed of wireless service (For example: interference, antenna type and environmental factors).**

A network is a group of computers that are connected to share hardware and software. In order for the computers to communicate with each other, they must share three elements: a network media and topology, a protocol, and a software client or service. In this chapter, we will focus on the first of these elements, the network media and topology.

While the basic concept of connecting computers hasn't changed much since the mid-1980s, the methods that we use to connect them have changed dramatically. Networking technologies have evolved dramatically over the last 20 years and will continue to evolve. The components that we use in our networks have also evolved because of these technologies.

When you connect computers, your main goal is to provide fast communication with as few errors as possible. You should understand that the type of media and topology you use in your network will largely determine your ability to reach this goal. In addition, you should know that the components that you choose for a network will also affect your capability to control network traffic. In this chapter, we will discuss several networking media and topologies and compare the features that they, and the components that use them, bring to your network design to help you control traffic within your network.

1.1 Recognizing Logical and Physical Network Topologies

Basically, a *topology* is a shape, so a network topology is the shape of a network. There is, however, a big difference between a physical network topology and a logical network topology. The physical network topology represents how the network looks to the naked eye—in other words, the way the components are arranged. The logical network topology represents how the flow of information works its way through the network. This may not be the same as it looks to the naked eye. You should understand the main network topologies as well as the difference between a physical network topology and a logical one. In this section, we discuss the most common network topologies.

Critical Information

Recognizing the major differences in regard to the shape and the components that are used in the most common topologies is important. You should be able to recognize these differences given a diagram, schematic, or description. In the following paragraphs, we discuss each network topology in greater detail.

Star

A *star* topology is a group of computers that are connected to a central location such as a hub or a switch. This is the most common topology in use today. The computers may be physically located next to each other or spread throughout an entire building, but the flow of information from each computer to the other computers must go through the central location. In a star topology, each computer has its own cable or connection to the hub. Since each computer has its own connection, the failure of one computer will not affect the other computers in the network; however, if the hub or switch should fail, then all of the computers on that hub or switch will be affected. Figure 1.1 is an illustration of a star topology.

FIGURE 1.1 A star topology

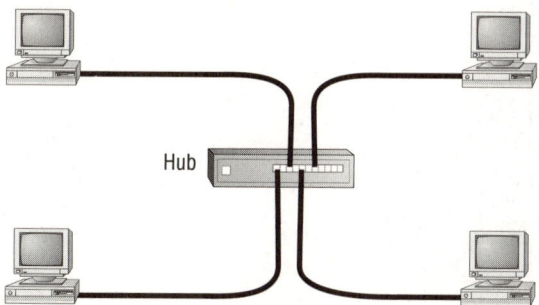

Bus

The *bus* topology was commonly used in earlier networks but is not seen much today. In a bus topology, a single cable connects all the computers. A coaxial cable is used with special connectors called BNC and T connectors. (We will discuss cables and connectors in the next section.) The T connectors provide an independent connection for each computer on the bus. In addition, the bus only works if both ends of the cable have a special resistor installed called a terminator. Figure 1.2 shows a bus topology; Figure 1.3 shows the T connector used to connect the computers to the bus.

FIGURE 1.2 A bus topology

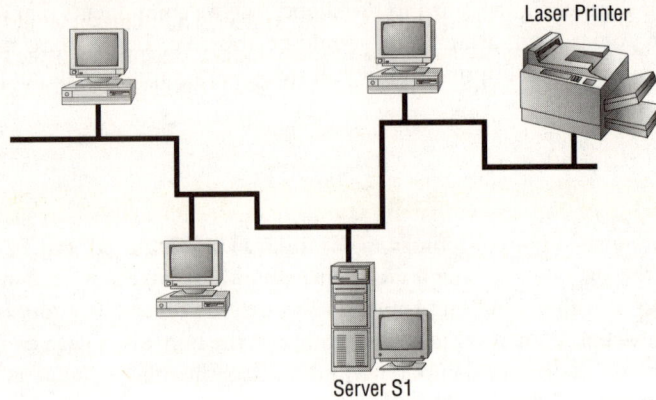

FIGURE 1.3 A T connector

Mesh

The *mesh* topology is not often used and is almost never used for individual computers. In a full-mesh topology, all of the components in the mesh have independent connections to all of the other components in the mesh. For example, if four computers are connected with a "full mesh," then the number of connections can be determined by the following formula:

n(n – 1) = total number of connections

In this case:

4(4 – 1) = 12

In other words, there are a total of 12 connections and each computer has to contain three network interface cards.

Actually, any network with multiple or redundant connections to network components can be considered a mesh topology, but because of the expense involved in creating this type of network, they are rarely created for individual computers. A mesh, and even a full mesh, would most likely be found connecting multiple networks in an organization. In fact, the Internet is the best and biggest example of a mesh topology. Figure 1.4 shows a full-mesh topology with four computers.

FIGURE 1.4   A mesh topology

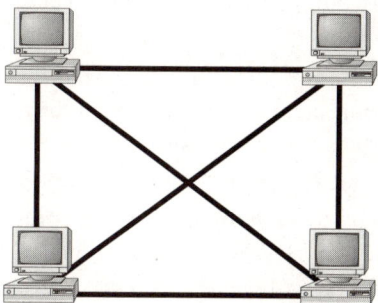

Ring

A *ring* topology (see Figure 1.5) looks exactly like a star topology to the naked eye. The real difference between a ring topology and a star topology lies in the technology used. Computers in a ring topology generally use an IBM Token Ring technology. Other components can also be arranged in a ring topology and use different technologies. The computers involved in a ring topology are not generally arranged in a physical ring. In fact, just as with a star topology, they can be located next to each other or spread throughout a building. The difference is that the central component that connects them contains the logical ring that facilitates communication on the network using the ring technologies. (We will discuss ring technologies in the next section.)

FIGURE 1.5   A ring topology

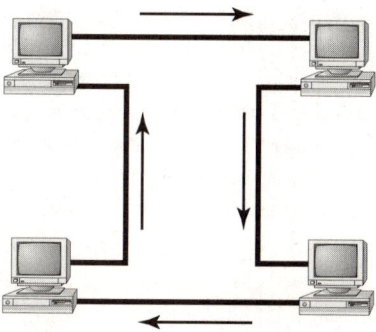

Exam Essentials

Know the difference between a physical topology and a logical topology. The physical topology of the network is simply what it looks like or how the components are arranged. The logical topology, on the other hand, represents the flow of information in the network.

Be able to list the main features of a star topology. Be able to recognize a star topology from a diagram, schematic, or description. A star topology contains a central hub (or switch) and all information must flow through the hub. A star topology is considered fault tolerant, since each device has its own network connection.

Describe the main features of a bus topology. A bus topology uses a coaxial cable, and all computers are connected to the same cable. T connectors are used to attach the computers. Resistors called terminators must be used at both ends of a bus. Keep in mind that the failure of one computer will generally not affect the entire segment, but a break in the cable will.

Summarize the main features of a mesh topology. A mesh topology provides multiple connections for the devices in the mesh. A full mesh requires $n(n-1)$ connections, where n is the number of devices in the mesh. A mesh topology is most often used with networks and not with individual computers.

Describe the main features of a ring topology. A ring topology looks like a star topology; the real difference is in the way that the information is transferred through the network. The IBM Token Ring is the most common type of ring topology, but is quickly being replaced by the star topology and Ethernet.

1.2 Specifying the Main Features of Networking Technologies

Whereas the topology of a network is the shape of the network, the technology is the method of putting information onto the network and controlling it based on the physical components that are used and how they operate within the network. Some technologies have evolved over time, some have been all but discontinued, while others have been improved and refined.

In February 1980, the Institute of Electrical and Electronics Engineers (IEEE) developed a set of standards called the 802 project. Each of the standards was given a number beginning with 802 (the 80th year and the second month). These standards have been refined over the last two decades, but (in general) are still used to represent the main networking technologies of the past, present, and future. In this section, we discuss each of these technologies in detail.

Critical Information

Familiarize yourself with the new technologies as well as some of the older, less used technologies. You should be able to specify the main features of each technology, such as speed, access method, topology used, and media used. In the paragraphs that follow, we discuss each of the technologies with which you should be familiar.

Ethernet

Ethernet is by far the most common technology in use today. The Internet operates using Ethernet technology. It was first developed by Xerox at the Palo Alto Research Center (PARC) and was defined as 802.3 by the IEEE. Ethernet began production at a speed of only 3Mbps, but common speeds today include 10Mbps, 100Mbps, and 1000Mbps. The speed of the network is dependent on the devices that are used and on the slowest devices in the network. (We will discuss types of network devices later in this chapter.)

Ethernet uses an access method known as Carrier Sense Multiple Access with Collision Detection (CSMA/CD). This method of putting data "on the wire" works by first sensing the wire to determine whether there is currently any data flowing on it, indicated by a fluctuation in electrical current. If no data is flowing on the wire, then the Ethernet device can send its data. Sometimes two devices might try to send data at the same time, resulting in a collision. If this happens, then the network is "stalled" until the devices have sent their data again with no collision. One of the responsibilities of a network designer is to control traffic in order to reduce or eliminate collisions.

Ethernet networks began as bus topologies that used coaxial cable. These networks used a large coaxial cable as a backbone and a smaller coaxial cable to connect the computers and hubs to the backbone. Today, Ethernet networks typically use unshielded twisted-pair (UTP) cable in a star topology. Some networks use wireless connections that require no cable at all. (We will discuss media types in greater detail later in this chapter.) Table 1.1 highlights the main features of the Ethernet topology.

TABLE 1.1 Ethernet Topology Features

Speed	10Mbps, 100Mbps (Fast Ethernet), 1000Mbps (Gigabit Ethernet), and 10,000Mbps (10G Ethernet)
Access Method	CSMA/CD
Topology	Star, bus (bus is not widely used today)
Media	Copper wire and fiber-optic cable

Logical Link Control (LLC)

Logical Link Control (LLC) is a networking technology defined by the IEEE as 802.2. It does not provide a complete networking model, but instead defines the standards for controlling the data sent and received by a system. LLC specifies the protocols, or rules, that perform flow control and error checking. These protocols are the essential foundation for all of the other networking standards.

Token Ring

Token Ring was introduced by IBM in the mid-1980s. Since it virtually eliminated collisions and thereby increased the speed of networks, it became the network topology of choice for those companies who could afford the best and most expensive networks. Defined by the IEEE as 802.5, Token Ring uses a token-passing access method. A token is a unique electronic signal that must be attached to a message in order for the message to enter the network or travel on it. Because there is only one token on each ring, only one message can travel on the network at any given point in time, thereby eliminating the possibility of collisions.

Token Ring uses a physical star topology but the logical topology is a ring. The ring is actually created inside special hubs called multiple-station access units (MSAUs). The media used in Token Ring is twisted-pair cable. Typically, Token Ring networks run at either 4Mbps or 16Mbps. While Token Ring had a huge following in the 1980s, it has been all but eliminated from modern network designs due to advancements in technology that increased the speed and reliability of Ethernet. Table 1.2 highlights the main features of the Token Ring topology.

Wireless

Today's networks have the capability to eliminate the cables for many of the computers. The IEEE 802.11 wireless standard was originally defined in the 1980s by the "forward-thinking" representatives of the IEEE. Nowadays, many individuals and companies are adopting the technology for portions of their networks. Because of the conveniences that they offer, wireless networks will likely continue to grow in popularity.

TABLE 1.2 Token Ring Topology Features

Speed	4Mbps, 16Mbps
Access Method	IBM token passing
Topology	Ring
Media	Copper wire

1.2 Specifying the Main Features of Networking Technologies

The 802.11 standard has two common levels: 802.11b and 802.11g. The 802.11b standard offers speeds up to 11Mbps, and the 802.11g standard increases the speed to 54Mbps. Both use an access method referred to as Carrier Sense Multiple Access with Collision Avoidance CSMA/CA. This access method is similar to CSMA/CD except that the device that wants to send its message must first send a very small message to make sure that the signal can be received without any collisions or other problems. If the short message is transmitted successfully, then the long message is sent next. The media that 802.11 wireless networks use is the 2.4GHz radio wave band. Table 1.3 highlights the main features of the wireless topology.

TABLE 1.3 Wireless Topology Features

Speed	11Mbps, 54Mbps
Access Method	CSMA/CA
Topology	Star (WAP is central point)
Media	2.4GHz radio band

FDDI

Fiber Distributed Data Interface (FDDI) was developed by the American National Standards Institute (ANSI) in the mid-1980s. It uses a token-passing access method and a dual-ring topology. Figure 1.6 shows an example of an FDDI topology. The media used by FDDI is typically fiber-optic cable, but it can also use shielded twisted-pair (STP) or unshielded twisted-pair (UTP) cable. (We will discuss cable types in greater detail later in this chapter.) FDDI communicates at a speed of 100 Mbps on copper wire, but can communicate much faster on fiber-optic cable. (FDDI on copper wire is sometimes referred to as CDDI.) Table 1.4 highlights the main features of the FDDI topology.

TABLE 1.4 FDDI Topology Features

Speed	100Mbps–620Mbps
Access Method	Token passing
Topology	Dual-ring
Media	Copper wire and fiber-optic cable

FIGURE 1.6 An FDDI topology

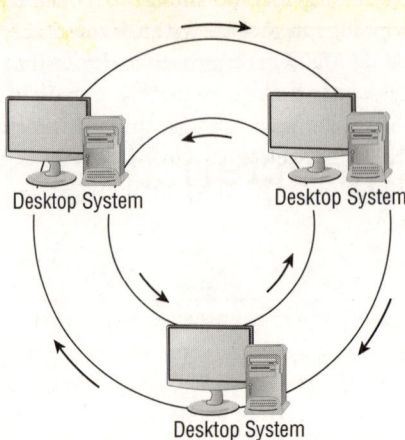

Exam Essentials

Know the difference between a topology and a technology. A network's topology represents the way that it is shaped logically and physically, but its technology represents the methods that it uses to introduce data onto the media and transfer it to other computers.

List the characteristics of Ethernet. Ethernet, the most common technology in use today, uses the CSMA/CD access method to put data onto the wire. Ethernet has evolved over time and has many different speeds, including 10Mbps, 100Mbps, 1000Mbps, and 10,000Mbps. Ethernet is defined by the IEEE 802.3 specification.

Describe the characteristics of LLC. LLC is a standard defined by the IEEE 802.2 specification. It is not a complete networking model, but it does define the standards for controlling data sent and received by systems. LLC defines the rules and standard for flow control and error checking.

Know the characteristics of Token Ring. Token Ring is a technology developed by IBM and defined by the 802.5 specification standard. Token Ring uses a token-passing method of carrier access to eliminate the possibility of collisions. The two main speeds of Token Ring are 4Mbps and 16Mbps. Token Ring is used on copper wire for local area networks (LANs).

List the characteristics of the wireless topology. The wireless topology is defined by the 802.11 specification standard. The two most common standards of wireless communication are 802.11b and 802.11g; both use the 2.4GHz radio band. Keep in mind that 802.11b operates at 11Mbps and 802.11g operates at 54Mbps. Wireless communications use a CSMA/CA method of media access, which tests the communication channel before sending data onto it.

Describe the characteristics of FDDI. FDDI is a topology that is used in wide area networks (WANs) rather than LANs. FDDI uses a token-passing method similar to Token Ring, but its method is more advanced. It uses a dual-ring topology to provide for fault tolerance. The speed of FDDI is generally 100Mbps, but some forms of FDDI can transmit much faster.

1.3 Specifying the Characteristics of Cable Standards

The cables that connect our networks today have evolved from earlier standards. Although some of these standards are no longer in common use today, understanding them will assist you in appreciating the advantages of the cables that we use today. You should know the characteristics of these standards. In this section, we discuss each of these cable standards in detail.

Critical Information

You should know the speeds, maximum lengths, topology, and cable types associated with each of the main cable standards. In the paragraphs that follow, we discuss each of these characteristics in detail.

10BASE-T and 10BASE-FL

The most common cable standard used in the early 1990s was 10BASE-T. The "10" represents the maximum speed of 10Mbps; "BASE" represents a baseband type of transmission in which only one signal can be on the wire at any given time; "T" indicates that a twisted-pair cable was used. The maximum length of any network segment using 10BASE-T is 100 meters.

As you can imagine, some organizations needed to have a network segment that was longer than 100 meters. In the mid- to late 1990s, 10BASE-FL was developed to provide the solution. It used a fiber-optic cable to transmit the signal rather than the copper twisted-pair cable. The fiber-optic cable can transmit much further without suffering a loss of signal due to the media itself (a problem referred to as *attenuation*). The speed of 10BASE-FL was still 10Mbps, but the maximum transmission length could be up to 20 kilometers! Many of these networks are still in use today where speed is not a concern but maximum distance is a factor. Table 1.5 shows the characteristics of 10BASET and 10BASE-FL.

TABLE 1.5 Characteristics of 10BASE-T and 10BASE-FL

	Speed	Max. Length	Topology	Cable Type
10BASE-T	10Mbps	100 meters	Star	Copper wire Category 3+
10BASE-FL	10Mbps	20 kilometers	Star	Fiber-optic

100BASE-TX and 100BASE-FX

100BASE-TX is by far the most common networking standard in use today. The "100" represents the maximum speed of 100Mbps; "BASE" represents a baseband type of transmission; and "TX" represents twisted-pair cable of the type that will support 100Mbps transmission. (We will discuss cable types in greater detail later in this chapter.) Although 100BASE-TX is 10 times faster than 10BASE-T, it is still limited to 100 meters per network segment.

To provide a solution for longer network segments, 100BASE-FX was developed. It uses fiber-optic cable to increase the distance that the signal can be transmitted without suffering from attenuation. Some devices that use 100BASE-FX can transmit up to 20 kilometers! Table 1.6 shows the characteristics of 100BASE-TX and 100BASE-FX.

TABLE 1.6 Characteristics of 100BASE-T and 100BASE-FX

	Speed	Max. Length	Topology	Cable Type
100BASE-T	100Mbps	100 meters	Star	Copper wire Category 5+
100BASE-FX	100Mbps	20 kilometers	Star	Fiber-optic

1000BASE-TX, 1000BASE-CX, 1000BASE-SX, and 1000BASE-LX

The next fastest cable standard is 1000BASEX, Gigabit Ethernet. The "1000" represents 1000Mbps, or 1 Gbps, and "BASE" represents a baseband type of transmission in a star topology. While this standard is implemented in many forms, the only main difference is the cable type used and therefore the maximum distance. Table 1.7 shows the difference in cable types and maximum transmission distance possible for each form of 1000BASEX.

TABLE 1.7 1000BASEX Cable Standards

	1000 BASE-TX	1000 BASE-CX	1000BASE-SX	1000BASE-LX
Cable Type	Unshielded twisted-pair	Shielded copper (STP)	One fiber-optic cable	Two fiber-optic cables
Maximum Distance	100 meters	25 meters	550 meters	5000 meters

10GBASE-SR, 10GBASE-LR, and 10GBASE-ER

The newest and fastest cable standard is the 10G standard. As you may have guessed, the 10G standard allows a maximum transmission speed of 10Gbps, or 10 billion bits per second, in a star topology. The 10G standard is currently subdivided into three standards: 10GBASE-SR,

1.3 Specifying the Characteristics of Cable Standards

10GBASE-LR, and 10BASE-ER. All of these 10G standards use fiber-optic cable. The major difference between the standards is the maximum transmission distance. Table 1.8 shows the maximum transmission distance for each standard.

TABLE 1.8 10GBASEX Cable Standards

	10GBASE-SR	10GBASE-LR	10GBASE-ER
Maximum Distance	82 meters	10 kilometers	40 kilometers

Exam Essentials

Recognize the terminology used when identifying cable standards. You should be able to determine the speed and transmission type of a cable standard solely based on its name.

Know the characteristics of the 10BASE-T standard. The 10BASE-T standard indicates a 10Mbps baseband signal that uses a twisted-pair copper wire. This means that the maximum distance for this technology, without the use of repeaters, is 100 meters. 10BASE-T uses a star topology.

List the characteristics of the 10BASE-FL standard. The 10BASE-FL standard indicates a 10Mbps baseband signal that uses a fiber-optic cable. This means that the maximum distance for a run is about 20 kilometers. 10BASE-FL uses a star topology.

Describe the characteristics of the 100BASE-TX standard. The 100BASE-TX standard indicates a 100Mbps (Fast Ethernet) baseband signal that uses a twisted-pair copper cable. This means that the maximum distance for a run is 100 meters, without the use of repeaters. 100BASE-FX uses a star topology.

Know the characteristics of the 100BASE-FX standard. The 100BASE-FX standard indicates a 100Mbps (Fast Ethernet) baseband signal that uses a fiber-optic cable. This means that the maximum distance for a run is 20 kilometers. 100BASE-FX uses a star topology.

Be familiar with the characteristics of the 1000BASE-TX standard. The 1000BASE-TX standard indicates a 1000Mbps (1Gbps) baseband signal that uses unshielded twisted-pair cable. This means that the maximum distance for a run is 100 meters, without the use of repeaters. 1000BASE-TX uses a star topology.

List the characteristics of the 1000BASE-CX standard. The 1000BASE-CX standard indicates a 1000Mbps (1Gbps) baseband signal that uses Category 5 shielded twisted-pair cable. It is therefore more immune to electrical interference, but it has a maximum distance of only 25 meters. 1000BASE-CX uses a star topology.

Describe the characteristics of the 1000BASE-SX standard. The 1000BASE-SX standard indicates a 1000Mbps (1Gbps) baseband signal that uses one fiber-optic cable. This means that it has a maximum distance of 550 meters, without the use of repeaters. 1000BASE-SX uses a star topology.

Know the characteristics of the 1000BASE-LX standard. The 1000BASE-LX standard indicates a 1000Mbps (1Gbps) baseband signal that uses two fiber-optic cables. This means that it has a maximum distance of 5000 meters, with the use of repeaters. 1000BASE-LX uses a star topology.

List the characteristics of the 10GBASE-SR standard. The 10GBASE-SR standard indicates a 10,000Mbps baseband signal that uses fiber-optic cable. Due to the type of fiber-optic cable that it uses, it has a maximum transmission distance of 82 meters. 10GBASE-SR uses a star topology.

Describe the characteristics of the 10GBASE-LR standard. The 10GBASE-LR standard indicates a 10,000Mbps baseband signal that uses fiber-optic cable. Due to the type of fiber-optic cable that it uses, it has a maximum transmission distance of 10 kilometers. 10GBASE-LR uses a star topology.

Know the characteristics of the 10GBASE-ER standard. The 10GBASE-ER standard indicates a 10,000Mbps baseband signal that uses fiber-optic cable. Due to the type of fiber-optic cable that it uses, it has a maximum transmission distance of 40 kilometers. 10GBASE-ER uses a star topology.

1.4 Recognizing Media Connectors

No matter what type of cable you are using, it won't be very effective unless it has the proper connectors on each end. The type of connectors that you use will depend on the cable as well as on your intended use for the cable. In other words, you need to have the proper connectors to plug into the devices that you are trying to use. In this section, we discuss the most common types of media connectors used in networks.

Critical Information

You should be able to recognize by sight the most common types of cable connectors and describe their main use. In this section, we will discuss the purpose of the major types of connectors and provide a photograph of each type.

RJ-11

"RJ" stands for *registered jack*. Chances are good that you have held an RJ-11 connector in your hand, since they are used on all of the telephone connections in the United States and most other countries. An RJ-11 connector can contain and connect two pairs of wires. In regard to computers, you are most likely to use an RJ-11 connector when you attach a modem to a telephone line. In fact, you plug an RJ-11 into the wall and another one into the modem. Figure 1.7 shows an RJ-11 connector on the left.

RJ-45

The RJ-45 connector is the most common network connector. It is used to connect network interface cards (NICs) to hubs and/or switches. RJ-45s can also be used to connect network devices together for communication as well as control. The RJ-45 connector can contain and connect four pairs of wires. For example, RJ-45 connectors are used to connect computer cables to a patch panel, a patch panel to a switch, and then to connect the switch to a router in order to supply a user connection to the Internet. Figure 1.7 shows an RJ-45 connector on the right.

FIGURE 1.7 An RJ-11 connector (left) and an RJ-45 connector (right)

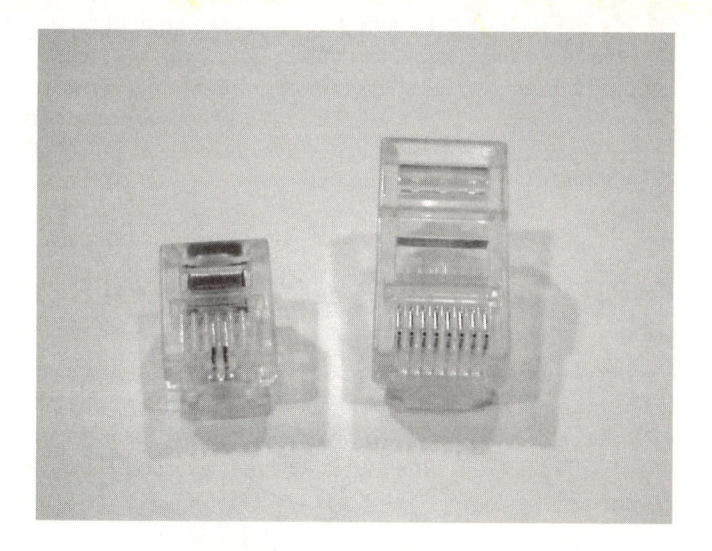

F-Type

Although coaxial cables are rarely used for computer network backbones, they have experienced a resurgence of growth because they are used to connect a cable modem to an NIC to provide a computer with a broadband Internet connection. Many of the newest coaxial cables use a new connector that slides onto the coaxial cable connection on a device with just one quick push. This new connector is referred to as an F-type connector. F-type connectors make connecting cable modems to the cable company's connections much easier than with previous connectors that had to be twisted many times to secure the connection. Figure 1.8 shows an F-type connector.

FIGURE 1.8 An F-type connector

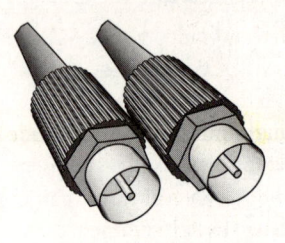

ST

The ST (straight tip) connector is a type of fiber-optic cable connector. It uses a half-twist bayonet type of lock to hold it in place securely. ST connectors are most commonly used with single-mode fiber-optic cable that runs long distances. For example, an ST connector might be used on either side of a fiber backbone between two buildings on a corporate campus. Figure 1.9 shows an ST connector.

FIGURE 1.9 An ST connector

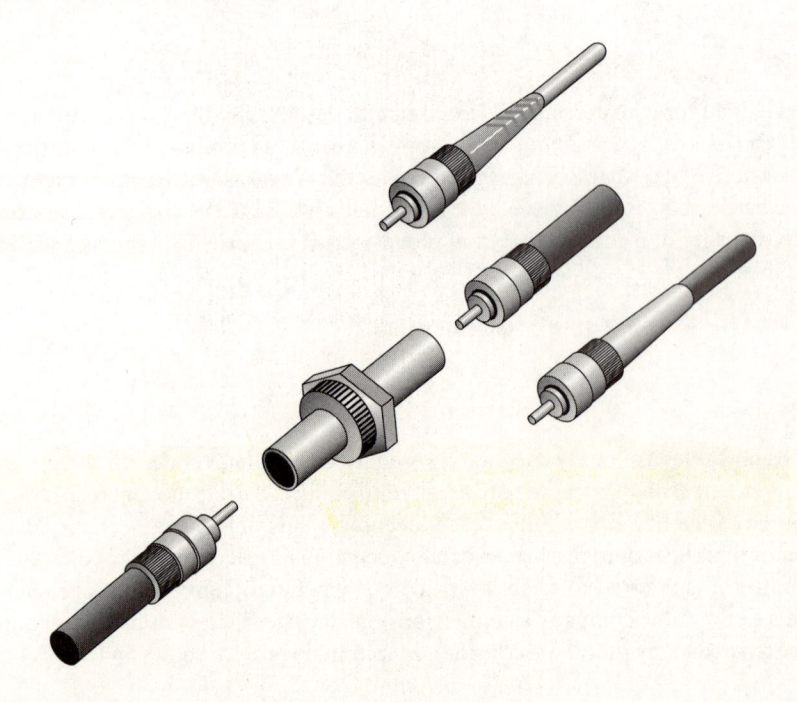

SC

The SC (standard connector) connector is a type of fiber-optic cable connector. It uses a push-pull connector mechanism that is similar to common audio and video plugs. SC connectors are most often used with multimode fiber-optic cable that is providing a backbone segment for a LAN. For example, SC connectors might be used on either side of a fiber backbone that runs between the floors of a single building. (We will discuss single-mode and multimode fiber-optic cable later in this chapter.) Figure 1.10 shows an SC connector.

FIGURE 1.10 An SC connector

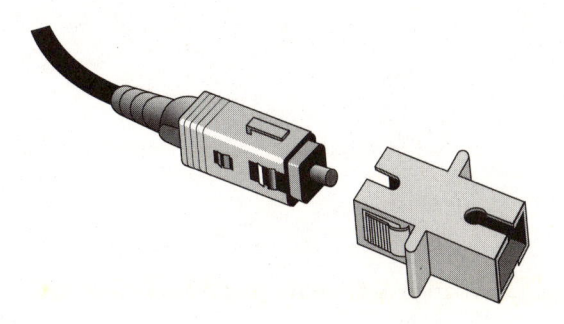

IEEE 1394

Specially developed for transferring pictures and video, the IEEE 1394 standard (also known as FireWire) has its own type of connector. You can recognize an IEEE 1394 connector by its small and distinctive "D" shape. This type of connector is now found on many types of video and multimedia devices. For example, you might use an IEEE 1394 connector to connect a digital video recorder to a computer to download pictures. Figure 1.11 shows an IEEE 1394 connector cable.

FIGURE 1.11 An IEEE 1394 connector cable

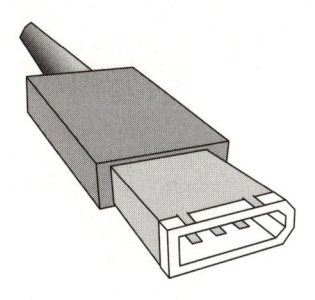

LC

The LC (local connector) connector is a fiber connector that is built into the body of an RJ-style jack. The LC connector is used for local connections. This type of connector is generally found on a fiber-optic patch cord that is used to connect fiber-optic equipment within the network closet itself. Figure 1.12 shows an LC connector.

FIGURE 1.12 An LC connector

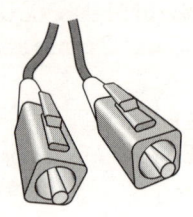

MTRJ

The MTRJ connector is one of the newest designs for connecting fiber-optic cable. The new connector is easier to use and smaller that the older types of connectors. Due to their rugged and durable design, they are becoming the connector of choice for use in the network and telecom closet of an organization. Figure 1.13 shows an MTRJ connector.

FIGURE 1.13 An MTRJ connector

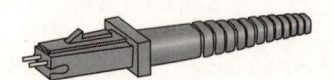

Exam Essentials

Be able to recognize the main types of connectors used in networks.   Be able to recognize a photo of the most common media connectors that we described in this chapter and discuss its normal use.

Know the characteristics of the RJ-11 connector.   RJ stands for registered jack, and the RJ-11 connector is the connector that is commonly used with regular telephone lines. The RJ-11 connector contains four wires to be used as two pairs of wires. RJ-11 connectors are used to connect modems to telephone lines for communication on the Internet.

Describe the characteristics of the RJ-45 connector.   The RJ-45 connector is the most common network connector. It is used to connect various types of network equipment, including patch panels, hubs, switches, and routers. The RJ-45 connector contains eight wires, or four pairs of wires.

List the characteristics of the F-type connector. The F-type connector is a new connector developed for use with coaxial cable connections. It provides a faster connection than the older type (BNC) connectors that were used for coaxial cable. The main use for coaxial cable these days is to connect cable modems to the cable company's outlet to create a connection to the Internet.

Know the characteristics of ST connectors. The ST connector is a type of fiber-optic cable connector that uses a half-twist bayonet type of lock. The ST connector is typically used with single-mode fiber-optic cable that runs long distances.

List the characteristics of SC connectors. The SC connector is a type of fiber-optic connector. It is a push-pull connector that is similar to audio and video plugs. The SC connector is most often used to connect a fiber-optic backbone segment within a LAN.

Be familiar with the characteristics of IEEE 1394 connectors. IEEE 1394 is a video and multimedia connector that is commonly referred to as FireWire. The IEEE 1394 connector has a distinctive "D" shape. The main purpose of the IEEE 1394 standard is increased speed of data transfer for video and multimedia applications.

Know the characteristics of LC connectors. The LC connector is a type of fiber connector. It is used to connect fiber-optic equipment within the network closet. This type of connector is generally found on patch cords that are used to connect fiber-optic equipment for short distances.

Describe the characteristics of MTRJ connectors. The MTRJ connector is a type of fiber connector. It is typically used to connect fiber-optic equipment for short distances in the network and telecom closet, as is the LC connector. The MTRJ connector is beginning to replace the LC connector because of its rugged design and durability.

1.5 Recognizing Media Types

The *media* is the wired or wireless connection that allows one computer to communicate with another computer. When you choose a cable standard and a connector type, you are also choosing a media type. It's important that you understand your choices in regard to connector type and media type.

Critical Information

You should be able to recognize the most common media types and describe their use. In this section we discuss each media type and its most common use.

Category 3, 5, 5e, and 6 Twisted-Pair Cables

The category of a twisted-pair cable indicates the tightness of the twist applied to the wire pairs in the cable. The twist in wire pairs prevents an electrical interference called crosstalk from affecting the communication. Crosstalk occurs when a signal bleeds over from one wire to another (even through the insulation of the wire). The tighter the twist, the faster you can transmit information through a cable without suffering from crosstalk. Table 1.9 shows the maximum speed of the main cable categories.

Category 5e (enhanced) is the cable type that is currently recommended as a minimum for all new installations. Cable is generally used to connect each computer to a central point, typically a hub or a switch, that is contained in a network closet. Ensuring that each computer has its own cable creates redundancy in the network and thereby provides fault tolerance.

TABLE 1.9 Cable Categories and Speeds

	Category 3	Category 5	Category 5e	Category 6
Maximum Speed	10Mbps	100Mbps	1000Mbps	1000Mbps

UTP

Unshielded twisted-pair (UTP) cable is the most common type of cable used today. UTP is offered for all of the categories of cable that we have discussed. It is most often used because it is far easier to install than STP (which we will discuss next). The only protection from electrical interference provided by UTP is the fact that the pairs of wires within the cable are twisted, which is usually enough.

STP

Shielded twisted-pair (STP) resembles UTP except that it includes a foil shield that covers the wires and adds another layer of protection against outside magnetic interference. In order for this protection to be effective, the connections have to be properly grounded. This adds to the complexity of installations, so most organizations have opted to use fiber-optic cable instead of STP when electromagnetic interference is a problem. For example, if a cable is passing by a large electrical motor or fluorescent light ballast, STP might be used to provide greater resistance from electromagnetic interference (EMI). STP cable was often used for communication connections through elevator shafts, prior to fiber-optic cable. Figure 1.14 shows an STP cable.

FIGURE 1.14 An STP cable

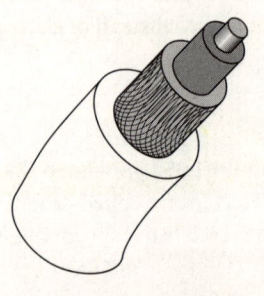

Coaxial Cable

In the late 1980s, coaxial cable was used as the backbone of network segments and to connect computers to the bus topology that made up the network. Coaxial cable is rarely used anymore for network backbones or to connect computers, but it is being used today to connect cable modems to the cable provider's connection to provide a computer with a broadband Internet connection. Coaxial cable consists of an inner core wire and an outer braid of insulating wire. The entire signal is carried by the inner core wire. Figure 1.15 shows the components that make up a coaxial cable.

FIGURE 1.15 A coaxial cable

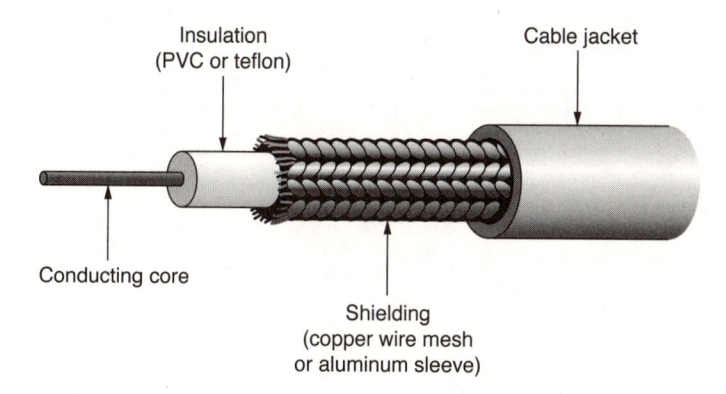

Single-Mode Fiber

Single-mode fiber-optic cable (SMF) is a very high speed and very high distance media. It consists of a single strand of fiberglass that carries the signals. The light source that is generally used with single-mode fiber is a laser, although light-emitting diodes (LEDs) might also be used. With single-mode fiber, a single light source is transmitted from end to end and pulsed to create communication. Single-mode fiber is used for long runs because it can transmit data 50 times further than multimode fiber and at a faster rate. For example, single-mode fiber might be used on an organization's corporate campus between buildings. Since the transmission media is glass, the installation of single-mode fiber can be a bit tricky. There are other layers protecting the glass core, but the cable still should not be crimped or pinched around any tight turns. It is, however, completely immune to electrical interference since light is used instead of electrical signals. Figure 1.16 illustrates the layers included in single-mode fiber-optic cable

Multimode Fiber

Multimode fiber-optic cable (MMF) also uses light to communicate a signal, but the light is dispersed into numerous paths as it travels through the core and is reflected back by cladding that lines the core. Multimode fiber provides high bandwidth at high speeds over medium distances (up to about 3000 feet) but can be inconsistent for very long runs. Because of this, multimode fiber is generally used within a smaller area of a building whereas single mode might be used between buildings. Multimode fiber is available in glass or in a plastic version that makes installation easier and increases installation flexibility. As with single-mode fiber, multimode fiber can be used when electrical interference is present, since it is completely immune to that interference. For example, multimode fiber might be used today to provide communication connections in a building that go through an elevator shaft. Figure 1.17 shows the how light is split into multiple paths in a multimode fiber-optic cable.

FIGURE 1.16 Single-mode fiber-optic cable

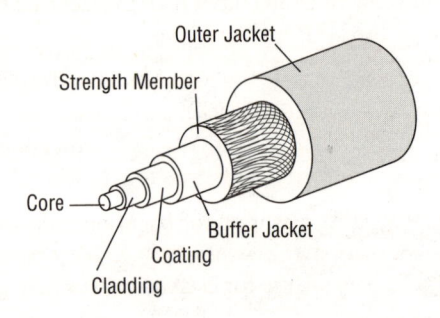

FIGURE 1.17 A multimode fiber-optic cable

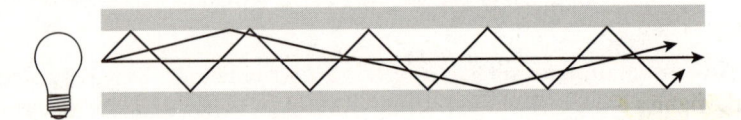

Exam Essentials

Know and be able to recognize common media types. The most common media types are twisted-pair cable, coaxial cable, and fiber optic cable. You should be able to recognize the most common media types given a picture or description.

Describe how common media types are used. You should know how the most common media types are used to transfer data throughout the network. You should be able to differentiate between copper based twisted-pair cables and fiber-optic cables. You should also know how each type might be used in a network.

Know the characteristics of Category 3 cable. Category 3 cable is a copper twisted-pair cable that can carry signal at a maximum of 10Mbps without suffering from crosstalk. This type of cable is rarely used in networks today.

Describe the characteristics of Category 5 cable. Category 5 cable, the most common cable type today, is a copper twisted-pair cable that can carry signals at a maximum rate of 100Mbps without suffering from crosstalk. Category 5 cable is used to connect computers and many other devices within a LAN.

List the characteristics of Category 5e cable. Category 5e cable is a copper twisted-pair cable that can carry signals at a maximum rate of 1000Mbps without suffering from crosstalk. This is one of the most commonly installed cables today.

Know the characteristics of Category 6 cable. Category 6 cable is a copper twisted-pair cable that can carry signals at maximum rate of 1000Mbps without suffering from crosstalk. This is also one of the most commonly installed cables today.

Describe the characteristics of UTP. Unshielded twisted-pair (UTP) cable is the most common type of cable used today. It does not provide any shielding other than the fact that the wires are twisted. Most of the cable standards include the UTP type of cable.

Know the characteristics of STP. Shielded twisted-pair (STP) cable is used to reduce the effect of EMI on cables in environments that contain large sources of EMI, such as electric motors or fluorescent light ballasts. STP includes a foil shield that provides that added protection. STP is rarely used in today's networks because it has been replaced by fiber-optic cable.

List the characteristics of coaxial cable. Coaxial cable was used for backbone segments and for bus topology networks in the late 1980s. The entire signal on a coaxial cable is transmitted through the core wire in the center of the cable. The main use for coaxial cable today is to connect cable modems to the cable provider's connection.

Know the characteristics of single-mode fiber. Single-mode fiber optic cable is a very high speed and high distance media. It generally uses a laser beam to concentrate and pulse light on a single strand of fiber. Single-mode fiber is typically used to provide a backbone for buildings on an organization's campus.

List the characteristics of multimode fiber. Multimode fiber-optic cable also uses light to transmit a signal, but the light is dispersed within the cable, causing it to travel numerous paths called modes. Each of these modes is part of the communication process that is used. Multimode fiber can provide very high bandwidth for short distances, but it can become inconsistent for very long runs, over 3000 feet. This fiber is most often used as a backbone for a LAN within a single building.

1.6 Identifying Network Components

As we said, the components that are used in a network have a tremendous effect on the capabilities of the network and on your ability to control traffic within the network. Network components have evolved with time because of the need to create fast, efficient network designs for many computers. In this section we discuss the major types of network components and their effect on your network design.

Critical Information

You should be able to identify the purpose, features, and functions of each of the main network components. In this section, we discuss each of these components in detail.

Hubs

A *hub* is a device that has multiple ports into which connections can be made. All connections made to a hub are also connected to each other. A hub does not filter any communication or provide any intelligence in regard to the data stream; it simply lets all of the information flow through it and connects anything and everything that is connected to it. Hubs are generally used to connect network segments of computers that are physically close to each other, such as all of the computers on one floor of a building or in a computer classroom. There are two major types of hubs: active and passive. An *active* hub is generally plugged into a power source so that it can amplify signals as well as connect them. A *passive* hub provides connectivity but no power. An example of a passive hub is a patch panel in a network closet.

Switches

A *switch* (also called a LAN switch) resembles a hub from the outside, but that is where the resemblance stops. Switches are considerably more expensive than hubs because of the advantages they offer. Whereas a hub simply lets traffic flow through it, a switch controls traffic through it to automatically optimize traffic flow on your network. A switch learns the physical address (MAC address) of all of the devices that are connected to it and then uses it to control traffic flow. Rather than forwarding all data to all of the connected ports, a switch can forward data only to the port where the computer with the destination address actually exists. This process automatically segments the network and dramatically decreases the traffic in the segments that are less used. Because of this, switches are often used to connect departments of a company so that communication between departments does not affect the other departments that are not involved in the communication. Also, large files can be transferred within in the same department without affecting the traffic in any of the other departments. In addition, switches can be used to create virtual local area networks (VLANs), which improve the flexibility of a network design. (We will discuss VLANs in Chapter 3, "Domain 3 Network Implementation.")

Bridges

Bridges are similar to switches in that they can provide some intelligence to segment a network. Bridges, like switches, can learn the MAC address of each of the hosts connected to them and use that address to control traffic to each of the host's ports. Bridges, however, are slower than switches, so they have been largely replaced by switches as a device that is used to segment traffic. You should be aware of two main types of Ethernet bridges:

Transparent bridge   A transparent bridge can connect two dissimilar networks but is "invisible" to both networks and does not provide translation of any kind. For example, if your network contained two Ethernet segments with one Token Ring segment between them, a transparent bridge could connect communication from one of the Ethernet segments, through the Token Ring segment, to the other Ethernet segment. The Ethernet traffic would not be interpreted by the Token Ring segment.

Translational bridge   A translational bridge, as you might expect, actually performs a translation between two dissimilar networks. For example, if you wanted to translate data from an Ethernet segment to a Token Ring segment, you could use a translational bridge.

Routers

Routers are devices that forward traffic from one network (or subnet) to another. Routers first determine whether the traffic belongs on their network; then they deliver the traffic that belongs on their network to the appropriate network hosts and forward the traffic that does not belong on their network to another router. Routers determine where to forward traffic by consulting a routing table. The routing table can be manually entered by an administrator, or it can be learned by the router by using routing protocols. Routers are the devices that connect the Internet and make the World Wide Web possible. They use a higher level of intelligence than that of bridges or switches. (We will discuss routing in greater detail in Chapter 2, "Domain 2 Protocols and Standards.")

Gateways

Actually, the term *gateway* refers more to a network role than a network device. Any device that is used to translate data from one format to another can be called a gateway. For example, a router that can route data from an Internetwork Package Exchange (IPX) network to an Internet Protocol (IP) network so that it can be understood by the IP network can be considered a gateway. Gateways can also be special servers whose main job is to translate protocols between two networks, such as a Systems Network Architecture (SNA) gateway between an IBM mainframe network and a Microsoft Windows network. The gateway is always positioned logically between the two networks that it will translate.

CSU/DSU

Channel Service Unit/Data Service Unit (CSU/DSU) is a converter used between a LAN and a WAN. Conversion of information is necessary because the technologies that are used in the WAN environment are very different from those used in a LAN environment. The CSU/DSU changes signal from one digital format to another. Originally, the CSU/DSU was always a separate component, but now many routers have this function built into them.

NICs

Network interface cards (NICs) are used to connect a computer to the network. A network interface card is like a small computer in itself. Its job is to translate a stream serial data (one bit at a time) into several streams of parallel data that will be used by the computer. The network interface card also examines every packet on the network cable to determine if the packet has a destination MAC address that matches its MAC address. If it does not, then the NIC does nothing more with the packet, but if the address does match then the NIC will forward the packet to the appropriate port of the computer based on the information contained in the packet. (We will discuss ports in greater detail in Chapter 2.)

ISDN Adapters

Integrated Services Digital Network (ISDN) is a service that was developed by telephone companies in the early 1990s. It was originally intended to provide individuals with a type of simultaneous voice and data communications capability. Since the Internet was in its infancy, and the World Wide Web did not exist, ISDN was ahead of its time. Today's networks use ISDN as a backup line for other communication lines that provide greater bandwidth. The device that connects an organization's equipment to the telephone company's ISDN line and converts the signal so that it can be sent over the line is called an ISDN terminal adapter. These devices are often built into the latest network equipment.

Wireless Access Point

A *wireless access point (WAP)* is a hub that is used by wireless devices. Typically, a WAP looks just like any other hub except that it has an antenna. The WAP is connected to the wired network of an organization so that any devices that can make a wireless connection to it will also be connected to the wired network. Wireless devices typically connect to the WAP using the 2.4GHz radio frequency. Since wireless networks are continuing to grow in popularity, you're likely to see many more WAPs. (We will discuss wireless connectivity in greater detail later in this chapter.)

Modems

The term *modem* stands for modulator/demodulator. Modulation is the process of converting digital data into analog data, usually in the form of sound. Demodulation is the reverse of this process, whereby the transmitted sounds are converted back into digital data on the other side of the connection. Modems are typically used to communicate on normal telephone wires using computers. The most common types of modems used on standard telephone lines can communicate at a maximum speed of 56Kbps. It is also possible to use multiple telephone lines simultaneously to increase the speed of communication. A simple 56K modem is built into most of the computers sold today.

Transceivers

The term *transceiver* stands for transmitter/receiver. The transceiver is more of a role in a network than a specific device. Any device that receives data, converts it, and then sends it to another location can be called a transceiver. For example, an NIC is a type of transceiver since it converts serial data into parallel data and then sends it to a port.

Firewalls

A *firewall* is a hardware or software system that is used to separate one computer or network from another one. The most common type of firewall is used to protect a computer or an entire network from unauthorized access from the Internet. Firewalls can also be used to control the flow of data to and from multiple networks within the same organization. Firewalls can be programmed to filter data packets based on the information that is contained in the packets.

Exam Essentials

Know the major network components.   The major components in today's networks include hubs, switches, bridges, routers, gateways, CSU/DSUs, NICs, ISDN Adapters, WAPs, modems, transceivers, and firewalls. You should be able to describe the purpose of each network component and its role in the network.

Be able to describe the functionality of each network component.   You should know how each of the major network components function. For example, you should know whether a component has any intelligence or makes any decisions about the traffic flow within a network. You should be able to differentiate between the types of network components and their capability to control network traffic.

List the characteristics of a hub.   A hub is a device with multiple ports that is used to connect devices on a network. A hub only connects devices and does not provide any intelligence or filtering. Two types of hubs are generally used in networks: active hubs (which also serve as multiport repeaters) and passive hubs (which are generally called patch panels).

Know the characteristics of a switch.   Switches (also called LAN switches) resemble hubs on the outside but perform filtering that hubs cannot handle. The filtering that is performed by the switches is based on the MAC address of the devices that are connected through the switch. The switches build a table of the MAC addresses and then use it to segment network traffic. Switches can be used to create VLANs, which can improve the flexibility of network design.

Describe the characteristics of a bridge.   Bridges are similar to switches in that they filter network traffic based on the MAC addresses of devices that are connected through them. Bridges can be used to connect dissimilar networks. The two main types of bridges are transparent and translational.

List the characteristics of a router.   Routers are devices that forward traffic from one network to another. Routers use a logical address and a routing table to determine whether network traffic belongs on their network or on another network. The routing table can be entered by an administrator or it can be learned by using routing protocols.

Describe the characteristics of a gateway. The term *gateway* refers to a network role of translating data from one format or protocol to another. The gateway can be only one of many roles on a device, or the device can be dedicated to that one role. One of the most common gateways is the IBM SNA gateway, which connects a mainframe or mini-mainframe computer to a network environment.

Know the characteristics of a CSU/DSU. A CSU/DSU is a converter used between a LAN and a WAN environment. This conversion is necessary because of the difference in the technologies that are used in the two environments. The CSU/DSU was originally a separate device, but now many routers have this function built into them.

List the characteristics of an NIC. A network interface card (NIC) is used to connect a computer to the network and facilitate communication. The NIC converts serial and parallel data to and from the computer and is also responsible for examining every packet of a data stream to determine whether that packet has a destination address that matches its own address. If the address matches, then the NIC receives the information and sends it to the correct port in the computer. If it does not match, then the NIC simply ignores the packet and does not process it any further.

Know the characteristics of an ISDN adapter. ISDN adapters were originally developed by the telephone company to convert signals so that telephone and computer equipment could use their ISDN lines. Today's networks sometimes use ISDN but the adapters are often built into the network equipment.

Describe the characteristics of a wireless access point. A wireless access point (WAP) is a hub that is used by wireless devices to connect them to a wired network. Wireless devices generally use a wireless NIC to connect to the WAP, which in turn provides a connection to a network or to the Internet. Wireless technology is growing in popularity.

Know the characteristics of a modem. You should know that the term *modem* stands for modulator/demodulator because the purpose of a modem is to convert digital signals to analog signal in the form of sounds (modulation) and to convert the sounds into the form of digital signals on the other end (demodulation). The 56K modem is the most commonly used modem on regular telephone lines today. A 56K modem in generally built into most desktop and laptop computers that are sold today.

List the characteristics of a transceiver. The term *transceiver* stands for transmitter/receiver. A transceiver is more of a role for a device than a device itself. Any device that can receive data, convert it, and then transmit it can be considered a transceiver.

Identify the characteristics of a firewall. A firewall is a hardware or software system that is used to separate one computer network from another. Firewalls are often used to protect a computer network from the Internet and can be programmed to filter packets based on the information that is contained in the packets.

1.7 Specifying the Characteristics of Wireless Technologies

One of the newest and most exciting forms of communication is *wireless* communication. This type of communication is still in its infancy, and many competing standards exist. Wireless networks, if properly installed, can add to the flexibility on your network. To properly install a wireless network you must be familiar with wireless networking standards. In this section, we discuss wireless networking standards and their effect on your network design.

Critical Information

You should know about the most common wireless standards used in today's networks. Specifically, you should be familiar with their carrier speed, frequency, transmission type, and topology. In this section, we discuss these characteristics in regard to each of the most common wireless technologies.

802.11

802.11 is the IEEE specification created for wireless LAN technology. 802.11 specifies an over-the-air interface between a wireless client and a base station or between two wireless clients. The IEEE accepted the specification in 1997. The original 802.11 standard used a frequency hopping spread spectrum radio (FHSS) signal. There have been many revisions to the standard since then. The following are the major 802.11 standards in use today. 802.11x represents the family of standards that use the direct sequence spread spectrum (DSSS) radio signal. Table 1.10 compares the characteristics of 802.11 wireless technologies.

802.11a Uses orthogonal frequency division multiplexing to increase bandwidth. This standard uses the 5GHz radio band and can transmit at up to 54Mbps. It is not widely used today.

802.11b Uses DSSS in the 2.4GHz radio band. This standard can transmit at up to 11Mbps with fallback rates of 5.5Mbps, 2Mbps, and 1Mbps. It is one of the most commonly used standards today.

802.11g Uses DSSS and the 2.4GHz radio band. This standard enhances the 802.11b standard and can transmit at speeds up to 54Mbps.

Infrared

The term *infrared* means "below red." In other words, infrared communication is communication made possible by light that is below red in the color spectrum of light. Human beings cannot see this light, but we can build devices that can transmit and receive it. To make use of this light, a group of manufacturers known as the Infrared Data Association (IrDA) developed a standard in the late 1990s. Many manufacturers have adopted this standard for use with the devices that they manufacture. Because of this, many devices now have the distinctive infrared port that allows them to communicate with other devices without the use of wires. The biggest difference between infrared and other wireless technologies is that infrared requires "line of sight" communications between devices. Also, infrared does not work well in bright sunlight.

Bluetooth

Bluetooth is a short-range radio technology that was developed by Ericsson, IBM, Intel, Nokia, and Toshiba. Many products sold today use Bluetooth technology, including printers, mice, keyboards, scanners, and many more. All products must pass interoperability testing by the Bluetooth Special Interest Group prior to their release.

Exam Essentials

Be familiar with the main types of wireless networks. The main types of wireless networks are 802.11, Infrared, and Bluetooth. You should be familiar with the each of these types of networks and where they might be used.

Know the main characteristics of the main types of wireless networks. You should know the main characteristics such as carrier speed, frequency, transmission type, and topology for the main types of wireless networks.

List the characteristics of 802.11x components. The 802.11x specification refers to the family of standards that use DSSS, usually on the 2.4GHz radio band. The most common of these are the 802.11b and 802.11g standards.

Know the characteristics of 802.11a. 802.11a is a standard for wireless communication that uses OFDM on the 5GHz radio band. 802.11a, which can communicate at a maximum rate of 54Mbps, is rarely used in today's networks.

Describe the characteristics of 802.11b. 802.11b is a standard for wireless communication that uses DSSS on the 2.4GHz radio band. 802.11b, which can communicate at a maximum rate of 11Mbps, is in common use in many networks today.

List the characteristics of 802.11g. 802.11g is a standard for wireless communication that uses DSSS on the 2.4GHz radio band. 802.11g, which can communicate at a maximum rate of 54Mbps, is in common use in many networks today.

Know the characteristics of infrared. The term *infrared* means "below red." Infrared light is light that humans cannot see, but we can use it to control devices and to communicate to them. The standards for the use of infrared light have been developed by the Infrared Data Association (IrDA). Infrared devices require a line-of-sight connection with a device in order to communicate effectively. Many devices are now including infrared capability.

1.8 Identifying Wireless Service Performance Factors

Since wireless services are continuing to grow in popularity, we are beginning to see wireless devices used in many different types of environments. While most wireless protocols work properly in the "perfect environment," most of them also become challenged in the real world. In this section, we discuss the real-world factors that affect wireless communications.

Critical Information

You should know the factors that might affect the range and speed of wireless device that you use. In this section, we discuss the most common of these factors.

Radio Interference

To understand how radio interference can be a problem in a wireless network, you have to consider the access method that the wireless network uses: Carrier Sense Multiple Access with Collision Avoidance (CSMA/CA). This means that a device will wait until no other device appears to be using the frequency before it sends its data over the frequency. If the network is close to an operating 2.4GHz phone, a microwave oven, or a Bluetooth device, it might sense that the network is in use and wait for the offending interference to subside before it sends its data. Also, if the interference is sporadic, the communication might be interrupted during a transmission. This would cause the data to become corrupted and would force the device to resend the data. In this case, the device might still operate but much more slowly than normal. To keep radio interference from affecting your networks, identify the sources and try to eliminate them wherever possible. Also, keeping devices in close proximity to the WAP will help to reduce the effects of interference, since the true signal will overpower the interference.

Antenna Type

Because your wireless network operates using radio waves, the sensitivity of the antenna that is used in your network can increase the range and speed of the communication. A huge variety of antennas are available from commercial sources. These include directional and omni-directional models for indoor and outdoor use. Network enthusiasts have even developed operational antennae from common household objects such as a tin can or an emptied potato chip can. The type of antenna that you use in your network will depend on the placement of the computers that require connectivity to the network. Often, the antenna that is built into the WAP is the only antenna that you will need.

Environmental Factors

While radio waves do not require line of sight in order to communicate properly, they are affected by some environmental factors. Simple factors such as the materials with which the building was constructed can affect the range and speed of your wireless network. Since you cannot see the radio waves, you have to experiment a little to determine the best method of deploying your WAPs.

You can begin experimenting by placing WAPs in "best guess" locations and then walking around your network with a laptop equipped with a wireless NIC to determine where the signal is strongest and where it becomes weak. You can then change the location of a WAP or add another WAP as you begin to get a sense of the network's tendencies within your building.

Another way to optimize your network is to purchase equipment that will provide a spread spectrum analysis of radio transmissions in your building in a graphical format that allows you to "see" the radio waves as they travel through your building. This type of equipment can also identify and isolate other types of radio waves that might cause interference in your network. In either case, your goal is to eliminate as much interference as possible and keep signal strength to a maximum wherever possible.

Exam Essentials

Know the factors that might affect the range and speed of your wireless network communications. The range and speed of the network might be affected by interference, antenna types, and environmental conditions. You should be able to identify options that might improve these characteristics within your network.

Describe how wireless networks are affected. Wireless networks might be affected by such factors as interference, antenna type, and environmental factors. Be familiar with the methods of troubleshooting these factors to provide for the maximum range and speed of your wireless network.

Understand how radio interference can affect computer communication. Radio interference can keep wireless devices from communicating effectively. Part of the reason for this is the fact that the wireless devices use a CSMA/CA access method, which ensures that a medium is clear before trying to send information onto it. Know how to diagnose a problem caused by another wireless device, such as a Bluetooth device, and how to solve the problem by either removing the false signal or strengthening the real signal.

Know how antenna type can affect wireless communications. The type of antenna used in a wireless network can dramatically affect the range and direction of signal. Some antennas are designed to be very sensitive to signals in one direction only (directional), while others are designed to receive signals in the same manner in all directions (omni-directional). The antenna that is included on the WAP is often the only antenna needed for a wireless network.

Understand how environmental factors can affect wireless communications. Environmental factors such as the type of building or the construction of walls in a building can have a dramatic effect on a wireless network. You can optimize your network by experimenting with the best placement of WAPs in the building so as to avoid the pitfalls caused by the environmental factors. In addition, you can purchase special software that will give you a graphical representation of radio wave behavior in your building and assist you in finding other sources of interference.

Review Questions

1. Which logical network topology uses a hub as a central point of communication for all of the devices on a segment?

    A. Ring
    B. Star
    C. Mesh
    D. All of the above

2. Which network technology uses the CSMA/CD carrier access method to communicate?

    A. Ethernet
    B. Token Ring
    C. FDDI
    D. Bus

3. Which wireless standard uses the 2.4GHz radio band to communicate at speeds up to 54Mbps?

    A. 802.11a
    B. 802.11b
    C. 802.11x
    D. 802.11g

4. What is the maximum distance that a device can transmit a signal if it uses a 100BASE-FX standard?

    A. 2000 meters
    B. 2 kilometers
    C. 20 kilometers
    D. 200 kilometers

5. What is the name of the registered jack connector that is used on most network devices?

    A. RJ-11
    B. Category 5
    C. ST
    D. RJ-45

6. What IEEE specification is assigned to the FireWire cable standard?

    A. 802.11x
    B. Category 5e
    C. 1394
    D. 802.5

7. What is the maximum data transmission speed for Category 5e cable?
   A. 100Mbps
   B. 1000Mbps
   C. 10,000Mbps
   D. 100,000Mbps

8. Which type of device can be used to segment a network *and to* create VLANs?
   A. Bridge
   B. Router
   C. Hub
   D. Switch

9. Which type of wireless communication uses light and requires line of sight to operate properly?
   A. Infrared
   B. 802.11x
   C. DSSS
   D. 802.11g

10. Which type of carrier access method is used by 802.11 devices?
   A. CSMA/CD
   B. Token passing
   C. WAP
   D. CSMA/CA

11. In which of the following technologies would MSAUs be used?
   A. FDDI
   B. IBM Token Ring
   C. Ethernet
   D. Wireless

12. Which of the following are the principle speeds of the IBM Token Ring technology? (Choose all that apply.)
   A. 4Kbps
   B. 16Mbps
   C. 4Mbps
   D. 8Mbps

13. In the term 100BASE-TX, the "T" represents which of the following?
    A. Transmission speed
    B. Terminal adapter
    C. Twisted-pair cable
    D. Twin direction signals

14. Which of following media types uses twisted-pair cable with an extra foil shield to guard against EMI?
    A. Thinnet
    B. Thicknet
    C. UTP
    D. STP

15. Which of the following devices converts LAN technologies to WAN technologies, and vice versa?
    A. Router
    B. Switch
    C. Bridge
    D. CSU/DSU

Answers to Review Questions

1. B. A star topology uses a hub as a central point of communication. A ring topology uses a multiple station access unit. A mesh topology does not have a central hub.

2. A. Ethernet uses the CSMA/CD carrier access method to communicate. Token Ring and FDDI use a token-passing method. Bus is a topology, not a technology.

3. D. The IEEE 802.11g wireless standard uses the 2.4GHz radio band to communicate at 54Mbps. The 802.11a standard uses the 5Ghz band to communicate at 54Mbps, but is not widely used. The 802.11b standard uses the 2.4GHz band to communicate at 11Mbps. 802.11x is the general name for the widely used family that uses DSSS on the 2.4GHz band.

4. C. The maximum distance the 100BASE-FX can transmit is 20 kilometers.

5. D. The registered jack that is used on most network devices is called RJ-45. An RJ-11 is used for normal telephone connections. Category 5 is a cable standard, not a registered jack. ST is a connector used for fiber-optic connections, and is not a registered jack connector.

6. C. IEEE 1394 is widely known as FireWire. 802.11x is the family of wireless standards that use 2.4GHz radio band and a DSSS method of transmission. Category 5e is a cable standard used for Gigabit Ethernet. 802.5 is the IEEE standard used for IBM Token Ring networks.

7. B. The maximum transmission speed for Category 5e cable is 1000Mbps (1Gbps).

8. D. A switch is the only device listed that can be used to segment a network and create VLANs. A bridge can be used to segment a network, but it cannot be used to create VLANs. A router can be used to segment a network, but also cannot be used to create VLANs. A hub can neither segment a network nor create VLANs.

9. A. Infrared wireless communication uses light and requires line of sight to operate properly. 802.11x uses the 2.4Ghz radio band. DSSS is a signaling method used by most 802.11x devices. 802.11g uses the 2.4GHz radio band.

10. D. 802.11 devices use the Carrier Sense Multiple Access with Collision Avoidance (CSMA/CA) method of carrier access. This means that they send a small signal to check media before they send the main signal. Token passing is used by ring networks. A wireless access point (WAP) is a transceiver device that is used with 802.11.

11. B. Multiple-station access units (MSAUs) are special hubs that are used in the Token Ring technology.

12. B, C. The two principle speeds of Token Ring are 4Mbps and 16Mbps. You must set the network card for the appropriate speed when you install it on a Token Ring network.

13. C. In terms such as 100BASE-TX the "T" always represents that twisted-pair cable is being used.

14. D. Shielded twisted-pair (STP) cable uses twisted-pair wires (as the name implies) with an extra foil shield to guard against electromagnetic interference (EMI). Thinnet and thicknet are coaxial cable types. Unshielded twisted pair (UTP) does not use a foil shield.

15. D. A CSU/DSU is a device that converts local area network (LAN) technologies to wide area network (WAN) technologies, and vice versa. Routers are used in LAN and WAN environments, but are not converters. Switches and bridges are primarily used in a LAN environment and are not converters.

Chapter 2

Domain 2 Protocols and Standards

COMPTIA NETWORK+ EXAM OBJECTIVES COVERED IN THIS CHAPTER:

✓ **2.1 Identify a MAC (Media Access Control) address and its parts.**

✓ **2.2 Identify the seven layers of the OSI (Open Systems Interconnect) model and their functions.**

✓ **2.3 Identify the OSI (Open Systems Interconnect) layers at which the following components operate:**
  - Hubs
  - Switches
  - Bridges
  - Routers
  - NICs (Network Interface Card)
  - WAPs (Wireless Access Point)

✓ **2.4 Differentiate between the following protocols in terms of routing, addressing schemes, interoperability, and naming conventions:**
  - IPX/SPX (Internetwork Packet Exchange/Sequence Packet Exchange)
  - NetBEUI (Network Basic Input/Output System Extended User Interface)
  - AppleTalk/AppleTalk over IP (Internet Protocol)
  - TCP/IP (Transmission Control Protocol/Internet Protocol)

✓ **2.5 Identify the components and structure of IP (Internet Protocol) addresses (IPv4, IPv6) and the required setting for connections across the Internet.**

✓ **2.6 Identify classful IP (Internet Protocol) ranges and their subnet masks (For example: Class A, B and C).**

✓ **2.7 Identify the purpose of subnetting.**

- ✓ **2.8 Identify the differences between private and public network addressing schemes.**
- ✓ **2.9 Identify and differentiate between the following IP (Internet Protocol) addressing methods:**
  - Static
  - Dynamic
  - Self-assigned (APIPA (Automatic Private Internet Protocol Addressing))
- ✓ **2.10 Define the purpose, function and use of the following protocols used in the TCP/IP (Transmission Control Protocol/Internet Protocol) suite:**
  - TCP (Transmission Control Protocol)
  - UDP (User Datagram Protocol)
  - FTP (File Transfer Protocol)
  - SFTP (Secure File Transfer Protocol)
  - TFTP (Trivial File Transfer Protocol)
  - SMTP (Simple Mail Transfer Protocol)
  - HTTP (Hypertext Transfer Protocol)
  - HTTPS (Hypertext Transfer Protocol Secure)
  - POP3 / IMAP4 (Post Office Protocol version 3 / Internet Message Access Protocol version 4)
  - Telnet
  - SSH (Secure Shell)
  - ICMP (Internet Control Message Protocol)
  - ARP / RARP (Address Resolution Protocol / Reverse Address Resolution Protocol)
  - NTP (Network Time Protocol)
  - NNTP (Network News Transport Protocol)
  - SCP (Secure Copy Protocol)
  - LDAP (Lightweight Directory Access Protocol)
  - IGMP (Internet Group Multicast Protocol)
  - LPR (Line Printer Remote)
- ✓ **2.11 Define the function of TCP / UDP (Transmission Control Protocol / User Datagram Protocol) ports.**

✓ **2.12 Identify the well-known ports associated with the following commonly used services and protocols:**
- 20 FTP (File Transfer Protocol)
- 21 FTP (File Transfer Protocol)
- 22 SSH (Secure Shell)
- 23 Telnet
- 25 SMTP (Simple Mail Transfer Protocol)
- 53 DNS (Domain Name Server)
- 69 TFTP (Trivial File Transfer Protocol)
- 80 HTTP (Hypertext Transfer Protocol)
- 110 POP3 (Post Office Protocol version 3)
- 119 NNTP (Network News Transport Protocol)
- 123 NTP (Network Time Protocol)
- 143 IMAP4 (Internet Message Access Protocol version 4)
- 443 HTTPS (Hypertext Transfer Protocol Secure)

✓ **2.13 Identify the purpose of network services and protocols (For example: DNS (Domain Name Service), NAT (Network Address Translation), ICS (Internet Connection Sharing), WINS (Windows Internet Name Service), SNMP (Simple Network Management Protocol), NFS (Network File System), Zeroconf (Zero Configuration), SMB (Server Message Block), AFP (Apple File Protocol), and LPD (Line Printer Daemon)).**

✓ **2.14 Identify the basic characteristics (For example: speed, capacity, and media) of the following WAN (Wide Area Networks) technologies:**
- Packet switching
- Circuit switching
- ISDN (Integrated Services Digital Network)
- FDDI (Fiber Distributed Data Interface)
- T1 (T Carrier level 1) / E1 / J1
- T3 (T Carrier level 3) / E3 / J3
- OCx (Optical Carrier)
- X.25

✓ **2.15 Identify the basic characteristics of the following internet access technologies:**
- xDSL (Digital Subscriber Line)
- Broadband Cable (Cable Modem)
- POTS / PSTN (Plain Old Telephone Service / Public Switched Telephone Network)
- Satellite
- Wireless

✓ **2.16 Define the function of the following remote access protocols and services:**
- RAS (Remote Access Service)
- PPP (Point-to-Point Protocol)
- SLIP (Serial Line Internet Protocol)
- PPPoE (Point-to-Point Protocol over Ethernet)
- PPTP (Point-to-Point Tunneling Protocol)
- VPN (Virtual Private Network)
- RDP (Remote Desktop Protocol)

✓ **2.17 Identify the following security protocols and describe their purpose and function:**
- IPSec (Internet Protocol Security)
- L2TP (Layer 2 Tunneling Protocol)
- SSL (Secure Sockets Layer)
- WEP (Wired Equivalent Privacy)
- WPA (Wi-Fi Protected Access)
- 802.1x

✓ **2.18 Identify authentication protocols (For example: CHAP (Challenge Handshake Authentication Protocol), MS-CHAP (Microsoft Challenge Handshake Authentication Protocol), PAP (Password Authentication Protocol), RADIUS (Remote Authentication Dial-In User Service), Kerberos, and EAP (Extensible Authentication Protocol)).**

As we mentioned in Chapter 1, "Domain 1 Media and Topologies," three components are essential in any network in order for computers to be able to communicate: a network media and topology, a common protocol, and a network client or service. In this chapter, we discuss the second component: the protocol. While many different types of protocols are in use today, all protocols have one thing in common: they are a set of rules by which a network or a group of components behave in order to communicate.

The types of protocols that you utilize will depend largely on the type of network you are using. Some protocols are much more common than others. Many protocols can stand on their own, whereas others are part of a larger suite of protocols. You can use protocols to facilitate communication as well as to secure communication, but you must understand protocols in order to make effective use of them. You should be aware of the many different protocols in use today and understand how they work together—and in some cases how they don't work together.

In this chapter, we start by discussing the factors that protocols have in common and how we can identify different types of protocols. We will also identify the types of network components that are most likely to use each type of protocol. After we have discussed the commonalities of protocols, we will then turn our attention to the differences in various protocols. We will also define each of the protocols as it relates to the entire model of communication, namely the Open System Interconnection (OSI) model. You should understand protocols in general terms as well as the many specific protocols in various protocol suites.

2.1 Identifying a MAC Address and Its Parts

A unique *Media Access Control (MAC) address* is "burned into" each *network interface card (NIC)* (pronounced "nick") by the manufacturer of the NIC. The MAC address is a six-byte hexadecimal address that consists of two distinct parts. Each byte of the address consists of two hexadecimal digits. Bytes are separated by a hyphen (-). The first three bytes identify the manufacturer that created the NIC. The last three bytes should be unique for each NIC that the manufacturer produces. The purpose of this unique address is to identify the NIC, and therefore the computer in which it is installed. Identifying each computer uniquely allows computers and software to address packets directly to that computer. Other NICs will then identify the packets as not being intended for the computer to which they are installed. In this section, we discuss how to identify a MAC address on a computer and the two components associated with the MAC address.

> **NOTE:** For more information on MAC addresses, see Chapter 2 of the *Network+ Study Guide, Fourth Edition* (ISBN: 0-7821-5506-3) from Sybex.

Critical Information

You should understand that the MAC address is also referred to as a physical address of a component. This is partially because it's usually burned into the device at the factory. Every NIC has its own unique MAC address that identifies it on the network. When it is installed in a computer, it becomes the unique identifier for that computer in the network. You should also understand that a MAC address has two distinct parts, and you should know what each part signifies.

Identifying a MAC Address

You can identify the MAC address of your local Windows 98, Windows NT, Windows 2000, Windows XP, or Windows Server 2003 computer by typing **ipconfig /all** at the command prompt. The physical address that is listed in the output is the MAC address. As you can see in Figure 2.1, the MAC address of the computer shown is 00-05-1B-00-4B-F6. On a Linux computer, you should use a similar command called `ifconfig`, which shows configuration information and allows you to change it as well.

FIGURE 2.1 An `ipconfig /all` output showing the physical (MAC) address of a computer

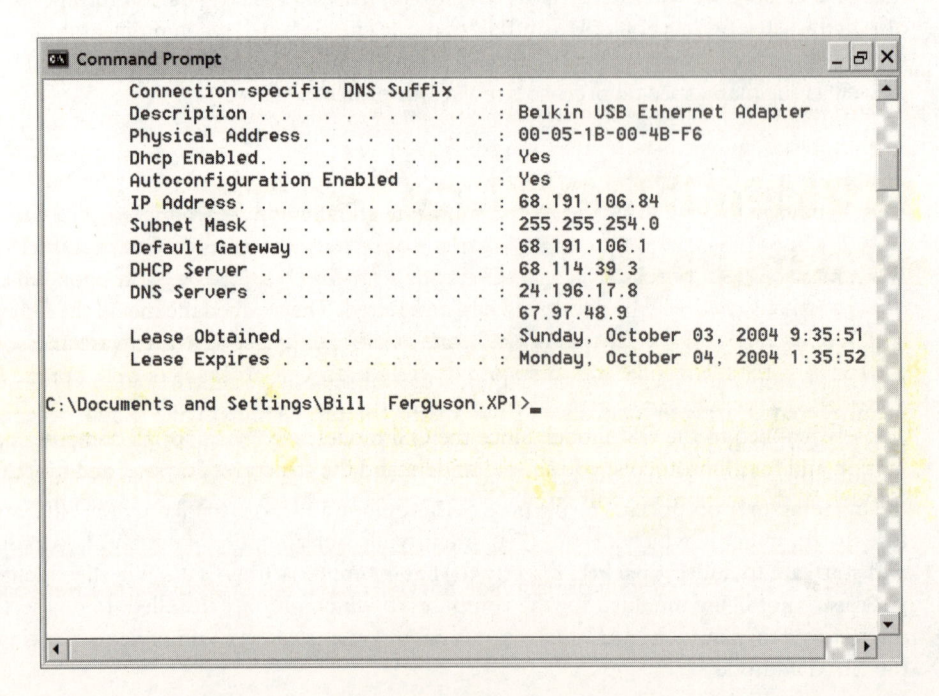

```
Connection-specific DNS Suffix  . :
Description . . . . . . . . . . . : Belkin USB Ethernet Adapter
Physical Address. . . . . . . . . : 00-05-1B-00-4B-F6
Dhcp Enabled. . . . . . . . . . . : Yes
Autoconfiguration Enabled . . . . : Yes
IP Address. . . . . . . . . . . . : 68.191.106.84
Subnet Mask . . . . . . . . . . . : 255.255.254.0
Default Gateway . . . . . . . . . : 68.191.106.1
DHCP Server . . . . . . . . . . . : 68.114.39.3
DNS Servers . . . . . . . . . . . : 24.196.17.8
                                    67.97.48.9
Lease Obtained. . . . . . . . . . : Sunday, October 03, 2004 9:35:51
Lease Expires . . . . . . . . . . : Monday, October 04, 2004 1:35:52

C:\Documents and Settings\Bill Ferguson.XP1>
```

Components of a MAC address

A MAC address is a six-byte hexadecimal address. Hexadecimal numbers are used because of the tremendous number of combinations of addresses that are possible and yet the relative ease of which the number can be read. (A six-byte MAC address can yield 281,474,976,710,655 addressing possibilities.) The first three bytes of the MAC address indicate the manufacturer of the NIC (in Figure 2.1, 00-05-1B is an Organizational Identifier [OI] for Belkin). (Some manufacturers use more than one OI.) The last three bytes are a unique number from that manufacturer. This address should be unique in the world!

Exam Essentials

Know what a MAC address is and how to identify the MAC address on a computer. A MAC address is a hexadecimal address that is burned into every NIC by the manufacturer. The MAC address is also referred to as a physical address, which you can identify on a local computer by typing `ipconfig /all` on a command line.

Know the components of a MAC address. A MAC address is a six-byte hexadecimal address that uniquely identifies a NIC (pronounced "nick") and its manufacturer. The first three bytes represent the manufacturer of the NIC and the last three bytes should be unique to that manufacturer's Organizational Identifier (OI).

2.2 Identifying the Seven Layers of the OSI Model and Their Functions

To understand anything and then develop it you need a way to relate to it, and computer communication is no exception. As computer communication became a reality, we needed a common language that we could use to communicate about computer communication. In the early 1980s representatives from over 60 countries, collectively known as the International Standards Organization (ISO), decided on and developed a model of communication upon which hardware and software could be developed and connected. They named the model the *Open System Interconnection (OSI) model* and then began to use it to create new hardware and software.

Initially, the OSI model was supposed to include an OSI protocol as well, but the OSI protocol was never fully developed. Every protocol that has been developed, however, can be loosely mapped to the OSI model. Since the OSI model is the basis for all computer communication and for all protocols, you should understand the structure, purpose, and function of the model. In this section, we will discuss how each of the layers of the OSI model function.

> **NOTE** For more information on the OSI model, see Chapter 2 of the *Network+ Study Guide, Fourth Edition.*

Critical Information

You should understand that the OSI model is composed of seven layers. You should be able to describe the function of each layer and how each of the adjacent layers relate to each other. Finally, you should understand that the layers that are not adjacent to each other are independent of one another.

The Seven Layers of the OSI Model

The OSI model is composed of seven layers (see Figure 2.2). Each of the layers has a defined purpose. The layers are numbered from the bottom up. In the sections that follow, we will discuss the name, number, and function of each layer of the model, beginning with the top layer.

FIGURE 2.2 The OSI model

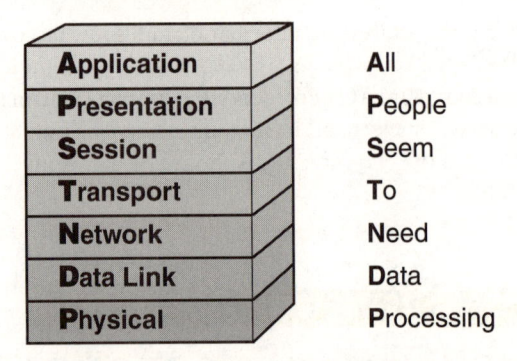

Layer	Mnemonic
Application	All
Presentation	People
Session	Seem
Transport	To
Network	Need
Data Link	Data
Physical	Processing

> **NOTE:** A good way to remember the layers of the OSI model is to remember the mnemonic, "All People Seem To Need Data Processing."

Application Layer

The Application layer, also called Layer 7, is the highest layer in the OSI model. It contains applications that facilitate network communication. These are not applications like Microsoft Word or Excel, but rather application protocols such as Hypertext Transfer Protocol (HTTP) for browsing the World Wide Web or File Transfer Protocol (FTP) for transferring files on networks and over the Web. At the Application layer, the data still resembles something that people can read and interpret.

Presentation Layer

At the Presentation layer (Layer 6) data is first converted into a form that can be sent over a network. At this layer data is compressed and decompressed and encrypted or decrypted, depending on which direction it's traveling. You can think of the Presentation layer as the "translation layer."

Session Layer

The Session layer (Layer 5) is responsible for establishing, synchronizing, maintaining, and then terminating the sessions between computers. It also handles error detection and notification. You can think of the Session layer as the "traffic cop" that directs the network traffic and lets the appropriate traffic flow at the appropriate time.

Transport Layer

The Transport layer (Layer 4) handles the actual processing of data between devices. This layer is responsible for resending any packets that do not receive an acknowledgment from the destination address. It's also responsible for any problems that are associated with fragmentation of packets.

Network Layer

The Network layer (Layer 3) is responsible for providing the mechanism by which data can be moved from computer to computer or from network to network. The Network layer does not actually move the data; instead it provides the addressing information and route discovery that are necessary to move the data to the appropriate location. The Network layer contains many protocols that facilitate these services, including Internet Protocol (IP), Internet Control Message Protocol (ICMP), Internet Group Management Protocol (IGMP), and Address Resolution Protocol (ARP).

Data Link Layer

The Data Link layer (Layer 2) is responsible for sending data to the Physical layer so that it can be put onto the "wire" or network media. The Data Link layer is subdivided into two other layers: the Logical Link Control (LLC) and the Media Access Control (MAC) layers. The LLC connects the Data Link layer to the higher-level protocols such as IP at the Network layer. The MAC layer connects the Data Link layer to the physical connection and provides the MAC address. The Data Link layer also defines the technology that is used for the network. This layer can also perform *checksums,* which are calculations that the system uses to make sure that packets are not damaged in transit.

Physical Layer

The Physical layer (Layer 1) defines the physical characteristics of the network such as the type of cable that must be used as well as the voltage that will be used to transmit data through the network. Since the Physical layer defines these characteristics, it also establishes the topology of the network. Many standards are defined at this layer, such as the IEEE 802.3 standard for Ethernet as well as the IEEE 802.5 standard for Token Ring networks.

Exam Essentials

Be able to list the names and the order of each of the layers of the OSI model. The OSI model has seven layers as follows:

7. Application
6. Presentation

5. Session

4. Transport

3. Network

2. Data Link

1. Physical

Understand the purpose of each layer of the OSI model. You should understand the main purpose and functions of each layer of the OSI model. In addition, you should be familiar with the types of protocols that are found in each layer.

2.3 Identifying the OSI Layers at Which Various Components Operate

Some of your most important responsibilities as a network designer and administrator are to control traffic, keep communication speeds to a maximum, and maintain as much available bandwidth as possible. In order to accomplish these tasks, you must understand the differences in the devices that you can use to construct a network and connect devices. The capabilities of various network devices are dependent in large part on the layer of the OSI model at which they operate. Typically the higher a device can operate in the OSI model, the more intelligence and filtering capabilities it has for the network.

> **Note:** For more information on where various components operate on the OSI model, see Chapter 2 of the *Network+ Study Guide, Fourth Edition*.

Critical Information

You should understand the basic workings of each device, and you should know the layer of the OSI model at which it operates. In this section, we discuss each of the most common devices and the layer of the OSI model at which they operate.

Hubs

A *hub* is a component that operates at the Physical layer. It connects devices but does not provide any intelligence or filtering. Most hubs have a power supply and can therefore also provide amplification of signal, but they do not change the signal in any way except to make it stronger.

Switches

A *switch* is a component that operates at the Data Link layer. As discussed in Chapter 1, switches provide filtering and network segmentation by automatically building a table of MAC addresses and the corresponding port on the switch. After a switch has built its table, it has the effect of creating a permanent virtual circuit (PVC) for each device connected through the switch. By using Layer 2 MAC addresses, switches help you control traffic and make the most of the bandwidth in your network while reducing or eliminating collisions.

Bridges

A *bridge* is a component that operates at the Data Link layer. Bridges can also segment traffic, but they do it using software rather than the faster circuitry that is used by switches. You can also use bridges to connect dissimilar networks or connect similar networks through a dissimilar network. For example, you can use a bridge to connect two Ethernet networks through a Token Ring network. Bridges accomplish this filtering and connecting using a minor level of intelligence based on Layer 2 MAC addresses.

Routers

A *router* is a component that operates at the Network layer. Routers are primarily responsible for two things. They determine whether each packet belongs on their network; then they either deliver the packet if it does belong or they consult their tables to determine where to send the packet. Routers typically communicate with other routers to update their tables so that they can pass packets in any efficient manner. Routers operate at a higher level of intelligence using the Layer 3 IP addresses configured on the network.

Network Interface Card (NIC)

A *network interface card (NIC)* is a component that operates at the Data Link layer and the Physical layer. A NIC is like a little computer within itself. It examines every packet that comes down the wire and determines whether that packet is addressed to it. If it is, then it passes the packet up the OSI model and into the ports of the computer. If it is not, then the NIC ignores the packet. At the same time the NIC converts parallel data coming out of the computer into serial data that can be passed down the network cable.

Wireless Access Points

A *wireless access point (WAP)* is a component that operates at the Physical layer. It connects a device that uses a wireless NIC to a wired network and the resources that the network provides. Wireless access points give you greater flexibility of network design, but you should also consider the inherent security risks.

Exam Essentials

Know the layer of the OSI model at which each network component operates. Hubs and WAPs operate at the Physical layer of the OSI model. Switches and bridges operate at the Data Link layer. Routers operate at the Network layer. NICs operate at the Physical and Data Link layers.

Know the level of intelligence that each of the network components use at their level in the model. You should know the level of intelligence or addressing schemes used by each of the most common network components. In addition, you should know about any filtering, segmentation, or routing that the components can provide for the network based on their respective levels of intelligence.

2.4 Differentiating Between Network Protocols

Protocols are rules of expected behavior in a given circumstance. Many types of network protocols have been established over time for devices that communicate on a network. It is these rules of expected behavior that allow communication to take place on the network. In order for two devices to communicate effectively, they both must be using the same protocol. In this section, we will examine the most common network protocols.

> **NOTE** For more information on protocols, see Chapter 3 of the *Network+ Study Guide, Fourth Edition*.

Critical Information

You should be able to differentiate between the following network protocols in terms of routing, addressing schemes, interoperability, and naming conventions.

IPX/SPX

Internetwork Packet Exchange/Sequenced Packet Exchange (IPX/SPX) is a proprietary protocol developed by Novell for NetWare servers. It is a routable protocol that was popular for many years prior to the Internet and the World Wide Web. It has now been largely replaced by TCP/IP to the point that the last few versions of Novell NetWare have used TCP/IP as their default protocol and have allowed IPX/SPX to be used only if needed. IPX/SPX is interoperable with the newer Microsoft operating systems through a protocol called NWLink that was developed by Microsoft to emulate the IPX/SPX protocol.

IPX/SPX is actually a suite of protocols, much like TCP/IP. You should know the major protocols in the IPX/SPX suite. In the following paragraphs, we will discuss the protocols that compose the IPX/SPX suite and their functions.

IPX

Not surprisingly, *Internetwork Packet Exchange (IPX)* is one of the major protocols in the IPX/SPX suite. IPX is primarily responsible for logical network addressing, route selections, and connection services. Route selections are determined by tables created by other protocols in the IPX/SPX suite. IPX is not a routable protocol and it is connectionless; therefore, it works in conjunction with SPX to provide reliability of communication.

IPX addressing is somewhat less complex than IP addressing, since IPX addresses automatically make use of the MAC address on a computer. The IPX address is a routable address that is a combination of an eight-character hexadecimal address, which is automatically assigned by the first server on the network, and the MAC address assigned to the NIC. In addition, the leading zeros in the network portion of the address are generally dropped. For example, a computer that is installed on the 00AC33CD network and has a NIC installed in it with a MAC address of 00-05-1B-04-02-06 would have an IPX address of AC33CD:00051B040206.

SPX

Sequenced Packet Exchange (SPX) is a routable protocol that adds reliability to IPX. SPX is a connection-oriented protocol, which means that it relies on acknowledgments of packets received. SPX is responsible for fragmenting packets of data and sequencing the data to ensure that the receiving device knows the correct order for the data. SPX is also responsible for reassembling the data on the other side of a connection.

RIP

Routing Information Protocol (RIP) is responsible for the establishment of routes for IPX addressing. It facilitates communication between routers to calculate the most efficient routes between the source and destination on the IPX/SPX network. This communication is usually based on periodic broadcasts and is an older and less efficient method of calculating routes.

NLSP

NetWare Link State Protocol (NLSP) is a newer method of calculating routes that can also be used by IPX/SPX networks. It facilitates the communication between routers so that they can each build a map of the network, and then keeps them up to date about the health or "link state" of each of the paths in the network. Routers can use this information to pass packets from the source address to the destination address in the most efficient manner. Since NLSP does not rely on periodic broadcasts, it makes more efficient use of network bandwidth than does RIP.

SAP

Service Advertising Protocol (SAP) is a protocol used by NetWare to allow systems that provide network services (such as file and print servers) to announce their services and their address to the network. It broadcasts about every 60 seconds. In today's tighter security environment, this type of service advertising may not be as popular as it was before.

NCP

NetWare Core Protocol (NCP) is a connection-oriented protocol that is primarily responsible for providing a connection between the clients and the services on a Novell network.

NetBEUI

NetBEUI stands for NetBIOS with an Extended User Interface. NetBIOS stands for Network Basic Input Output System. Therefore, NetBEUI stands for Network Basic Input Output System with an Extended User Interface. In other words, the NetBEUI protocol is the NetBIOS service with a GUI interface. NetBEUI uses the NetBIOS names assigned by network administrators. These names can be a maximum of 15 characters in length.

NetBEUI is a simple, fast protocol with a very low overhead. It is self-configuring and is therefore sometimes used for very small networks. Its biggest downfall is that it is not routable and therefore cannot be used by larger networks or on the Internet. Table 2.1 highlights the main characteristics of NetBEUI.

TABLE 2.1 Characteristics of NetBEUI

Routable (Yes or No)	Addressing Schemes	Interoperability	Naming Conventions
No	NetBIOS names assigned by administrator	Not interoperable with other protocols, since it is not routable	Uses NetBIOS names that can be a maximum of 15 characters

AppleTalk

The *AppleTalk* protocol suite, as you may have guessed, was designed specifically for Apple computer networks. The AppleTalk suite is made up of several protocols. It is not necessary that you know all of the protocols, but you should know about the following main protocols in the suite:

AppleShare AppleShare provides Application layer services.

AppleTalk over IP AppleTalk over IP allows Macintosh clients to connect to an Apple Remote Network Server (ARNS) using IP over the Internet.

Name Binding Protocol (NBP) NBP maps computer names to Network layer addresses.

EtherTalk Link Access Protocol (ELAP) ELAP is a communications protocol that is compatible with Ethernet.

TokenTalk Link Access Protocol (TLAP) TLAP is a communications protocol that is compatible with the IBM Token Ring protocol.

Zone Information Protocol (ZIP) ZIP divides network devices into logical groups called zones.

AppleTalk node addresses are automatically generated by the computer when it is booted. The network administrator assigns the network number. The full address is a combination of a 16-bit network address followed by an 8-bit node address. Networks with large numbers of users can also use zones to divide the network for administrative purposes.

Because AppleTalk is a proprietary protocol, it is not very interoperable at all. In fact, it can only be used by Macintosh systems. Other systems, such as Microsoft Windows, can provide special support communication with AppleTalk.

AppleTalk is a routable protocol. Routing is enabled by a distance vector routing protocol, much like RIP, called Routing Table Maintenance Protocol (RMTP). RMTP creates and maintains the tables by which routers make decisions.

AppleTalk systems can be assigned names to make it easier for users to locate resources in the network. Naming functionality is provided by NBP, which handles the name resolution of computer names to network addresses. Table 2.2 highlights the main characteristics of AppleTalk.

TABLE 2.2 Characteristics of AppleTalk

Routable (Yes or No)	Addressing Schemes	Interoperability	Naming Conventions
Yes – RTMP	8-bit network address assigned by administrator. 16-bit random node address automatically assigned by system.	Not interoperable with other protocols. Microsoft systems can install special software to communicate.	Naming system functionality is provided by NBP.

TCP/IP

In the late 1970s and early 1980s, the Department of Defense needed to develop a reliable system of communication for its mainframe computers. The Advanced Research Projects Agency (ARPA) began to experiment with communications protocols and developed a network system known as ARPANET. The original ARPANET protocol was NCP but, due to limitations, another protocol was soon needed. Transmission Control Protocol/Internet Protocol (TCP/IP) was developed to be a robust, reliable, and scalable protocol. It soon became the protocol of choice for the ARPANET, which eventually grew into what we now know as the Internet.

The TCP/IP suite of protocols includes protocols that work at various layers of the OSI model. We will discuss the details of each of these protocols later in this chapter. TCP/IP is an open standard protocol, which makes it interoperable with all operating systems. In fact, the interoperability of TCP/IP is one of the factors that is largely responsible for its growth.

The IP protocol of the TCP/IP suite is most responsible for the addressing function.

We will discuss IP addressing in detail later in this chapter. In general, each node of a network is identified by a unique address, and so is each network segment. The *IP address* consists a 32-bit address made up of four sets of eight bits (referred to as octets), which are expressed as decimal numbers, such as 192.168.0.1. These addresses can be manually configured by administrators or automatically configured by special servers called *Dynamic Host Configuration Protocol (DHCP)* servers.

TCP/IP nodes are generally referred to as hosts. They can be referred to by their IP address or by their hostname. Name resolution can take place through a text file (`hosts.txt`) or a dynamic database referred to as Domain Name System (DNS). We will discuss name resolution services in greater detail later in this chapter.

TCP/IP is fully routable, which makes it perfect for networks of all sizes. The TCP/IP suite contains routing protocols such as Routing Information Protocol (RIP) and Open Shortest Path First (OSPF). RIP is a distance vector protocol and OSPF is a link-state protocol. Distance vector protocols require frequent communication between routers to maintain routing tables. Link-state protocols build a map of the entire topology of a the routers that make up a network and only change the map when a change is made to that topology. Most large networks use a link-state protocol because of its lower overhead and greater intelligence for routing decisions. Table 2.3 highlights the main characteristics of TCP/IP.

TABLE 2.3 Characteristics of TCP/IP

Routable (Yes or No)	Addressing Schemes	Interoperability	Naming Conventions
Yes	32-bit IP address. 4 octets in decimal form. Can be configured by administrators or automatically configured by DHCP servers.	Open standard protocol is fully interoperable with all vendors and operating systems.	Can use IP address or host address. Host addresses are resolved by `hosts.txt` file or by DNS servers.

Exam Essentials

Know the routability of each of the major protocols. TCP/IP and IPX/SPX are routable protocol suites. NetBEUI is not a routable protocol. RIP is a routing protocol used for communication between routers to populate routing tables.

Define the addressing schemes of each of the major protocols. You should know the addressing schemes used by the most common protocols. In addition, you should be able to differentiate between the addressing schemes used.

Know the interoperability of each of the major protocols. You should know which of the major protocols are interoperable with other systems. In addition, you should know by what means they can become interoperable.

Know the naming conventions used by each of the major protocols. You should know the naming conventions that are used by each of the major protocols. In addition, you should know about any name resolution mechanisms that they use.

2.5 Identifying the Components and Structure of IP Addresses

In order to communicate effectively on a network, each device must be assigned a unique IP address. The IP address consists of two parts: a network address and a host address. You can think of the network address as a street name and the host address as a house on the street. As you can imagine, it would be very confusing for the mail carrier if multiple houses on the same street had the same number. In the same way, every host on a TCP/IP network must have a unique address for that network.

The IP addressing version that we use today is the same version that was developed in the early 1980s, IPv4. Since IPv4 offers more than 4 billion addressing possibilities, it was originally assumed that we would never run out of addresses (or that it would take a very, very long time). Because of the growth of the Internet and an inefficient use of IP addresses, we are in danger of running out of addresses in the not-too-distant future. Due to this fact, a new version of IP addressing, IPv6, is being developed. IPv6 will offer more than just an expanded number of possible addresses; it also promises improved security. In this section, we will discuss IPv4 and IPv6 in greater detail.

> **NOTE** For more information on IPv4 and IPv6, see Chapter 3 of the *Network+ Study Guide, Fourth Edition*.

Critical Information

You should know the components and structure of IPv4 and IPv6. In addition, you should know the required settings for connections across the Internet.

IPv4

IPv4 addressing is based on the *binary system, which uses a series of ones and zeros to represent numbers and all other characters used by a computer.* The reason that we have to use binary bits is that the computer only knows two states: on and off. (Actually, it only knows a fluctuation of voltage based on a timing signal.) With this method we can create numbers ranging from 0 to 255. This is the basis for all IP addressing as we know it today.

An IPv4 address (which we will refer to as an IP address from now on) is made up of four sets of 8 bits, called octets. Each bit in each octet has a value depending on its position in the octet. The leftmost bit of each octet has a value of 128, followed by 64, 32, 16, 8, 4, 2, and 1 as you move from left to right. Each bit can either be a 1 or a 0. If it is a 1, then its value counts based on its decimal value. If it is a 0, then its value does not count. Table 2.4 illustrates this method and creates the decimal value of 167 with binary bits.

You can facilitate communication of computers on your network or even on the Internet by configuring their active interfaces with the following:

TABLE 2.4 Using Binary Bits to Create Decimal Values

Bit Value	128	64	32	16	8	4	2	1	
Binary Digit	1	0	1	0	0	1	1	1	
	128		+32			+4	+2	+1	=167

A valid IP address An IP address that is unique and valid for the network or subnet in which it is configured.

A subnet mask A 32-bit binary address, expressed in decimals, that defines which parts of the IP address refer to the network address and which parts refer to the host address.

A default gateway The address of the inside interface of the router that is on your network or subnet and can give you access to or toward an Internet connection.

A DNS address The address of a DNS server that can resolve requests and thereby provide access to Web information.

> **NOTE** We will discuss IP address configuration in greater depth later in this chapter.

IPv6

When *IPv6* was first developed many experts thought we would be moving to it sooner than we have. Because of advancements in technology, which make network address translation easier and more prevalent in organizations, we have found ways to conserve the remaining IPv4 addresses and make more efficient use of them. We will, however, have to move to IPv6 addressing at some point in the future. In fact, the newest operating systems—Windows XP and Windows Server 2003—have the capability already.

The good news is, if we move to IPv6 within your lifetime, there is very little possibility that we will have to change again. This is because of the tremendous number of addresses that are available with IPv6. Whereas IPv4 is based on a 32-bit binary address, IPv6 will be based on a 128-bit hexadecimal address. This system will yield an astounding 340,282,366,920,938, 463,463,374,607,431,768,211,456 address possibilities.

IPv6 addresses will be expressed in a different format than IPv4. A 128-bit hexadecimal address is expressed as an 8-octet pair in hexadecimal separated by colons. The following is an example of an IPv6 address:

    62CE:9D66:23FC:34D2:84CD:F5D1:9DC2:62CD

As you can see, hexadecimal addresses use only numbers and the letters A–F to express the values. This creates a system that has a tremendous number of possibilities. IPv6 will eventually provide greater numbers of addresses as well as enhanced security and traffic control, but it will require some re-education for those who use it. Like IPv4, a complete configuration for use of

IPv6 on the Internet will require an IP address, subnet mask, default gateway, and a DNS server address.

Exam Essentials

Know the difference between IPv4 and IPv6. We are currently using IPv4, which is based on a 32-bit binary system. We will eventually move to IPv6, which is based on a 128-bit hexadecimal system.

Explain the requirements for connections on the Internet. Connecting to the Internet requires a valid IP address, subnet mask, default gateway, and an address of a DNS server.

2.6 Identifying Classful IP Ranges and Their Subnet Masks

When the Internet and TCP/IP were first developed, 4 billion addresses seemed like an awful lot of addresses and nobody really envisioned running out. For this reason, the founders of the Internet gave some of the larger organizations address spaces that would actually support millions of hosts. Medium-sized companies were later given address spaces that would support thousands of hosts. Small companies were given address spaces that would support hundreds of hosts. No real thought was given to the minimum that an organization could possibly use, because after all we had a "virtually unlimited" supply of addresses, or so we thought.

The addressing scheme that resulted from this is known as *classful addressing*. While purely classful addressing is rarely used today, it is still essential to your understanding of IP addresses. In this section, we discuss classful IP address ranges and their subnet masks.

> For more information on IP ranges and subnet masks, see Chapter 3 of the *Network+ Study Guide, Fourth Edition*.

Critical Information

You should be able to identify the address class of an IP address based on the first octet of the address. In addition, based on the address class, you should know the default subnet mask for the classful address. Finally, you should know the addresses that are not valid for IP addressing.

Classful IP Address Ranges

As we mentioned before, the subnet mask actually controls which bits of an IP address are network bits and which are host bits. Using the subnet mask, we can control the number of hosts that a given network can contain. Classful addressing aligns the first octet of an IP address with a default subnet mask in ranges called *classes*. IP addresses are actually divided into five classes, but we only use the first three for normal addressing. Table 2.5 illustrates the relationship of the first octet, the class, and the subnet mask.

TABLE 2.5 IP Address Classes and Subnet Masks

First Octet Address	Class	Default Subnet Mask
1–126	A	255.0.0.0
128–191	B	255.255.0.0
192–223	C	255.255.255.0

You may have noticed that the number 127 is missing. This is because the 127 network is reserved for diagnostics and testing. The most notable address on this network is the loopback address 127.0.0.1, which we will discuss in later chapters. Also, note that class D addresses are reserved for multicasts and that class E addresses are reserved for experimentation and future development.

Exam Essentials

Know how to determine the class of an IP address based on the its first octet.   The address class ranges based on the first octet of a classful address can be determined as follows:

> 1–126 Class A
>
> 128–191 Class B
>
> 192–223 Class C

Note: 127 is reserved for diagnostic purposes, such as loopback.

Know the default subnet mask for each class of address.   The default subnet masks for each class are as follows:

> A 255.0.0.0
>
> B 255.255.0.0
>
> C 255.255.255.0

Know which addresses are not valid for normal IP address assignment   Only class A, B, and C addresses are valid for normal IP address assignment; the 127 network is reserved for diagnostics and testing. The 127.0.0.1 address is commonly used for a loopback address to test TCP/IP.

2.7 Identifying the Purpose of Subnetting

If you use a classful network address with a default subnet mask, then you have one and only one network. This might be fine if you only have one location, but what if you have many locations? Do you have to be assigned another classful network address for each location? You do unless you can divide your network into multiple networks so that you can use the network addresses in a more efficient manner. In addition, if you are using two different technologies, such as Ethernet and Token Ring, then you would need to maintain them on two separate networks for security and control. These are the main reasons for *subnetting*. In this section, we discuss subnetting in greater detail.

Critical Information

You should understand the purpose of subnetting a network. In addition, you should know the procedure that is applied to a registered address to create subnets. Finally, you should be able to determine the number of subnets and the number of hosts per subnet that are created by changing a subnet mask from the default to a custom subnet mask.

Subnetting Basics

Subnetting allows an organization to have one registered public network address and yet use many addresses from that address for each of its locations. This is accomplished by changing the subnet mask to something other than the default. Based on the subnet mask assignment, you can create more networks with fewer hosts in each network. For example, a Class B network address such as 174.23.0.0 would have a default subnet mask of 255.255.0.0. This means that 16 bits are used for the network and 16 bits can be used for hosts. With 16 bits used for hosts, you can have a maximum of 65,534 hosts. You can determine this by the formula 2^n-2, where n is the number of bits. In this case $2^{16}-2 = 65,534$.

Now if you have a building that will hold 65,534 users, then you are all set, but chances are your users are located in more than one geographical location. Suppose you have six locations and you have thousands of users at each location. You can't have the same network address on both interfaces of the router that connects them, so you need more networks.

Since you have 16 bits for hosts, why not "borrow" some of those to create some subnets? Using a related formula to the one we just discussed, you can determine the amount of bits that you need to borrow to create six subnets by solving for n in the equation $2^n-2 \geq 6$. Solving for n, you get the number 3 or higher. This means that if you borrow the first three bits after the network bits, then you can use them to create six new subnets. Looking back at Table 2.4, you can see that the total value of the first three bits is 224 (128+64+32). This means that if you change the default subnet mask to a custom subnet mask of 255.255.224.0, you will be able to create six subnets. Since each of the subnets can now use the remaining bits, you can have $2^{13}-2$ hosts in each subnet, or 8,190 hosts per subnet.

> **Note:** This is really just the beginning of an entire subnetting exercise, but it is the only part that you will need to know for the exam. If you decide to continue in a networking track, you will then calculate the subnet address ranges and broadcast addresses for each subnet.

> **Note:** For more information on subnetting, see Chapter 3 of the *Network+ Study Guide, Fourth Edition*.

Exam Essentials

Describe the main reasons that subnetting is used. Subnetting is used to create more network addresses to provide greater control and greater security, and to use one registered network address for multiple geographical locations of an organization.

Understand how to use 2^n-2. Be able to use the formula 2^n-2 to determine the appropriate subnet mask that can be used with a specified classful network address to create a certain number of subnets with a specified number of hosts in each subnet.

2.8 Identifying the Differences Between Public and Private Addressing Schemes

As we discussed earlier, one of the most important aspects of TCP/IP is that each client that is using it must have a unique IP address on the network on which they are using it. If the network is a small one that you control, then that may not be much of an issue, but the same rule holds true no matter how large the network gets. If you control all of the addresses on your own network (behind a firewall) and they do not come into contact with any of the Internet addresses, then you can decide which addressing scheme to use. You can use some addresses that are set aside for that purpose, or you can use your own scheme, but you should be aware of the risks associated with using your own scheme. If the addresses that you choose should conflict with any other addresses, then your communication and their communication will be affected adversely until the address conflicts are resolved.

As you can imagine, a network the size of the Internet can become very challenging in regard to making sure that all of the addresses are unique. For this reason, the assignment of addresses on the Internet is tightly controlled by organizations that were developed specifically for this purpose. These addresses are referred to as public or registered addresses.

2.8 Identifying the Differences Between Public and Private Addressing Schemes

> **NOTE** For more information on public and private addresses, see Chapter 3 of the *Network+ Study Guide, Fourth Edition*.

Critical Information

In this section, we discuss the differences between public and private network addressing schemes. You should know what options you have in regard to your own private network addressing and the inherent risks associated with each option. In addition, you should know what a registered address is and how to obtain one.

Private IP Addressing

It's your network, so it only makes sense that you can use the IP addresses of your choice, right? Well, this is only partially true because you have to take into consideration what would happen if your network were to suddenly find itself on the Internet. If you always maintain your IP network behind a firewall, this will not be of concern, but if something went wrong with the firewall and your network was exposed to the Internet, then you could have IP addresses that conflict with those of another organization. The result would most likely be that neither you nor the other organization would be able to communicate effectively.

To prevent this scenario from occurring, *private IP address ranges* have been developed and defined by RFC 1918. These private IP address ranges are filtered by all of the routers that support the Internet, so if they leak out of your network they will immediately be filtered and will not affect communication or cause IP address conflicts. There is no law that says you have to use these private IP address ranges, but it is highly recommended and it only makes sense to use them.

Private IP address ranges are defined for Class A, B, and C addresses. Table 2.6 shows the private IP address ranges for each class. You should be familiar with these ranges for the real world as well as for the test. The table shows the default subnet mask, but you can subnet within these ranges as well.

TABLE 2.6 Private IP Address Ranges

Class	Address Range	Default Subnet mask
A	10.0.0.0–10.255.255.255	255.0.0.0
B	172.16.0.0–172.31.255.255	255.255.0.0
C	192.168.0.0–192.168.255.255	255.255.255.0

Public IP Addressing

Unique IP address assignment on the Internet was originally the responsibility of the Internet Assigned Numbers Authority (IANA), but it has been handed over to other organizations that coordinate with one another to ensure that addresses are unique. The current three major organizations for the entire world are divided geographically as follows:

American Registry for Internet Numbers (ARIN)   Serves the North American continent and parts of the Caribbean

Asia Pacific Network Information Centre (APNIC)   Serves the Asia Pacific region

Reseaux IP Europeans Network Coordination Centre (RIPE NCC)   Serves Europe, the Middle East, and parts of Africa

Addresses that are assigned by these authorities are referred to as registered or *public addresses*. If you are connecting a computer to the Internet, then you must use an address that has been assigned by one of these authorities. Now, you may be thinking, "I'm connected to the Internet and I never contacted any of those organizations." That's probably because you use an address that is provided by your Internet service provider (ISP), who obtained the address from one of these authorities. ISPs have large blocks of IP addresses that they can assign to their clients, thereby giving them a valid and unique IP address to use on the Internet. Some large organizations still go through the process of registering for their own address blocks, but most organizations simply get whatever addresses they need from their ISP.

Exam Essentials

Describe the difference between a private IP address and a public IP address.   Private IP addresses are used by an organization inside its firewall and are not exposed to the Internet, whereas pubic IP addresses are used on the Internet and therefore must be registered to assure their uniqueness.

Know the private IP address ranges.   You should know the private IP address ranges for each class. Private IP address ranges are highly recommended because they are filtered on the Internet routers. There is no requirement or law that forces an organization to use these address ranges.

List the organizations that register public IP addresses.   You should know the names of the three organizations that are responsible for dispensing unique IP addresses to organizations and to ISPs. In addition, you should know the area of the world for which each organization is responsible.

Explain the method that most people use to obtain access to the Internet.   Most organizations and most users do not use the registry organizations to obtain an IP address, but instead use an ISP who has obtained the IP addresses for its clients. The ISP is then responsible for ensuring that each client is assigned a unique address.

2.9 Identifying and Differentiating Between Addressing Methods

So once you have your unique IP address, how do you go about configuring it on a computer? Even more importantly, if you are in charge of configuring hundreds or even thousands of devices with appropriate IP addresses, how do you configure all of the devices in your network? In this section, we discuss your options in regard to IP address configuration. The methods that you use will depend on your network and the various devices within it.

Critical information

The three main methods used to configure IP addresses are static, dynamic, and self-assigned. You should be familiar with these three methods of configuration. In addition, you should know when each method is appropriate.

> **NOTE** For more information on addressing methods, see Chapter 3 of the *Network+ Study Guide, Fourth Edition*.

Static IP Address Configuration

Every device that works on a network can be assigned a *static IP address*. This, however, does not mean that static addressing is the best method to use for all devices. You should typically assign a static IP address to devices such as routers, printers, and servers. You should rarely assign client computers a static IP address, but instead they should receive an IP address automatically. Having said this, let's now discuss how to configure a static IP address on the most common Microsoft Windows clients and servers.

The process of configuring an IP address on a client or server is rather straightforward. First, you access the controls for the connection and then you assign the IP address for the TCP/IP protocol. A valid static address should include the IP address and subnet mask. These are the only two requirements for intranet communication within one subnet of an organization.

In most cases, the computer will also need access to other subnets and to the Internet. In this case, in addition to the IP address and subnet mask, the configuration should include a default gateway and a valid DNS server address. The *default gateway* should be the address assigned to the router interface that is within the computer's subnet.

After a valid static address is configured on a computer, it should be able to communicate within its network. The only way to change a static configuration is to access the same tool again and change the settings. Figure 2.3 shows the IP address configuration for a connection in a Windows Server 2003 computer.

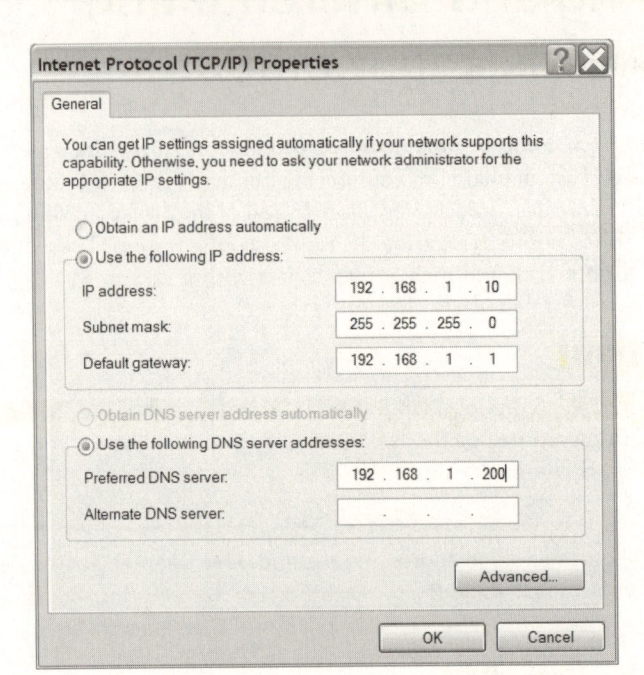

FIGURE 2.3 A static IP configuration on Windows Server 2003

> **Note:** Static addresses can also be assigned to devices such as routers and printers. The precise method of static assignment will vary with the vendor, but the basic elements of IP address, subnet mask, and default gateway will remain the same.

Dynamic IP Address Assignment

As we discussed earlier, most clients, Microsoft and non-Microsoft, should not be assigned a static IP address but rather should obtain the IP address automatically. This is because automatic assignment of IP addresses to clients drastically improves the security and manageability of a network. This method also makes changing an IP configuration much easier.

Automatic configuration is usually accomplished using a Dynamic Host Configuration Protocol (DHCP) server. A DHCP server can automatically configure clients with an IP address, subnet mask, default gateway, DNS server address, and much more. The configuration of the DHCP server is generally the responsibility of the network administrator.

After a DHCP server is configured, clients should be configured to obtain their IP addresses automatically from the DHCP server. If the clients are configured properly, they will broadcast on the network when they are first started to obtain an address from a DHCP server. Figure 2.4 shows Windows XP client connection that is set to obtain an IP address automatically.

FIGURE 2.4 A Windows XP client set to obtain an IP address automatically

> All Windows operating systems after Windows 98 are set by default (when first installed) to obtain an IP address from a DHCP server.

Self-Assigned

Now you may be thinking, "What if a client is set to obtain an address automatically but no DHCP server is available to fulfill the request? What happens then?" Well, it depends on which operating system you are using. Microsoft clients prior to Windows 98 would simply leave the IP address configured to 0.0.0.0 with a subnet mask of 0.0.0.0. Microsoft Windows 98 clients and later Microsoft clients have a service called *Automatic Private IP Address Assignment (APIPA)*. This service automatically assigns each client a unique address in the 169.254.0.0 network when they are configured to obtain an address automatically and a DHCP server is not available. This is useful if you just want to attach the computers to a hub to form a small network and you don't want to bother with assigning IP addresses. If all of the computers are set to obtain an address automatically, then they will in essence create their own subnet so that communication can take place between them without any additional configuration. The computers would, of course, have no access to another network or to the Internet. Figure 2.5 shows the `ipconfig` output of a computer that has been assigned an APIPA address.

FIGURE 2.5 The `ipconfig` output of a computer that has been assigned an APIPA address

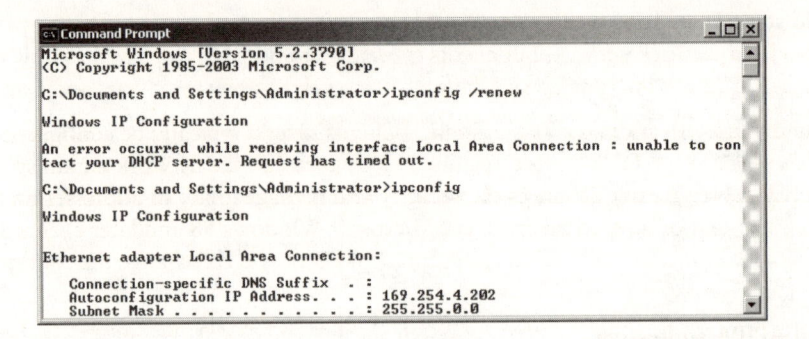

```
Command Prompt
Microsoft Windows [Version 5.2.3790]
(C) Copyright 1985-2003 Microsoft Corp.

C:\Documents and Settings\Administrator>ipconfig /renew

Windows IP Configuration

An error occurred while renewing interface Local Area Connection : unable to con
tact your DHCP server. Request has timed out.

C:\Documents and Settings\Administrator>ipconfig

Windows IP Configuration

Ethernet adapter Local Area Connection:

        Connection-specific DNS Suffix  . :
        Autoconfiguration IP Address. . . : 169.254.4.202
        Subnet Mask . . . . . . . . . . . : 255.255.0.0
```

Windows XP and Windows Server 2003 offer one more service, called *Alternate Configuration*. With Alternate Configuration, you can assign an address that will be used in the event that a DHCP server is not available. This is particularly useful for a user who uses a laptop computer at work and at home. If the configuration at work relies on a DHCP server but the configuration at home requires a specific address, the user would have to change the setting from Obtain an IP Address Automatically to a static address every time he changed the location of the computer. With Alternate Configuration, the computer will find the DHCP server at work and it will configure the alternate address at home when it does not find a DHCP server, without requiring additional configuration from the user. Figure 2.6 shows using Alternate Configuration on a Windows XP computer.

FIGURE 2.6 Using Alternate Configuration on a Windows XP computer

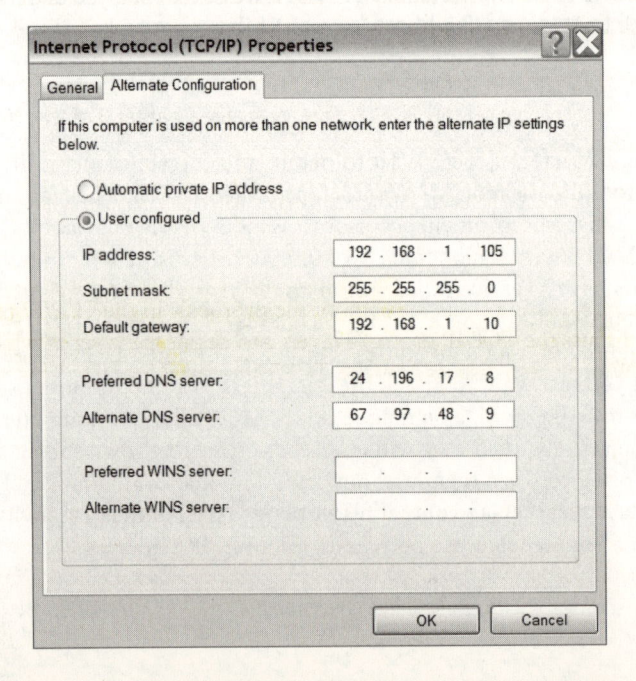

```
Internet Protocol (TCP/IP) Properties                    [?][X]

 General  Alternate Configuration

  If this computer is used on more than one network, enter the alternate IP settings
  below.

     ○ Automatic private IP address
     ● User configured

     IP address:              192 . 168 .   1 . 105
     Subnet mask:             255 . 255 . 255 .   0
     Default gateway:         192 . 168 .   1 .  10

     Preferred DNS server:     24 . 196 .  17 .   8
     Alternate DNS server:     67 .  97 .  48 .   9

     Preferred WINS server:      .     .     .
     Alternate WINS server:      .     .     .

                                        [  OK  ] [ Cancel ]
```

Exam Essentials

Understand static IP address configuration. Servers, printers, and routers should usually be configured with a static IP address, but clients typically should not. You should know how to configure a static address on the latest Windows operating systems for clients and computers.

Understand dynamic IP address configuration. Clients should typically be configured with their IP addresses using a DHCP server, which is configured by the network administrator. Using a DHCP server greatly enhances the security and manageability of addresses on a network, since users do not have to be involved. Microsoft Windows 98 and later clients are configured by default to obtain an IP address automatically, but you can change the configuration to assign a static IP address when necessary.

Understand APIPA addressing. APIPA addressing is available on Microsoft Windows 98 and later clients. This type of addressing automatically assigns a client an IP address in the 169.254.0.0 network when the client is set to obtain an IP address from a DHCP server and a server is not available. Windows XP and Windows Server 2003 have an additional feature in APIPA that automatically assigns a specified address instead of an address in the 169.254.0.0 network. This can be useful for a person who utilizes a laptop in a network at home and at work.

2.10 Using Protocols in the TCP/IP Suite

As we mentioned before, the TCP/IP protocol suite contains many protocols. These protocols work together to provide communication, management, diagnostics, and troubleshooting for a network that uses the TCP/IP protocol. In order to understand TCP/IP, it is essential that you understand all of the protocols in the suite. In this section, we examine each of these protocols in detail.

> For more information on the TCP/IP protocols, see Chapter 3 of the *Network+ Study Guide, Fourth Edition.*

Critical Information

We will define the purpose, function, and use of each of the protocols in the TCP/IP protocol suite. In addition, we will discuss the TCP/IP protocol layers and define the layer at which each of the protocols operates. We will also discuss how the TCP/IP protocol loosely aligns with the OSI model of communication.

Internet Protocol (IP)

Internet Protocol (IP) is a protocol that is used to transport data from one node on a network to another node. A node can be a computer or a router interface. IP is considered to be a connectionless protocol, which works at the Network layer of the OSI model. Because it is connectionless, it does not establish a session with another computer and does not guarantee the delivery of packets; it only makes an effort to deliver them. To guarantee delivery of packets, a higher-level protocol such as TCP is required.

IP also performs the task of fragmenting and reassembling packets when needed. Fragmentation is sometimes necessary because devices that make up the network have a maximum transmission unit (MTU) size that is smaller than the packet to be delivered. In this case, the packet must be "broken up" into smaller pieces and then reassembled on the other side of the transmission. This is an important role that IP provides for the network.

Probably the most widely known role that IP provides is addressing of packets. IP marks each packet with a source address and a destination address. As we discussed in the section "Identifying Classful IP Ranges and Their Subnet Masks," this IP addressing is essential to the success of network communications.

> **NOTE** We will discuss more IP addressing functions later in this chapter.

Transmission Control Protocol (TCP)

Transmission Control Protocol (TCP) is a connection-oriented protocol that works at the Transport layer of the OSI model. It uses IP as its transport protocol and assists IP by providing a guaranteed mechanism for delivery. TCP requires that a session first be established between two computers before communication can take place. TCP also adds features such as flow control, sequencing, and error detection and correction.

TCP works by a process referred to as a three-way handshake. The TCP three-way handshake works as follows:

1. TCP sends a short message called a SYN to the target host.

2. The target host opens a connection for the request and sends back an acknowledgment message called an ACK or SYN ACK.

3. The host that originated the request sends back another acknowledgment, confirming that it has received the ACK message and that the session is ready to be used to transfer data.

A similar process is used to close the session when the data exchange is complete. The entire process provides a reliable protocol. TCP extends its reliability by making sure that every packet that it sends is acknowledged. If a packet is not acknowledged within the timeout period, the packet is resent automatically by TCP.

User Datagram Protocol (UDP)

User Datagram Protocol (UDP) also operates at the Transport layer of the OSI model and uses IP as its transport protocol, but UDP does not guarantee delivery of packets. The reason that it doesn't guarantee delivery of packets is that UDP does not establish a session. UDP is instead known as a "fire and forget" protocol because it just assumes that the data sent will reach its destination and does not require acknowledgments. Because of this, UDP is also referred to as a connectionless protocol.

Now, you might be wondering why anyone would want to use UDP instead of TCP. Well, the advantage of UDP is its low overhead in regard to bandwidth and processing effort. Whereas a TCP header has 14 fields of information that have to be processed, a UDP header only has 4 fields. Applications that can handle their own acknowledgments and that do not require the additional features of the TCP protocol might use the UDP protocol to take advantage of the lower overhead. Often, multimedia presentations that are broadcast or multicast onto the network use UDP since they can be monitored to make sure that the packets are being received. Services such as the Domain Name System (DNS) service also take advantage of the lower overhead provided by UDP.

File Transfer Protocol (FTP)

File Transfer Protocol (FTP), as its name indicates, provides for the transfer of files through a network environment. It can be used within an intranet or through the Internet. FTP is more than just a protocol; it is an application as well, and thus FTP works at the Application layer (Layer 7) of the OSI model and uses the TCP protocol as a transport mechanism. FTP allows a user to browse a folder structure on another computer (assuming that the user has been given the permissions to authenticate to the computer) and then to download files from the folders or to upload additional files.

Many organizations use FTP to make files available to the general public and therefore allow users to log onto the FTP server anonymously. In other words, the users do not have to utilize a username and password to authenticate to the server. Since the files are there for the public, the users are allowed to access them without authenticating. Organizations also use FTP to transfer files within an organization. Typically, these servers require authentication by the user, either by supplying an additional username and password or by a pass-through authentication provided by a previous logon such as to *Active Directory*.

You can use FTP through most browsers and even from a command line, but it is typical for users to purchase a third-party software such CuteFTP or SmartFTP instead. Using FTP to transfer files allows you to transfer much larger files than are generally allowed as an attachment by most ISPs. Using the third-party tool allows you to see that the file was transferred to the intended location. Figure 2.7 shows a connection to the FTP server at Sybex. This is one of the servers to which authors send completed work.

Trivial File Transfer Protocol (TFTP)

Trivial File Transfer Protocol (TFTP) is similar to FTP in that it allows the transfer of files within a network, but that's where the similarity stops. Whereas FTP allows for the browsing of files and folders on a server, TFTP requires that you know exactly the name of the file that you want to transfer and exactly where to find the file. Also, whereas FTP uses the connection-oriented TCP protocol, TFTP operates at the Application layer (Layer 7) and uses the connectionless UDP protocol. TFTP is most often used for simple downloads such as transferring firmware to a network device such as a router or a switch. Its main advantage is its speed, since it does not require the overhead that FTP does.

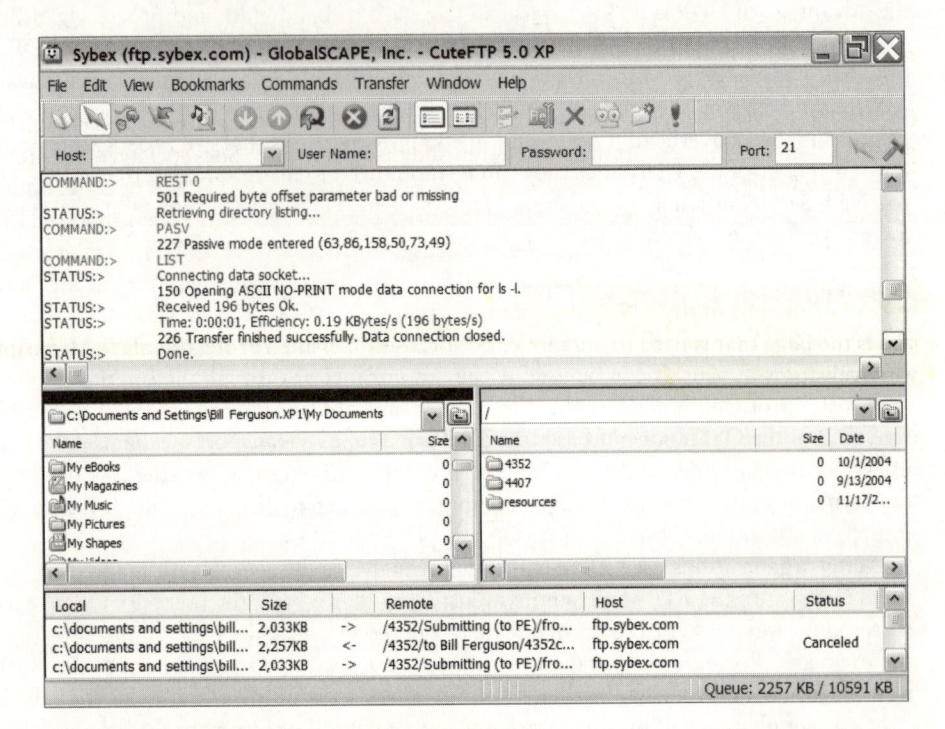

FIGURE 2.7 A connection to an FTP server at Sybex

Simple Mail Transfer Protocol (SMTP)

Simple Mail Transfer Protocol (SMTP) defines how e-mail messages are sent between hosts on a network. You can remember SMTP as "Sending Mail To People." SMTP works at the Application layer (Layer 7) of the OSI model and uses TCP to guarantee error-free delivery of messages to hosts. Since SMTP requires that the destination host always be available, mail systems spool the incoming mail and display it in a user's mailbox so that the user can read it at another time. How the user reads the mail is determined by what protocol he uses to access the SMTP server.

Hypertext Transfer Protocol (HTTP)

Hypertext Transfer Protocol (HTTP) is the Application layer (Layer 7) protocol that users utilize to browse the World Wide Web. HTTP clients use a browser to make special requests from an HTTP server (web server) that contains the files that they need. The files on the HTTP server are formatted in Hypertext Markup Language (HTML) and are located using a uniform resource locator (URL). The URL contains the type of request being generated (for example `http://`), the DNS name of the server to which the request is being made, and optionally the path to the file on the server. For example, if you type `http://micosoft.com/support` in a browser, you will be directed to the Support pages on Microsoft's servers.

Hypertext Transfer Protocol Secure (HTTPS)

One of the disadvantages of using HTTP is that all of the requests are sent in clear text. This means that the communication is not secure and therefore unsuited for web applications such as e-commerce or the exchanging of sensitive or personal information through the Web. For these applications, *Hypertext Transfer Protocol Secure (HTTPS)* is an Application layer (Layer 7) protocol that provides a more secure solution and that uses Secure Sockets Layer (SSL) to encrypt information sent between the client and the server. In order for HTTPS to operate, both the client and the server must support it. All of the most popular browsers now support HTTPS, as do web server products such as Microsoft Internet Information Server (IIS), Apache, and most other web server applications. To use a URL to access a website using HTTPS and SSL, start with `https://` instead of `http://`—for example, `https://partnering.one.microsoft.com/mcp` is the page that is used to authenticate Microsoft Certified Professionals to Microsoft's private website.

Post Office Protocol Version 3 (POP3)

Post Office Protocol Version 3 (POP3) is one of the protocols used to retrieve mail from SMTP servers. Using POP3, clients connect to the server, authenticate, and then download their mail. Once they have downloaded their mail, they can read it. Typically, the mail is then deleted from the server, although some systems hold a copy of the mail for a period of time specified by an administrator. One of the drawbacks of POP3 authentication is that it is generally performed in clear text. This means that an attacker could sniff your POP3 password off the network as you enter it.

Internet Message Access Protocol Version 4 (IMAP4)

Internet Message Access Protocol Version 4 (IMAP4) is another Application layer (Layer 7) protocol that is used to retrieve mail from SMTP servers, but IMAP4 offers some advantages over POP3. To begin with, IMAP4 provides a more flexible method of handling e-mail. You can read your e-mail on the e-mail server and then determine what you want to download to your own PC. Since the mail can stay in the mailbox on the server, you can retrieve it from any computer that you wish to use, provided that the computer has the software installed to allow you to access the server. Microsoft Hotmail is a good example of an IMAP4 type of service. You can access your Hotmail from any browser. You can then read, answer, and forward mail without the need to download the messages to the computer that you are using. This can be very convenient for users who travel.

Telnet

Telnet is a virtual terminal protocol that has been used for many years. Originally, Telnet was used to connect "dumb terminals" to mainframe computers. It was also the connection method used by earlier Unix systems. Today, Telnet is still used to access and control network devices such as routers and switches. It operates at the Application and Presentation layers (Layer 6 and Layer 7) of the OSI model.

Telnet can be used for remote control and remote configuration of servers in network environments. The main problem with Telnet for today's environment is that it is not a secure protocol; everything is transmitted in plain text. For this reason, Telnet is being replaced by more secure methods such as Secure Shell and Microsoft's Remote Desktop Connection, which provide encrypted communication.

Secure Shell (SSH)

First developed by SSH Communications Security Ltd., *Secure Shell (SSH)* is a program that allows you to log in to another computer over a network, execute commands, and move files from one computer to another. SSH provides strong authentication and secure communications over insecure channels. It protects networks from attacks such as IP spoofing, IP source routing, and DNS spoofing. The entire login session is encrypted; therefore, it is almost impossible for an outsider to collect passwords. SSH is available for Windows, Unix, Macintosh, and OS/2, and it also works with RSA authentication. SSH operates at Application and Session layers (Layer 7 and Layer 5) of the OSI model.

Internet Control Message Protocol (ICMP)

Internet Control Message Protocol (ICMP) is a protocol that works at the Network layer (Layer 3) of the OSI model. ICMP provides error checking and reporting functionality. Although it provides many functions, the most commonly known is the ping utility provided by ICMP. The ping utility is most often used for troubleshooting. In a typical "ping scenario," an administrator uses a hosts command line and the ping utility to send a stream of packets called an echo request to another host. When the destination host receives the packets, ICMP sends back a stream of packets referred to as an echo reply. This confirms that the connection between the two hosts is configured properly and that the TCP/IP protocol is operational.

ICMP can also send back a message such as "Destination Host Unreachable" or "Time Exceeded." The former is sent when the host cannot be located on the network, and the latter is sent when the packets have exceeded the timeout period specified by TCP. Still another function of ICMP is the sending of source quench messages. These messages are sent by ICMP when the flow of data from the source is larger than that which can be processed properly and quickly by the destination. A source quench message tells the system to slow down and therefore prevents the resending of many data packets.

Address Resolution Protocol (ARP)

Address Resolution Protocol (ARP) is a protocol that works at the Network layer of the OSI model. It is used to resolve IP addresses to MAC addresses. This is an extremely important function, since the only real physical address that a computer has is its MAC address; therefore, all communication will have to contain a MAC address before it can be delivered to the host. This is accomplished in a series of steps as follows:

1. A computer addresses a packet to another host using an IP address.
2. Routers use the IP address to determine whether the destination address is in their network or on another network.

3. If a router determines that the address is on another network, it forwards the packet to another router based on the information that is contained in its routing table.

4. When the router that is responsible for the network that contains the destination address receives the packet, it checks the ARP cache to determine if there is an entry that resolves the IP address to a MAC address. If there is an entry, it uses the MAC address contained in the entry to address the packet to its final destination.

5. If there is no entry in the ARP cache, the router resolves the IP address to a MAC address by using ARP to broadcast onto the local network. It asks the computer with the IP address contained in the destination address of the packet to respond with its MAC address. The router also gives the computer its own MAC address to use for the response.

6. The broadcast is "heard" by all of the computers in the local network, but it will only be responded to by the computer that has the correct IP address. All other computers will only process the request to the point that they determine that it is not for them.

7. The computer that is configured with the IP address in question responds with its MAC address.

8. The router addresses the packet with the MAC address and delivers it to its final destination.

> In Chapter 4, "Domain 4 Network Support," we will discuss the arp utility that you can use to examine and control the ARP cache.

Reverse Address Resolution Protocol (RARP)

Reverse Address Resolution Protocol (RARP), as its name implies, is the opposite of ARP. RARP resolves a MAC address to an IP address. RARP was first used by diskless workstations to obtain an IP address from a server before DHCP servers were available. It simply presented its MAC address and was given an IP address based on its MAC address. RARP is sometimes used as a very rudimentary form of security on applications.

Network Time Protocol (NTP)

Network Time Protocol (NTP) is a protocol that works at the Application layer of the OSI model and synchronizes time between computers in a network. In today's distributed networks, ensuring that the time is synchronized between clients and servers is essential. Authentication protocols such as the Kerberos protocol used with Microsoft's Active Directory use keys that are valid for only about five minutes. If a client and a server are not synchronized, the keys could be invalid the very second that they are issued. In many of today's networks, an authoritative time source such as the Internet is first used and configured onto a time server (perhaps a domain controller), then that server uses NTP to synchronize time with other computers in the network. Some computers may be a receiver of the correct time as well as a sender of the time to other computers in the network.

Network News Transport Protocol (NNTP)

Network News Transport Protocol (NNTP) runs at the Application layer and is used to connect computers to newsgroup servers that use the Usenet system. (Usenet is a worldwide bulletin board system that can be accessed through the Internet or through many online services.) NNTP replaced the original UUCP protocol.

Secure Copy Protocol (SCP)

Secure Copy Protocol (SCP) runs at the Application layer and is used to copy files securely within a network or between networks. SCP is often used in high-security networks.

Lightweight Directory Access Protocol (LDAP)

Lightweight Directory Access Protocol (LDAP) is a set of protocols for accessing information directories. It is based on the standards within the X.500 standard, but it is significantly simpler. LDAP also supports TCP/IP, so it has become the standard for Windows Active Directory. LDAP operates at the Session layer (Layer 5) of the OSI model.

Internet Group Multicast Protocol (IGMP)

Internet Group Multicast Protocol (IGMP) is the standard for IP multicasting on intranets. It is used to establish host memberships in multicast groups on a single network. The mechanisms of the protocol allow a host to inform its local router, using Host Memberships Reports, that it wants to receive messages addressed to a specific multicast group. IGMP operates at the Network layer (Layer 3) of the OSI model.

Line Printer Daemon/Line Printer Remote (LPD/LPR)

Line Printer Daemon/Line Printer Remote (LPD/LPR) is a printer protocol that operates at the Session layer (Layer 5) and uses TCP/IP to establish connections between computers and printers on a network. The technology was first developed for use with Unix and has since become the de facto cross-platform printing protocol. The LPD software is typically stored in the printer or print server. The LPR software must be installed on the client computer. The LPR software sends a print request to the LPD printer/server, which in turn queues the file and prints it as soon as the printer is available.

Table 2.7 highlights the main characteristics of each of the protocols that we discussed.

TABLE 2.7 Characteristics of Protocols in the TCP/IP Protocol Suite

	Purpose	Function	Use
IP	Addresses and transports data from one network node to another.	Connectionless protocol, "fire and forget." Performs fragmenting and assembling of packets. Works at the Network layer (Layer 3) of the OSI model.	IP addresses are assigned to computers and to router interfaces. These addresses are used to transfer a packet into the proper network so it can be delivered to a host.

TABLE 2.7 Characteristics of Protocols in the TCP/IP Protocol Suite *(continued)*

	Purpose	Function	Use
TCP	Responsible for flow control and error recovery.	Waits for receipt of acknowledgments from the destination that packets have been delivered without errors. Resends packets that are not acknowledged within a specified time frame. Works at the Transport layer (Layer 4) of the TCP/IP suite.	Works by a process of a three-way handshake. Sends SYN messages and waits for an ACK response.
UDP	Broadcasts packets through a network making a "best effort" to deliver them to the destination	Connectionless protocol. Works at the Transport layer (Layer 4) of the OSI model.	Used for applications that can provide their own acknowledgments or that can be monitored, such as multimedia over the Internet.
FTP	Provides the rules of behavior for transferring files through an intranet or over the Internet.	Works at the Application layer (Layer 7) of the OSI model. Provides a protocol as well as an application for transferring files.	Used to browse file structures on a remote computer and to transfer files between computers in intranets and on the Internet.
TFTP	Provides for transferring files within a network.	Connectionless protocol that works at the Application layer (Layer 7) of the OSI model. Uses UDP for low overhead without a guarantee of delivery.	Typically used for simple file transfers such as those between a computer and a router or a switch for management purposes.
SMTP	Provides for the delivery of mail messages within a network or between networks.	Works at the Application layer (Layer 7) of the OSI model and uses TCP to guarantee delivery of mail to remote hosts.	Typically used to transfer e-mail messages within a network and between networks.
HTTP	Provides for browsing services for the World Wide Web.	Works at the application layer (Layer 7) of the OSI model and uses provides access to files on web servers through the use of URLs to pages that are formatted with HTML.	Typically used to browse information on the many servers that interconnect the World Wide Web.

TABLE 2.7 Characteristics of Protocols in the TCP/IP Protocol Suite *(continued)*

	Purpose	Function	Use
HTTPS	Provides for access to resources on the Internet in a secure fashion.	Works at the Application layer (Layer 7) of the OSI model and uses SSL to encrypt data traffic so communications on the Internet can remain secure.	Used for Internet communications that must remain secure, such as banking, e-commerce, and medical transactions.
POP3	Allows the storage and retrieval of user e-mail on servers. Allows users to access and download e-mail from servers.	Works at the Application layer (Layer 7) of the OSI model. Users can connect to the server and download messages to a client. The messages can then be read off the client.	Used for many e-mail applications. Users can check their e-mail boxes and download messages that have been placed in them.
IMAP4	Allows the storage and retrieval of user e-mail on servers. Allows users to access e-mail on servers and either read the e-mail on the server or download the e-mail to the client to read it.	Works at the Application layer (Layer 7) of the OSI model. Allows a user to read messages on an e-mail server without having to download the messages off the server.	Typically, this method of e-mail retrieval is very convenient for users who travel and therefore might access their e-mail from more than one location. The mail remains on the server until they delete it, so they can gain access to it from multiple locations.
Telnet	Provides a virtual terminal protocol for connecting to a managing server.	Works at the Application layer (Layer 7) of the OSI model. Provides a connection using an authentication method that is performed in clear text. This protocol and application are not considered secure.	Has been used in the past for "dumb terminals" that connected to mainframe computers. Now is used to connect computers to servers, routers, switches, etc., for remote management.
SSH	Provides the capability to log onto a computer remotely, execute commands, and move files in a secure and encrypted environment.	Works at the Application layer (Layer 7) of the OSI model. Provides for a secure logon and a secure environment in which to execute commands.	Typically used to manage servers from clients and to move sensitive files from one server to another within the same network or between networks.

TABLE 2.7 Characteristics of Protocols in the TCP/IP Protocol Suite *(continued)*

	Purpose	Function	Use
ICMP	Provides error checking and reporting functionality.	Works at the Network layer (Layer 3) of the OSI model. Provides background services that can be used to provide information to an administrator and to request a "quench" of the information flow in the network.	Typically used as part of the ping tool to test network connectivity. Can send back an echo reply when an echo request message is sent to it. Can also send back a message such as "Destination Host Unreachable" and "Time Exceeded" when the connection to the pinged host is not possible.
ARP	Resolves IP addresses to MAC addresses.	Works at the Network layer (Layer 3) of the OSI model. Includes a cache that is checked first. If the entry is not found in the cache, then ARP uses a broadcast to determine the MAC address of the client.	Typically used by the system as a background service, but also includes a utility that can be used for troubleshooting.
RARP	Resolves IP addresses to MAC addresses.	Works at the Network layer (Layer 3) of the OSI model. It assigns an IP address when presented with a MAC address.	Used with diskless workstations to automatically assign an IP address. Also sometimes used as very rudimentary security for computer authentication.
NTP	Synchronizes time between computers in a network.	Works at the Application layer (Layer 7) of OSI model. Can synchronize time between clients and servers.	Used to synchronize time to assure that authentication protocols such as the Kerberos protocol work properly and that applications that require collaboration operate properly.
NNTP	Provides access to Usenet newsgroups on news servers.	Works at the Application layer of the TCP/IP suite. Provides a set of standards for accessing and opening news articles on a Usenet-based news server.	Typically used by individuals and organizations to research information about a variety of topics. News servers do not provide for "browsing" but instead just provide lists of articles for specified topic.

TABLE 2.7 Characteristics of Protocols in the TCP/IP Protocol Suite *(continued)*

	Purpose	Function	Use
SCP	Provides the capability to copy and transfer files securely in a network.	Works at the Application layer (Layer 7) of the OSI model. Provides the capability to transfer or copy files within a network while keeping them encrypted and secure.	Typically used to transfer and/or copy files within a high-security network.
LDAP	Provides a service to access directories.	Based on the X.500 standard of Directory Access Protocols, but much simpler. It works at the Application layer (Layer 7) of the OSI model.	Used as the basis for network directory services such as Windows Active Directory and Novell Directory Services.
IGMP	Provides a standard for multicasting on an intranet.	Allows a host to inform its local router, using Host Memberships Reports, that it wants to receive messages addressed to a specific multicast group. It works at the Network layer (Layer 4) of the OSI model.	Used to establish host memberships in multicast groups on a single network.
LPD/ LPR	A printer protocol that uses TCP/IP to provide connections between computers and printers.	LPD software is stored in the printer or print server while LPR software must be installed on the client computer. The LPR software sends a print request to the LPD printer/server, which in turn queues the file and prints it as soon as the printer is available. These protocols work at the Application layer (Layer 7) of the OSI model.	Originally developed for Unix, LPD/LPR has now become the de facto standard for TCP/IP-based printing. Many OSs use this protocol to "capture" a printer and configure a server or client to print to it.

Exam Essentials

Know the purpose of each of the protocols in the TCP/IP protocol suite.   You should know the general purpose for each of the protocols in the TCP/IP protocol suite. In addition, you should understand how the protocols work together.

Describe the function of each of the protocols in the TCP/IP protocol suite.   You should know the function for each of the protocols in the TCP/IP protocol suite. In addition, you should know the level of the OSI model at which each protocol functions.

Explain how each of the protocols in the TCP/IP protocol suite is used.   You should know the general use of each of the protocols in the TCP/IP protocol suite. In addition, you should understand how some of the protocols work together with other protocols.

2.11 Defining the Function of TCP/UDP Ports

If we performed only one task at a time with each computer, we might not need ports, but the fact is that computers can perform many tasks at one time. Therefore, we need a way to identify packets so that they will be processed by the computer in the correct manner. By identifying each packet with a port number, we ensure that the computer will direct the packet to the right area within it where the appropriate processes can be performed.

TCP and UDP port numbers are used to identify packets in regard to the services that they require. You can also filter traffic using these port numbers to restrict only specific types of traffic from a network. You should understand how TCP and UDP ports can be used to facilitate and control traffic. In this section, we will discuss the various types of TCP and UDP ports and describe their general use.

> **NOTE**   For more information on the TCP/UDP ports, see Chapter 3 of the *Network+ Study Guide, Fourth Edition*.

Critical Information

You should be able to define the function of TCP and UDP ports. You should be able to list the three main designations of ports. In addition, you should understand the general use of each designation of ports.

Port Designations

TCP/IP has 65,536 ports available. As you can imagine, some ports are used much more than others. Ports are divided into three main groups or designations as follows:

Well-known ports   These port numbers range from 0 to 1,023. These are the most commonly used ports that have been used for the longest period of time. When CompTIA states that you should know the definition of well-known ports, they are referring to these ports.

Registered ports   These port numbers range from 1,024 to 49,151. Registered ports are used by applications or services that need to have consistent port assignments. These ports, like the well-known ports, are agreed upon by most organizations for standardization of use.

Dynamic or private ports   These port addresses range from 49,152 to 65,535. These ports are not assigned to any particular protocol or service and can therefore be used for any service or application.

It is common for applications to establish a connection on a well-known port and then move to a dynamic port for the rest of the conversation. It's important that you understand port numbers, because you may be configuring them for communication purposes as well as to provide filtering and therefore prevent communication of specified applications or services. In the next section, we will examine the most common specific port assignments more closely.

Exam Essentials

Know the port numbers and understand the use of well-known ports.   The range of addresses for well-known ports is from 0 to 1,023. The well-known ports are the most common port designation.

Be able to list the port numbers and describe the use of registered ports.   The range of addresses for registered ports is from 1,024 to 49,151. Registered ports are not used as often as well-known ports but are agreed upon for use by a specific service or application.

List the port numbers and undertand the use of dynamic or private ports.   The range of addresses for dynamic, or private, ports is from 49,152 to 65,535. These port numbers are not assigned to any specific protocol, service, or application and can therefore be used by any service or application.

2.12 Identifying Well-Known Ports Associated with Services and Protocols

Now that we have discussed the general nature of ports, let's look at much more specific information about well-known ports. Although there are 1,024 well-known ports, only a handful of these are commonly used on networks. The ones that are used most frequently are not arranged in any logical order in regard to their use, so unfortunately the only way to remember most of

2.12 Identifying Well-Known Ports Associated with Services and Protocols

them is to memorize them. In this section, we will pair up each of the most commonly used well-known ports with its protocol, service, or application.

Critical Information

You should be able to identify the port number that each of the most common network protocols, services, and applications use. You should know the port number when given a service as well as the service when given a port number.

Well-Known Port Numbers

As we said before, *well known* is the name given for the port designation, but not all of the numbers between 0 and 1,023 have a well-known service assigned to them. The good news is that you don't have to memorize 1,024 port assignments! The bad news is that you do have to memorize the port assignments in Table 2.8. As you can see, some of the ports are TCP (connection-oriented) ports and others are UDP (connectionless) ports. HTTP is an application that uses both types of ports.

TABLE 2.8 The Most Common Well-Known Port Numbers and Associated Services

Service, Protocol, or Application	Port Assignment	TCP, UDP, or Both
FTP (File Transfer Protocol)	20, 21	TCP
SSH (Secure Shell)	22	TCP
Telnet	23	TCP
SMTP (Simple Mail Transfer Protocol)	25	TCP
DNS (Domain Name System)	53	UDP
TFTP (Trivial File Transfer Protocol)	69	UDP
HTTP (Hypertext Transfer Protocol	80	Both
POP3 (Post Office Protocol version 3)	110	TCP
NNTP (Network News Transfer Protocol)	119	TCP
IMAP4 (Internet Message Access Protocol version 4)	143	TCP
SNMP (Simple Network Management Protocol)	161	UDP
HTTPS	443	TCP

You should memorize the port numbers in Table 2.8 so that you can recognize them when configuring servers, routers, switches, and other network equipment. You might use them to configure a service or protocol. In addition, you might use them to filter a protocol or service on a firewall. In either case, a familiarity with the port numbers will assist you in configuration as well as in communication about the services and applications themselves.

Exam Essentials

Understand the use of ports.   Ports are used so that a computer can work with many applications at the same time and through the same physical interfaces. A port is a logical location in a computer where a packet is sent for processing based on the information contained in packet. In this way, the packets are sent to the logical place in the computer that has the correct resources to process the packet.

Memorize the most common port numbers.   You should memorize the most common ports, such as HTTP, FTP, SMTP, and others. Be able to relate the port number to the application, and vice versa. This is essential information for troubleshooting as well as for general network knowledge.

2.13 Identifying the Purpose of Network Services and Protocols

As mentioned earlier, protocols are rules of behavior that network services and applications follow. Each service or application is designed for a specific purpose. As important as it is that you know the port number of the most common network services, it's equally important that you understand the purpose of each of the services and what they bring to the network. In this section we identify the most common network services and protocols and describe their purpose.

Critical Information

You should be glad that you don't have to know every one of the services in an average network, because there are hundreds of them. You should, however, be able to list the most common of these services and their purpose in the network.

Be able to identify the purpose of the most common protocols and services. In addition, you should know how the protocols and services work together in the network. In the following sections, we discuss the most common network services and describe the purpose of each one.

Domain Name System (DNS)

Domain Name System (DNS), as its name implies, is a service that resolves names in a network. Specifically, DNS resolves hostnames to IP addresses. This is an important service because the

IP addresses are then used to route packets into the correct network and finally to the correct computer or computers.

Network Address Translation (NAT)

Network Address Translation (NAT) is a service that translates one set of IP addresses to another set of IP addresses. NAT is most often used between a private network and the Internet, but it can also be used in other ways, such as to translate a group of global internal addresses to a group of global external addresses. NAT is a service that can be run on a computer, a router, or a specialized device that only provides network address translation.

Internet Connection Sharing (ICS)

Internet Connection Sharing (ICS) is a service that allows you to connect one computer (the host computer) to a network (such as the Internet) and then connect other computers to that computer to give them access to the Internet as well. ICS requires that the host computer contain two network interface cards. ICS can often act as a small DHCP server, issuing the clients an IP address. For example, if you have a small office that contains 10 client computers but no server, you can connect one host computer to the Internet and let the other computers connect to it to make their connection to the Internet.

Windows Internet Name Services (WINS)

Windows Internet Name Services (WINS) is a dynamic database that resolves NetBIOS names to IP addresses. It is used on Microsoft networks, but other clients can make use of a WINS database by employing a WINS proxy. NetBIOS names are registered by clients and servers in a Microsoft network and then used to determine the services that each computer can perform for the network. Microsoft networks can use multiple WINS servers for fault tolerance and load balancing.

Simple Network Management Protocol (SNMP)

Simple Network Management Protocol (SNMP) is a management protocol that you can use to gather information about a network. SNMP can gather information about the servers, routers, switches, and other network equipment. Typically, a server is installed with SNMP management software and then devices can be installed with SNMP agent software. The agent software can be programmed by the management software to gather information about devices in the network and report it back to a centralized *management information base (MIB)*. You can use SNMP software by itself on a command-line interface, or you can use third-party tools to make the process simpler.

Network File Systems (NFS)

Network File Systems (NFS) is a file system developed and used by Sun Microsystems that allows all network users to access shared files stored on computers of different types. NFS uses an interface called Virtual File Systems (VFS), which runs on top of the TCP/IP protocol suite. Users can work with the shared files as if they were stored locally on their hard disks. NFS standards are publicly available.

Zero Configuration (Zeroconf)

Zero Configuration (Zeroconf) is not intended for use on large networks, but it is a handy tool to use to form an ad hoc network to connect devices for a conference or meeting when tools to create a more proper configuration (such as Active Directory or DNS) are not available. Zeroconf should not be used if security is a concern, since it is very limited in this regard. Zeroconf can allocate addresses without a DHCP server and translate between domain names without a DNS server.

Server Message Block (SMB)

Server Message Block (SMB) is a message format used by DOS and Windows to share files, directories, and services. Many network products have used SMB in the past and continue to use SMB, including Windows for Workgroups, Windows NT, and LAN Manager. SMB is used as a "common denominator" by many products and applications to facilitate file sharing among different operating system platforms.

AppleTalk File Protocol (AFP)

AppleTalk File Protocol (AFP) is Apple's version of a client/server file sharing protocol to be used on an AppleTalk network. AFP servers and clients can talk to each other, but any other protocol first has to be translated to talk to an AFP client or server. AFP over TCP/IP allows Apple users to access AFP servers over TCP/IP networks.

Line Printer Daemon (LPD)

Line Printer Daemon (LPD) is software that is stored in a print server that receives the request to print from an LPR client and queues the file to be printed as soon as the print device becomes available. It was originally developed for Unix, but has since become the de facto cross-platform printing protocol.

Exam Essentials

Know the name resolution services. You should know the name resolution protocols and services that a network uses. DNS is used for hostname resolution and WINS is used for NetBIOS name resolution. You should also know when each of the name resolution services might be necessary in a network.

List the protocols used to share information in a network. You should know the major protocols that are used to share information in a network. SMB is primarily used for Microsoft networks but can be used by other platforms as well. NFS is used by Sun systems and AFP is used by Apple systems.

Understand the LPD printing protocol. The LPD printing protocol is the protocol that is used on print servers. It was first developed for use with Unix but has been adopted as a standard for remote printing. The client uses the LPR service and protocol to connect to print servers that use LPD.

Understand the SNMP management protocol. The SNMP protocol can be used to gather information about computers and other devices in a network. This protocol uses a management station to store data and agents to collect data. The SNMP protocol and service can be used by itself on a command-line interface or it can be incorporated into third-party software for easier use.

Describe the Zeroconf protocol. Zeroconf is a protocol that can be used in very small networks where security is not a concern. Zeroconf can allocate IP addresses without the use of a DHCP server and resolve hostnames without using a DNS server. Zeroconf is not considered secure and should not be used in an environment where security is a priority.

2.14 Identifying the Basic Characteristics of Various WAN Technologies

Generally speaking, a *wide area network (WAN)* is the result of connecting multiple local area networks (LANs). Another characteristic of a WAN is the fact that the organization rarely owns all of the lines of communication on which it is sending data. In addition, WAN technologies are typically much slower than LAN technologies. WAN technologies that are comparable in speed to LAN technologies are typically very expensive.

Critical Information

Since WAN communication uses completely different types of communication lines and equipment than LAN communication, it only makes sense that the technologies used would also be different. WAN technologies have evolved over time to provide remote office and remote access users with faster and more reliable communications methods and communications media. In this section, we will examine each of these types of communication technologies.

Packet Switching

Packet switching is a technology whereby each packet of a data communication can take a separate route to its destination. It has been used in the past with X.25 technology to ensure communication through a questionable network of communications. If packets should arrive out of order, special devices called packet assemblers and dissemblers are used to put the packets back into the correct order before presenting them to the computer. In today's more reliable networks, packet switching is used with frame relay to speed up communications by creating more available bandwidth on multiple permanent virtual circuits (PVCs).

Circuit Switching

Circuit switching is a technology whereby a single communication channel is opened at the start of a session and that single channel is used throughout the communication. All packets are sent over the same channel and the communication channel is closed when the session has ended. Normal telephone lines use a circuit switching method of communication.

Integrated Services Digital Network (ISDN)

Integrated Services Digital Network (ISDN) is an international standard for sending voice, data, and video over digital telephone lines or normal telephone wires. There are two types of ISDN, *Basic Rate Interface (BRI)* and Primary Rate Interface (PRI). BRI offers only 128Kbps bandwidth using two 64Kbps B (bearer) channels and one 16Kbps D (delta) channel. *Primary Rate Interface (PRI)* offers tremendously more bandwidth, using twenty-three 64Kbps B channels and one 64Kbps D channel in the United States and thirty 64Kbps B channels with one 64Kbps D channel in Europe. Originally, ISDN used baseband transmission on copper wire, but the new form of ISDN (B-ISDN) offers a broadband signal using a fiber-optic cable. ISDN is often used as a backup line in organizations that also have higher bandwidth and more expensive main connection lines.

Fiber Distributed Data Interface (FDDI)

Fiber Distributed Data Interface (FDDI) is a set of protocols used for sending digital data over a fiber optic cable. FDDI networks use a token-passing system and a dual-ring topology. They can support data rates up to 100Mbps using the new FDDI-2 extension. FDDI networks are typically used as a backbone for a WAN.

T Carrier Level 1 (T1)

A *T Carrier level 1 (T1)* is a United States–based dedicated line that can carry 1.544Mbps in 24 separate 64Kbps channels. Organizations can lease an entire T1 or only a part of a T1, referred to as Fractional T1. Each 64Kbps channel can be configured to carry voice or data transmissions. T1s are a popular choice for businesses connecting to the Internet and for Internet service providers (ISPs). They can also be used to directly connect multiple geographical locations of the same organization. Similar lines are available outside of the United States, such as the E1 in Europe and the J1 in Japan.

T Carrier Level 3 (T3)

A *T Carrier level 3 (T3)* is a United States–based dedicated line that can carry about 43Mbps on 672 separate 64Kbps channels. Each channel can be configured for voice or data transmissions. T3s are primarily used by ISPs that are connecting directly to the backbone of the Internet. T3s are also used to form the backbone of the Internet itself. Similar lines are available outside of the United States, such as the E3 in Europe and the J3 in Japan.

Optical Carrier (OCx)

Optical Carrier (OC) is a term used to describe the speed of networks that conform to the Synchronous Optical Network (SONET) standard, which allows data streams at different rates to be multiplexed. This adds greatly to the flexibility of data networks throughout the world. The term OCx covers a range of speeds, including the following:

- OC-1 = 51.85Mbps
- OC-3 = 155.52Mbps

- OC-12 = 622.08Mbps
- OC-24 = 1.244Gbps
- OC-48 = 2.488Gbps
- OC-192 = 9.952Gbps
- OC-255 = 13.21Gbps

X.25

X.25 was an original standard used for packet-switching networks. It allowed for reliable communication through a very unreliable medium at that time, namely the telephone companies' standard lines with analog switches. X.25 was very slow and has since been replaced by Frame Relay, which is much faster.

Exam Essentials

Be able to define the differences between packet switching and circuit switching. Packet-switching networks use multiple paths and might send each successive packet down a different path, depending on the traffic and the health of the network. In contrast, circuit-switching networks open a channel of communication and send all of the packets down that channel. Packet-switching networks might stay connected when no data is being sent, whereas circuit-switching networks terminate the connection when the communication in finished.

Be familiar with ISDN terminology. There are two basic types of ISDN: Basic Rate Interface (BRI) and Primary Rate Interface (PRI). Each ISDN channel can carry a maximum of 64Kbps. BRI uses two 64Kbps and one 16Kbps D channel, whereas PRI uses twenty-three 64Kbps D channels and one 64Kbps D channels. In both cases, only the B channels are counted for bandwidth.

Know the characteristics of FDDI. FDDI uses a fiber-optic cable and a token-passing method of access with a dual-ring topology. The newest FDDI-2 networks are capable of speeds up to 200Mbps. FDDI is typically used for the backbone of an organization's WAN.

Be familiar with T carrier levels. T1 lines can carry 1.544Mbps on twenty-four 64Kbps channels of communication. This type of line is usually used by an organized as a leased line to connect offices or to connect directly to the Internet without using an ISP. In contrast, T3 lines can carry about 43Mbps on 672 separate 64Kbps channels. This type of line is generally used by very large organizations or by ISPs that connect directly to the backbone of the Internet. These types of lines might also be used to build the backbone of the Internet itself.

Be able to describe OCx. OCx is a speed designation used for fiber-optic lines that conform to the SONET standard. Be familiar with the various speeds of fiber-optic communication.

Know the characteristics of the X.25 technology. X.25 was one of the original technologies used on packet-switching networks. X.25 offered very slow but reliable communication through the unreliable telephone lines in the 1980s. It has all but been replaced by Frame Relay.

2.15 Identifying the Basic Characteristics of Various Internet Technologies

The Internet has become a tool that most business cannot afford to be without. In addition, most U.S. households now have some form of Internet access. The question is no longer *whether* we will connect to the Internet, but rather *how* we will connect to it. Many technologies have been developed to give users more bandwidth on their Internet connections and thereby make the Internet an even more useful tool.

Critical Information

There are many technologies from which an individual or an organization can choose to provide access to the Internet. Some technologies are inherently much faster than others, but they all have advantages as well as disadvantages. In this section, we will discuss the characteristics of each of the main Internet access technologies. We will point out the main advantages as well as any disadvantages of each one.

Digital Subscriber Line (xDSL)

The term *Digital Subscriber Line (xDSL)* is used collectively to refer to all of the digital subscriber lines. The two main categories of xDSL are *Asymmetric Digital Subscriber Line (ADSL)* and *Symmetric Digital Subscriber Line (SDSL)*. Both types use technologies on common telephone lines to increase the bandwidth of the line. ADSL can provide data rates from 1.5 to 9Mbps when receiving data (referred to as downstream rate) but only 16 to 640Kbps when sending data (referred to as the upstream rate). ADSL allows the subscriber to use the telephone wires for voice as well as data simultaneously. SDSL can support data rates up to 3Mbps in both directions, but SDSL does not allow the use of telephone wires for both voice and data simultaneously. Both technologies are growing in popularity and are used by small- to medium-sized businesses as well as in homes for fast connections to an ISP and thereby to the Internet.

Broadband Cable (Cable Modem)

Many homes are currently wired with cable TV connections. The coaxial wire that cable TV providers use can provide significantly more bandwidth than a standard telephone line. Because of this, many cable TV companies have begun offering broadband Internet access as part of their packages. This requires a special device that converts the signal from the coaxial cable into a signal that the computer can understand (referred to as a cable modem). *Broadband cable* using cable modems currently offers data rates up to 2Mbps in many areas of the United States. This technology is expected to continue to grow. It is used primarily by individual households as part of a "cable package," but some small- to medium-sized businesses also use this technology for Internet access.

Plain Old Telephone Service (POTS)/Public Switched Telephone Network (PSTN)

Whether you use the more technical term *Public Switched Telephone Network (PSTN)* or the term that was coined by telephone company personnel, *Plain Old Telephone Service (POTS)*, you are referring to the normal telephone lines that are used to provide voice telephone service to millions of people all over the world. The main advantage of these types of lines is that they are available almost everywhere. You can use a PSTN line and a modem to connect to an ISP and gain a connection to the Internet that you can use to connect to servers all over the world. The main disadvantage of these lines is that they are very limited in bandwidth. Most PSTN lines offer a data rate of only about 52Kbps. It is possible to combine multiple modems and multiple lines into the same data stream (referred to as multilink), but this is rarely done nowadays because of the other broadband options. Still, many people use PSTN lines to obtain slow but inexpensive access to the Internet. (Most ISPs offer a PSTN price per month that is much lower than their broadband price per month.)

Satellite

A less common form of Internet access is through a satellite dish. Some satellite TV providers have bundled Internet access into their offerings along with TV packages. Typically, this service is only available as a download and the upload must be provided with a telephone line, DSL, or other type of media, but some companies are offering uploads to the satellites. Typically download speeds are between 1 and 2Mbps, but upload speeds are much slower (generally 128Kbps or less).

Wireless

It is also possible to connect to the Internet through completely wireless technologies. This is a different concept than wireless technologies that are used within networks to connect to wireless access points. In contrast, wireless Internet access is typically acquired from Personal Digital Assistant (PDA) devices and other mobile devices such as cell phones. CDMA and GPRS are the two main technologies used. Both of these offer data rates of 45 to 70Kbps.

Exam Essentials

Know the characteristics of xDSL. xDSL is a term used to refer to all of the digital subscriber line technologies, including ADSL and SDSL. The biggest difference between ASDL and SDSL is that ADSL has a much slower upstream rate relative to its downstream rate, whereas SDSL is capable of the same data rate in both directions. ADSL can support voice and data simultaneously on one line, whereas SDSL cannot. The data rate of xDSL varies between providers, but the downstream rate can usually exceed 1.5Mbps.

List the characteristics of broadband cable Internet access. Broadband cable Internet access is provided by cable TV companies through the coaxial cable that is located in a user's home. It requires a special piece of equipment called a cable modem, which is typically provided by the cable TV company. Broadband cable access can currently support data rates up to 2Mbps.

Describe the characteristics of the PSTN or POTS network. The PSTN or POTS network refers to the regular telephone lines that are installed throughout the United States as well as the rest of the world. Computers can be connected to these telephone lines with the standard modem included on most computers. The main advantage of using this type of network is the fact that it is available in most locations. The major disadvantage of using PSTN for Internet access is that it's very slow compared with other technologies.

Know the characteristics of satellite Internet access. Satellite Internet access is generally available from satellite TV providers. Downstream data rates with satellite are typically much faster than upstream data rates, and many satellite companies require that you use another media for upstream transmissions. Satellite Internet access downstream rates are currently advertised in the range of 1.5 to 3.0Mbps.

Describe wireless Internet access. Completely wireless Internet access is now available for use with cell phones and PDAs. The current technologies of CDMA and GPRS both offer 45 to 70Kbps speed.

2.16 Defining the Function of Remote Access Protocols and Services

Remote access protocols are protocols that are used to connect to a computer resource on a LAN from outside the LAN. The medium for these connections could be PSTN, xDSL, broadband cable, or another type of medium. Based on the medium used for the connection, a different set of protocols will be used than those that are typically used on the LAN. It is important that you understand the most common types of remote access protocols.

Critical Information

Be able to define the function of the most common remote access protocols and services. You should know which protocols are associated with each type of service. In addition, you should be able to define the advantages and disadvantages of each of the remote access protocols and services.

It stands to reason that a service that is designed to work on a totally different type of communication line from that of a LAN would have a protocol that is totally different as well. In this section, we will discuss the most common protocols and services and how each service relates to the protocol that supports it. We will also discuss the main advantages and disadvantages of each of the remote access protocols and services.

Remote Access Service (RAS)

Remote Access Service (RAS) is a remote access solution that is included with Microsoft Windows server products. Its main function is to give users access to the network from a remote location as if they were actually sitting at their desks, although sometimes the access is much

2.16 Defining the Function of Remote Access Protocols and Services

slower. RAS is implemented in Windows NT Server as RAS, and in Windows 2000 Server and Windows Server 2003 as *Routing and Remote Access Server (RRAS)*, but both product implementations offer the same basic functionality—remote access connectivity to a LAN environment. RAS servers can provide dial-up connections using modems as well as virtual private networking (VPN) connections using WAN miniports. Figure 2.8 shows an RRAS server on Windows Server 2003.

FIGURE 2.8 An RRAS server on Windows Server 2003

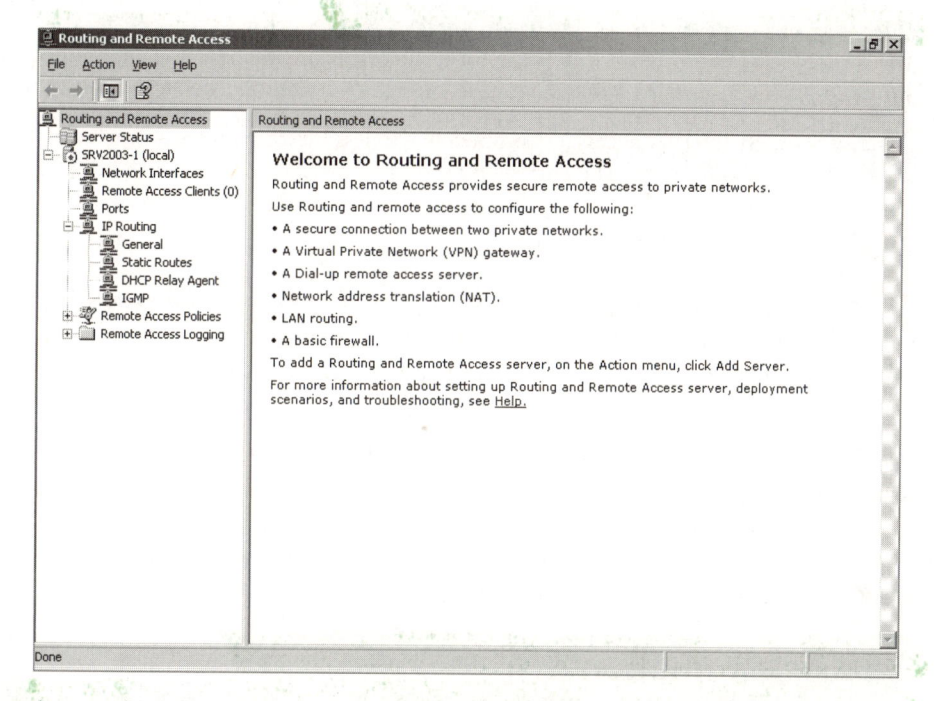

RAS is also capable of providing security using tunneling protocols such as Point-to-Point Tunneling Protocol (PPTP) and Layer 2 Tunneling Protocol (L2TP), although L2TP is only available on Windows 2000 or later servers. RAS and RRAS servers support remote connectivity to all of the major client operating systems in use today.

> **NOTE** We will discuss the details of these tunneling protocols and other security protocols later in this chapter.

Serial Line Interface Protocol (SLIP)

In the 1970s, graduate students at the University of California, Berkley, developed a protocol designed to allow TCP/IP communication to be transmitted over serial connections. This was the first protocol that allowed computers to communicate over normal telephone lines. *Serial*

Line Interface Protocol (SLIP) did its job in the early years, but it has some shortcomings, which have caused it to be replaced with newer protocols. To begin with, SLIP is not a secure protocol. All communications that establish as a session are transmitted in clear text. This does not provide the security required for today's network environments. In addition, no error-checking mechanism is built into SLIP. Finally, SLIP is limited to the TCP/IP protocol, so protocols such as IPX/SPX, NWLink, and AppleTalk over IP cannot be used with SLIP.

Point-to-Point Protocol (PPP)

Point-to-Point Protocol (PPP) is the standard remote access protocol used today. It addresses the shortcomings of SLIP by providing for authentication mechanisms, error checking, and multiple protocol support. You can choose among several authentication options, including Password Authentication Protocol (PAP), Challenge Handshake Authentication Protocol (CHAP), and Extensible Authentication Protocol (EAP).

> We will discuss each of these protocols in greater detail later in this chapter.

The PPP protocol establishes a session with a three-step process as follows:

1. Framing rules are established between the client and the server. These include the size of the frames allowed as well as the data rates that can be used.
2. The client is authenticated by the server using the configured authentication protocol.
3. Network control protocols (NCPs) configure the remote client for the correct LAN protocols TCP/IP, and so on.

After these three steps are successfully completed, the server and client can begin to exchange data.

Point-to-Point Protocol over Ethernet (PPPoE)

Point-to-Point Protocol over Ethernet (PPPoE) is a protocol that has become popular because of the growing number of people who use cable modems and DSL connections to access the Internet. PPPoE is a specification for connecting users on an Ethernet to the Internet through a common broadband medium such as a cable modem or DSL line. All of the users on the Ethernet can share one common connection to the Internet. The Ethernet principles apply to the connection (CSMA/CD) as well as the principles of PPP (authentication and error checking). PPPoE can also be implemented with wireless devices that connect multiple users in an Ethernet to the Internet.

Point-to-Point Tunneling Protocol (PPTP)

Point-to-Point Tunneling Protocol (PPTP) is a protocol used to create a secure tunnel between two points on a network over which other protocols such as PPP can be used. This tunneling functionality provides the basis for VPNs. While PPTP is a widely used tunneling protocol,

2.16 Defining the Function of Remote Access Protocols and Services

other tunneling protocols are available that provide even greater security, such as L2TP. We will discuss L2TP and other security protocols later in this chapter.

Virtual Private Network (VPN)

Virtual Private Network (VPN) is not as much of a technology as it is a term used to describe a form of networking. A VPN is a secure connection that is transmitted through a nonsecure medium, usually the Internet. To create a VPN, a tunneling protocol is used to encrypt the communication as it flows through the nonsecure medium. The communication is then decrypted on the other side of the connection. VPNs can be established using server software as well as routers. They are commonly used by businesses to provide connections to multiple locations of an organization without the use of expensive private leased lines.

Remote Desktop Protocol (RDP)

Remote Desktop Protocol (RDP) is a protocol used by Microsoft to establish remote display and remote control capabilities between servers and clients on a Microsoft network. It is the protocol on which Windows Terminal Services operates. Originally, Terminal Services offered two options during installation: Remote Administration and Application Server. In later versions of Terminal Services (Windows Server 2003), only Application Server is offered. This is because Remote Desktop Connection, which also uses the RDP protocol, is now included with Windows XP Professional client software and Windows Server 2003 server software. Figure 2.9 illustrates a Remote Desktop Connection interface that utilizes the RDP protocol.

FIGURE 2.9 The Remote Desktop Connection tool

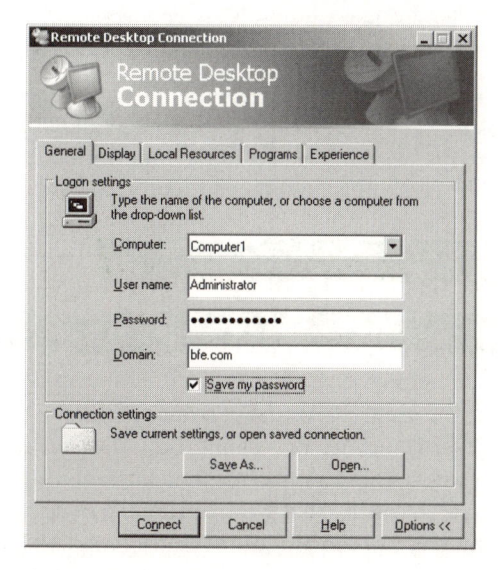

Exam Essentials

Describe the function of RAS. RAS provides the service that allows remote access connectivity to a Microsoft LAN. RAS servers can provide security as well as connectivity. RAS is implemented as RRAS in Windows 2000 Server and Windows Server 2003.

Explain the function of SLIP. The SLIP protocol was the first protocol used to provide a TCP/IP connection through normal telephone wires. This protocol is not commonly used today because of its shortcomings in regard to security, error checking, and flexibility of protocol use. The protocol that has replaced SLIP is PPP.

Know the function of PPP. PPP is the protocol that is most commonly used for remote access connections to today's networks. It offers several methods of authentication to provide a secure communication environment in any network. Be able to describe the three-step process that PPP uses to create a session between two computers.

Understand the function of PPPoE. PPPoE is a protocol used to connect an Ethernet to a common broadband medium. PPPoE has increased in popularity because of the growth of cable modems, DSL, and wireless devices that support it. PPPoE operates within the principles of Ethernet communication as well as PPP communication.

Know the function of PPTP. PPTP is a protocol used to establish a tunnel for secure communication through a nonsecure medium, such as the Internet. PPTP is the basis for VPNs. PPTP offers some security, but other tunneling protocols offer even greater security.

Describe the function of a VPN. A VPN is a network that is secure even though the communications are transmitted through a nonsecure medium, such as the Internet. VPNs are created using tunneling protocols such as PPTP and L2TP. Businesses use VPNs to connect multiple locations of their organization in a secure manner without having to lease expensive dedicated lines.

Explain the function of RDP. RDP is a remote display and remote control protocol used with Microsoft Terminal Services and Microsoft Remote Desktop Connection. It allows administrators to connect to and remotely administer servers and clients in their networks.

2.17 Identifying the Purpose and Function of Various Security Protocols

As we discussed earlier, a protocol is a set of standards or defined rules of behavior. In regard to computers, the protocol is somewhat like a language that defines how computers communicate. If two computers do not share the same set of rules, they cannot communicate with each other. When we are connecting computers, we ensure that we are using the same protocol so that the computers can communicate; however, we can also use protocols to create an environment that does not allow another computer to interpret the communication.

The purpose of security protocols is to create a secure communication channel by using a set of rules and standards that are known only by specific entities. Computers that are configured

2.17 Identifying the Purpose and Function of Various Security Protocols

with the correct protocols and other specific configuration can communicate, but other computers cannot interpret the communication. You can choose from several security protocols for your own environment. Some are designed to authenticate computers, while others are designed to encrypt or scramble data so that it cannot be read by others. Encryption protocols continue to evolve, but let's look at some protocols of which you should be aware for the test.

Critical Information

You should be able to identify the most common security protocols. In addition, be able to describe the purpose and function of each of the most common protocols used for authentication and encryption.

Internet Security Protocol (IPSec)

Internet Security Protocol (IPSec) is a protocol designed to encrypt data during communication between two computers. It operates at the Network layer of the OSI model and provides security for protocols that operate at the higher layers of the OSI model. Because of this, you can use IPSec to secure practically all TCP/IP-related communications.

The function of IPSec is to ensure that data on network is safe from being viewed, accessed, or modified by anyone except the intended receiver. IPSec can be used to provide security within networks as well as between networks. To be more specific, IPSec has three main security services:

Data verification Ensures that the data that is received is actually from the source from which it appears to have originated.

Protection from data tampering Ensures that the data has not been changed in any way during the transmission between the sending computer and the receiving computer.

Private transactions Ensures that the data that is sent is readable only by the intended receiver.

There are two main modes of IPSec: *transport mode* and *tunnel mode*. Transport mode is used to send and receive encrypted data within the same network. Tunnel mode is used to send encrypted data between networks. It includes an encryption mechanism as well as an authentication mechanism. The only Microsoft clients that can use IPSec are Windows 2000 Professional and later.

Layer 2 Tunneling Protocol (L2TP)

Layer 2 Tunneling Protocol (L2TP) is a tunneling protocol that is used to secure data transfer and prevent data from being modified during transit. It is considered more secure than PPTP, but it is limited in use to the very latest clients and servers. The only Microsoft clients that support L2TP are Windows 2000 Professional and later. Windows 2000 Server and later servers also support L2TP.

L2TP authenticates the client in a two-phase process. First, it authenticates the computer and then it authenticates the user. Authenticating the computer helps to prevent a *man-in-the-middle attack* where the data is first intercepted by another computer and then forwarded to the intended receiver. LT2P can also authenticate the end of the tunnel with an IP address, so that it doesn't send data to an unintended receiver. L2TP works by using digital certificates, which means the computers that use L2TP must support digital certificates.

Secure Sockets Layer (SSL)

Secure Sockets Layer (SSL) is a security protocol that is used on the Internet. It was originally developed by Netscape for use with its Navigator browser. SSL uses public key encryption to secure communications over the Internet. You can use SSL to connect to a website by using a secure Uniform Resource Locator (URL) that begins with `https://` instead of `http://`. You must also use a browser that supports SSL.

SSL secures communication over the Internet by providing three key services:

Server authentication   The user can confirm a server's identity. This is very useful if you are purchasing something on the Web. On the Internet Explorer browser, you can double-click on the "gold lock" at the bottom of a secure page to view a server's certificate of authentication.

Client authentication   The server can confirm a user's identity. This is for sensitive information such as banking information or medical information. The server can verify the identity of the requester before sending the information.

Encrypted connections   Data can be protected during transit. You can configure SSL to encrypt the data and to prevent the data from being tampered with or modified during transit.

Wired Equivalent Privacy (WEP)

As we discussed in Chapter 1, wireless networks are becoming increasingly popular in today's networks. Because of this, we need to secure communications on wireless networks just as we secure them on wired networks. One of the first attempts at wireless security was *Wired Equivalent Privacy (WEP)*, which attempted to secure wireless connections on 802.11b-based networks. WEP attempted to secure the connections by encrypting the data transfer, but WEP was found not to be "equivalent to wired" security because the security mechanisms that were used to establish the encryption were not encrypted. In addition, WEP only operates at the lower layers of the OSI model and therefore cannot offer end-to-end security for applications. Because of these shortcomings, many people have chosen newer and more sophisticated methods of securing wireless communications.

Wi-Fi Protected Access (WPA)

Wi-Fi Protected Access (WPA) was designed to improve on WEP as a means of securing wireless communications. It can usually be installed as an upgrade on systems that currently use WEP. WPA offers two distinct advantages over WEP:

- Improved data encryption through Temporal Key Integrity Protocol (TKIP), which scrambles the keys using a hashing algorithm. TKIP also provides an integrity-checking feature that ensures that the keys haven't been tampered with or altered.

- User authentication through the use of the EAP and user certificates. This ensures that only authorized users are given access to the network.

802.1x

The latest and most advanced form of wireless security is *802.1x*, which is the name for the IEEE standard that it supports. This type of wireless security is a standard feature of the latest operating systems such as Windows XP Professional. Access can be controlled per user and/or per port. 802.1x uses EAP to provide the following methods of authentication:

EAP Transport Level Security (EAP-TLS)   This is the strongest method of encryption. EAP-TLS requires a certificate-based security environment. In other words, a form of certificate authority must be used. It provides mutual authentication, negotiation of the encryption method, and encrypted key determination between the client and the authenticator.

Protected EAP (PEAP)   PEAP uses TLS to enhance the security of other authentication methods such as CHAP. PEAP can be used without certificates unless it is being used in conjunction with MS-CHAP v2, which requires certificates in order to provide mutual authentication between the client and the server.

Remote Authentication Dial-In User Services (RADIUS)   Clients can be authenticated to use a wireless connection based on a current logon that can be authenticated by a domain controller. This method is used only when the user has an account in a domain such as a Microsoft Windows Active Directory domain.

Exam Essentials

Describe the purpose and function of IPSec.   IPSec is a protocol designed to secure data communication between two computers. The function of IPSec is to ensure that the transmitted data has not been viewed accessed or modified by anyone except the intended receiver. IPSec can be used within networks (transport mode) and/or between networks (tunnel mode).

Explain the purpose and function of L2TP.   L2TP is a tunneling protocol that is considered more secure than PPTP. L2TP uses digital certificates to provide authentication of the client computer as well as the user of the connection. L2TP can protect against the man-in-the-middle attack by authenticating the client computer and the tunnel IP address before sending data down the tunnel.

Understand the purpose and function of SSL.   SSL is a security protocol for sending information over the Internet. You can access a secure website on a browser using `https://` at the beginning of the URL instead of `http://`. SSL uses public key cryptography to provide secure communication and to allow authentication of the server to the client, authentication of the client to the server, and encryption of the data transfer.

Know the purpose and function of WEP.   WEP was one of the first attempts to provide security for a wireless network. WEP provides security by encrypting the data traffic after the user has authenticated, but the authentication itself is in clear text and not secure. The shortcomings of WEP have resulted in its replacement by stronger methods of wireless security, such as WPA and 802.1x.

Describe the purpose and function of WPA. WPA is a wireless security protocol that was developed to strengthen the security of wireless systems that were already using WEP. WPA offers advantages, including improved encryption methods using TKIP and improved authentication methods using EAP.

Explain the purpose and function of 802.1x. 802.1x is the most advanced wireless protocol available today. It can control access on a per user and/or per port basis. 802.1x can be used in conjunction with certificate-based methods, standard methods (such as CHAP), or RADIUS authentication with a centralized authenticator.

2.18 Identifying Authentication Protocols

When two computers exchange information through a network, the only physical change that takes place is a fluctuation in current or radio signal (in the case of a wireless communication). Based on the precise way the fluctuation occurs, we can use authentication protocols that enable one computer or user to prove its identity to another user. In essence, authentication protocols are the way that a computer or a user communicates the concept, "I am who I say I am and I can prove it."

Authentication protocols have evolved over the last several years, and there are many from which you can choose depending on your network's security needs. We will discuss the common authentication protocols in use today.

Critical Information

Due to an ever-increasing need for stronger security, authentication protocols have evolved over the last several years—and they continue to evolve. Basically, there are only three ways that a user can prove his identity, something he knows, something he has, or something he is. The latest methods of security combine two or even all three of these factors, creating a new method referred to as *multifactor authentication*.

You should be able to identify the most common authentication protocols. You should know which clients can use each protocol and the type of network that is likely to use each type of protocol. In this section, we will discuss some of the older authentication protocols as well as the most common authentication protocols used in today's networks.

Password Authentication Protocol (PAP)

Password Authentication Protocol (PAP) is an older remote access authentication protocol that is not commonly used in today's networks. PAP uses a two-way handshake mechanism. In other words, the server asks the client for the password and the client provides the password in clear text. If anyone is "listening in" or *sniffing* the network, they can also see the password in clear text and use it. Because of this limitation, PAP is not considered a secure authentication protocol and would therefore only be used in networks that do not require security.

Challenge Handshake Authentication Protocol (CHAP)

Challenge Handshake Authentication Protocol (CHAP) is a remote access authentication protocol that uses a password that is a shared secret between the server and client, but the password is never sent in clear text. Instead, a three-way handshake is used in which the server sends the client a challenge to prove that it knows the password by inserting it into a challenge string sent by the server. When the server receives the password inserted into the challenge string, the server removes the challenge string and compares the password with the one that it knows. If the two are the same, then the communication can continue. If they are not the same, then the communication will be terminated. In this way, CHAP establishes authentication without having to send a password in clear text. CHAP is the strongest authentication method that can be used when there are a mixture of Microsoft clients and other types of clients such as Novell, Unix, or Apple.

Microsoft Challenge Handshake Protocol (MS-CHAP)

Microsoft Challenge Handshake Protocol (MS-CHAP) is Microsoft's variation on the CHAP protocol, which provides even greater security for authentication of Microsoft clients. Because MS-CHAP is specifically written for Microsoft, all clients must be running a Microsoft operating system. While it's possible for any Microsoft clients to use MS-CHAP, it is more likely that it will be used by Windows 95, Windows 98, and Windows NT Workstation clients. This is because the newer clients can use an even more secure protocol referred to as MS-CHAP v2.

Microsoft Challenge Handshake Protocol version 2 (MS-CHAP v2)

Microsoft Challenge Handshake Protocol version 2 (MS-CHAP v2) is a much stronger form of remote access authentication that can only be used by Windows 2000 Professional and later clients or Windows 98 clients using a VPN. There are many new features in MS-CHAP v2 that strengthen the security of the authentication mechanisms. The most important of these is the fact that MS-CHAP v2 offers a two-way authentication method. This means that a client can verify that the server is a legitimate server and not a rogue RAS server before it reveals its credentials to the server for authentication. This prevents an attacker from inserting a server into a network environment for the purpose of collecting user credentials for later use. MS-CHAP v2 is a good solution for networks with Microsoft Windows 2000 Server or Windows Server 2003 and clients that are Windows 2000 Professional or later.

RADIUS Authentication

As we discussed earlier in this chapter, RADIUS authentication occurs when a device such as a RADIUS server or a wireless WAP defer the authentication to a centralized authority such as a domain controller on a Microsoft Active Directory. The device that receives the remote access request simply acts as a go-between and the actual authentication occurs as the centralized authenticator. This is a viable method of authentication for remote access connections and wireless connections to a domain environment such as Microsoft Active Directory of Novell Directory Services.

Kerberos Authentication

Kerberos authentication is a form of local authentication that is used on most networks today. It was developed by the Massachusetts Institute of Technology (MIT) and has been adopted by many vendors, including Microsoft. Kerberos allows the private exchange of information and instruction in what would otherwise be an open network. Using Kerberos authentication, clients can log onto a Windows Active Directory or Novell's NDS and browse resources to which they are assigned permissions.

Kerberos is named for the mythical three-headed dog that guarded the gates of Hades. It uses a series of tickets, which allow a client to prove that it should have access to a resource. Since the tickets are valid only for a short period of time after they are issued, Kerberos prevents an internal attacker from "replaying" a conversation and thereby gaining access to a resource for which he does not have permission.

Extensible Authentication Protocol (EAP)

As the name suggests, *Extensible Authentication Protocol (EAP)* is an open set of standards that allows the addition of new methods of authentication. EAP can also use certificates from other trusted parties as a form of authentication. It is currently used primarily for smart cards, but it will soon evolve and be used for many forms of biometric authentication using a person's fingerprint, retina scan, and so on.

Exam Essentials

Know the characteristics of PAP. PAP is a remote access protocol that sends a password in clear text with a two-way handshake. The only networks that might use PAP today would be those in which security is of no concern.

Describe the characteristics of CHAP. CHAP is considered to be the strongest protocol that can be used on a server if the clients are not all Microsoft clients. CHAP uses a three-way handshake to verify that the user knows the password without sending the password in clear text.

List the characteristics of MS-CHAP. MS-CHAP is Microsoft's version of CHAP made specifically for use with Microsoft clients. MS-CHAP provides even greater authentication security, but it can only be used with Microsoft clients. All Microsoft clients can use MS-CHAP, but it will most likely be used by Windows 95, Windows 98, and Windows NT Workstation clients, since the newer client can use even more secure protocols, such as MS-CHAP v2.

Know the characteristics of MS-CHAP v2. MS-CHAP v2 is a remote access protocol that provides several features that make it more secure than MS-CHAP. The most important of these features is the mutual authentication, whereby the client authenticates the server as well as the server authenticating the client. MS-CHAP v2 is available only for Windows 2000 Professional and later clients, and Windows 98 clients on VPNs.

Describe how RADIUS authentication works. RADIUS authentication is a process of using a server or another device as a go-between that connects the client to the network after the client is authenticated by a central authenticator. RADIUS authentication can be used for remote access as well as wireless access to a network. A domain controller running Microsoft Active Directory can provide a centralized authenticator for RADIUS authentication.

Know the characteristics of Kerberos. Kerberos is a local security protocol that creates a secure communication channel using a series of tickets. The Kerberos tickets are valid only for a short period of time to prevent an internal replay attack. Kerberos is the default authentication protocol in Windows Active Directory as well as Novell Directory Services.

List the characteristics of EAP. EAP is a set of open standards that allows for the expansion of authentication protocols. EAP currently uses mostly smart card authentication and trusted certificate authentication, but it is quickly evolving to include biometric identification such as fingerprints, eye scans, and so on.

Review Questions

1. What is name of the unique physical address that is assigned to every network interface card?
   A. IP address
   B. Hostname
   C. MAC address
   D. NetBIOS name

2. At which layer of the OSI model is information from applications translated into a form of communication that can be sent over the network?
   A. Physical
   B. Transport
   C. Network
   D. Presentation

3. Which layer of the OSI model is responsible for resending packets that do not receive an acknowledgment from the destination address on the network?
   A. Application
   B. Transport
   C. Network
   D. Session

4. Which layer of the OSI model is divided into two sublayers?
   A. Session
   B. Application
   C. Data Link
   D. Physical

5. At which layer of the OSI model does a network bridge operate?
   A. Network
   B. Data Link
   C. Physical
   D. Session

6. At which layer of the OSI model does a router operate?
   A. Network
   B. Application
   C. Session
   D. Transport

7. Which of the following protocols is not routable?
   A. IP
   B. IPX
   C. AppleTalk
   D. NetBEUI

8. How many bits are used to create and IPv4 address?
   A. 8
   B. 6
   C. 32
   D. 64

9. In which address class is the classful IP address 191.222.232.254?
   A. A
   B. B
   C. C
   D. D

10. If you have a class B address with a default subnet mask and you need to create 8 subnets, then which of the following subnet masks should you use?
    A. 255.255.255.240
    B. 255.255.224.0
    C. 255.255.240.0
    D. 255.240.0.0

11. Which of the following IP addresses are valid for private IP addressing that is filtered from the Internet? (Choose two.)
    A. 10.1.1.1
    B. 172.17.255.254
    C. 11.1.2.4
    D. 193.168.2.1

12. You are troubleshooting a connection for a user. The user cannot connect to the network. You determine that the user has an IP address of 169.254.2.5. Which type of server is most likely the cause of the problem?
    A. WINS
    B. DNS
    C. Domain Controller
    D. DHCP

13. Which protocol in the TCP/IP protocol suite is responsible for managing the three-way handshake that establishes a session?

    A. IP
    B. UDP
    C. TCP
    D. ARP

14. Which of the following protocols is responsible for sending e-mail over the Internet?

    A. POP3
    B. IMAP4
    C. FTP
    D. SMTP

15. Which protocol is responsible for responding to a ping request?

    A. ICMP
    B. TCP
    C. ARP
    D. UDP

16. Which protocol resolves IP addresses to MAC addresses?

    A. DNS
    B. ARP
    C. NetBIOS
    D. TCP

17. Which information directory protocol is the standard for Windows Active Directory?

    A. TCP
    B. UDP
    C. LDAP
    D. IGMP

18. Which of the following are designated as well-known port numbers? (Choose two.)

    A. 80
    B. 49,150
    C. 1,011
    D. 8,080

19. Which of the following is the total available bandwidth of a T1 line?
    A. 128Kbps
    B. 2.544Gbps
    C. 1.544Mbps
    D. 56Mbps

20. Which of the following remote access protocols is used to establish connectivity in most of today's remote access networks?
    A. SLIP
    B. PPP
    C. PPTP
    D. L2TP

Answers to Review Questions

1. **C.** A Media Access Control (MAC) address is a unique physical address that is assigned to each network interface card. MAC addresses are "burned into" the card at the manufacturer.

2. **D.** The Presentation layer of the OSI model is responsible for converting and translating data into a form that can begin to be sent over the network. The Presentation layer provides compression and decompression as well as encryption and decryption. You can remember the Presentation layer as the translation layer.

3. **B.** The Transport layer of the OSI model contains the protocols that are responsible for resending packets that do not receive an acknowledgment from the destination address. These protocols include TCP, SPX, and other protocols.

4. **C.** The Data Link layer of the OSI model is divided into two sublayers: the Logical Link Control (LLC) layer and the Media Access Control (MAC) layer. The LLC connects the Data Link layer to the higher-level protocols such as IP at the Network layer. The MAC layer connects the Data Link layer to the physical connection and provides MAC address.

5. **B.** A network bridge operates at the Data Link layer of the OSI model. Bridges create a table using the MAC addresses of hosts that are connected to the bridge.

6. **A.** Routers operate at the Network layer using the logical addresses that are assigned at the Network layer. These include IP addresses, IPX addresses, and others.

7. **D.** NetBEUI is not a routable protocol. It is, however, a self-configuring protocol that is useful for a very small network that does not need access to the Internet.

8. **C.** An IPv4 address is a 32-bit address. It is composed of four sections of 8 bits each, called octets. Each octet is converted to decimal form for configuration purposes, but the computer uses the entire 32-bit address for communication.

9. **B.** The classful IP address of 191.222.232.254 is a class B address. All addresses in which the first octet is 128–191 are considered class B addresses.

10. **C.** If you have a class address with a default subnet mask, then the current subnet mask is 255.255.0.0. This means that you have 16 bits for networks and 16 bits for hosts. If you want to create 8 subnets, then you need $2^n-2 \geq 8$. Solving for n, you can determine that you need to use the first 4 bits from the network address to create the subnets ($2^3-2=6$, which is not enough, but $2^4-2=14$, which is more than enough). The values of the first 4 bits total 240 (128+64+32+16), so the new subnet mask is 255.255.240.0.

11. **A, B.** The valid private address ranges include the following:

    - 192.168.0.0–192.168.255.255
    - 172.16.0.0–172.31.255.255
    - 10.0.0.0–10.255.255.255

    Only answers A and B fall into these ranges.

12. D. The address 169.254.2.5 is an APIPA address that was generated by the computer because it is configured to obtain an IP address from the DHCP server and a DHCP server is not available.

13. C. Transmission Control Protocol (TCP) is responsible for managing the three-way handshake that creates a session between two computers. TCP establishes the session by sending a short SYN message, receiving an ACK message, and then sending another short acknowledgment (ACK) message indicating that it received the acknowledgment from the other computer.

14. D. Simple Mail Transfer Protocol (SMTP) is responsible for sending e-mail over the Internet. SMTP is used to send e-mail to e-mail servers that use the POP3 and/or IMAP4 protocols to receive mail and make it available for users.

15. A. Internet Control Message Protocol (ICMP) is responsible for responding to a ping echo request with an echo reply. Ping is a tool that you can use to check general network connectivity.

16. B. Address Resolution Protocol (ARP) is used to resolve IP addresses to MAC addresses on a network. A computer's only truly unique physical address is the MAC address on its NIC. The MAC address must be used before packets can be delivered to a host.

17. C. The standard protocol used for directory services in Windows Active Directory is Lightweight Directory Access Protocol (LDAP). It is based on the X.500 standard, but it is significantly simpler.

18. A, C. The port numbers that are designated as well-known port numbers are those in range of 0–1,023. Ports in the range of 1,024–49,151 are designated as registered ports. Ports in the range of 49,152–65,535 are designated as dynamic or private ports.

19. C. A T1 line is one of the most common types of leased line used by today's businesses for connectivity to remote offices and to the Internet. It is capable of 1.544Mbps on 24 independent 64Kbps channels.

20. B. Point-to-Point Protocol (PPP) is the most common remote access protocol used to establish connectivity in today's remote access networks. PPP has replaced SLIP because it is more secure and flexible. PPP can be further encrypted using tunneling protocols such as PPTP and L2TP.

Chapter 3

Domain 3 Network Implementation

COMPTIA NETWORK+ EXAM OBJECTIVES COVERED IN THIS CHAPTER:

✓ **3.1 Identify the basic capabilities (For example: client support, interoperability, authentication, file and print services, application support and security) of the following server operating systems to access network resources:**
  - UNIX / Linux / Mac OS X Server
  - NetWare
  - Windows
  - Appleshare IP (Internet Protocol)

✓ **3.2 Identify the basic capabilities needed for client workstations to connect to and use network resources (For example: media, network protocols and peer and server services).**

✓ **3.3 Identify the appropriate tool for a given wiring task (For example: wire crimper, media tester / certifier, punch down tool or tone generator).**

✓ **3.4 Given a remote connectivity scenario comprised of a protocol, an authentication scheme, and physical connectivity, configure the connection. Includes connection to the following servers:**
  - UNIX / Linux / MAC OS X Server
  - NetWare
  - Windows
  - Appleshare IP (Internet Protocol)

✓ **3.5 Identify the purpose, benefits and characteristics of using a firewall.**

- ✓ **3.6 Identify the purpose, benefits and characteristics of using a proxy service.**
- ✓ **3.7 Given a connectivity scenario, determine the impact on network functionality of a particular security implementation (For example: port blocking / filtering, authentication and encryption).**
- ✓ **3.8 Identify the main characteristics of VLANs (Virtual Local Area Networks).**
- ✓ **3.9 Identify the main characteristics and purpose of extranets and intranets.**
- ✓ **3.10 Identify the purpose, benefits and characteristics of using antivirus software.**
- ✓ **3.11 Identify the purpose and characteristics of fault tolerance:**
    - Power
    - Link redundancy
    - Storage
    - Services
- ✓ **3.12 Identify the purpose and characteristics of disaster recovery:**
    - Backup / restore
    - Offsite storage
    - Hot and cold spares
    - Hot, warm and cold sites

All of the theory and "book knowledge" in the world will do you no good if you don't know how to apply what you have learned. Likewise, it is much easier to remember facts for the test if you can connect them to some real-world understanding of a subject. Being able to put together and manage a network takes more than just an understanding of the pieces that make up the network; you also need to understand how the pieces work together.

In particular, you should understand the most common server and client operating systems and know how they work together. You should also be familiar with the components that create or control connectivity such as wiring, authentication and encryption protocols, proxies, and so on. Finally, you should know how to protect your network with firewalls, fault-tolerance strategies, and disaster-recovery methods.

In this chapter on network implementation, we discuss all of these concepts in detail. We also focus on how they relate to one another in the construction and management of a network. At the end of this chapter, you should be more familiar with each of these components and their relation to establishing and maintaining a functional network.

3.1 Identifying Server Operating System Access to Network Resources

Although Microsoft has most of the market in regard to server operating systems, they do not have it all. You should therefore understand the capabilities of various server operating systems in regard to interoperability with Microsoft and with each other. Server operating systems can be used for a variety of tasks on a network. They can also provide resources, such as a file server, application server, or print server.

Critical Information

You should be familiar with the means of accessing network resources located on the most common types of server operating systems. Be able to compare and contrast the differences between the methods used to access resources on each type of server operating system.

Unix/Linux/Mac OS X Server

Unix was one of the first server operating systems to be used to provide resources on a network. Many Unix servers are still in use today, due to the legacy programs that are still used on the servers and the relative flexibility of the Unix operating system in regard to the clients that it can use. You can connect to a Unix server using the Telnet program or SSH. Unix authentication and security is accomplished in much the same way as Microsoft's newer networks, with Remote Procedure Call (RPC) and the Kerberos protocol. Unix can also use the PPP protocol for remote access authentication.

Microsoft also provides a package for clients that allows Microsoft clients to connect to and use resources and printers on a Unix server, referred to as Services for Unix. Clients can use the Line Printer Requester (LPR) protocol to connect to Unix servers running the Line Printer Daemon (LPD) protocol. Despite Unix's flexibility in regard to clients, most companies do not use Unix servers anymore. This is partially due to the fact that much of the configuration of Unix server was originally accomplished through a "not so user friendly" command prompt, although newer versions of Unix, such as Solaris and AIX, now offer a robust GUI.

Linux is a "spin-off" of Unix, first developed by Linus Torvalds and a number of enthusiastic developers in 1991. Linux is an open source operating system, which means you can download the kernel for free. However, there are many distributors—such as Red Hat and SUSE—who offer installation help, online and telephone support, and other freeware applications on one convenient CD for a fee.

Linux boasts an open source architecture, which means that you can make real changes to the way that it operates. If you don't like something about Linux, you can just change a few things and make your own new version. While this fact has aided the growth of Linux, especially within the circles of computer software developers, it's also limiting the acceptance of the software by "big business." This is due to the fact that big business relies on standardization, which Linux (because of its open source nature) has been unable to provide. This is gradually changing and Linux may begin to give Microsoft a "run for their money" in the near future.

As with Unix, you can use Telnet to connect to and manage Linux servers; however, you can also use an array of GUI tools provided by Linux. Linux uses the TCP/IP protocol, which makes it largely interoperable with Microsoft and with AppleTalk for IP. It also uses Lightweight Directory Access Protocol (LDAP) for its databases, which makes it interoperable with Microsoft Active Directory as well as Novell Directory Services. In regard to security, like Unix, Linux is capable of using the Kerberos authentication protocol for local connections and PPP authentication for remote connections.

For file and print services, Linux clients can use Samba (from the Server Message Block protocol or SMB), which is a suite of programs that implement the SMB protocol on Linux. The SMB protocol is the foundation of Windows networking, or as Microsoft now calls it, the Common Internet File System (CIFS). The latest version of Samba, 3.0.10, includes many new features to increase compatibility with Windows 2000 and Windows Server 2003 domains.

Mac OS X Server is a Unix-based product from Apple computers. It is a newer server product that was designed for today's networks and for the use with the TCP/IP protocol rather than a proprietary protocol from Apple. Mac OS X Server can also act as a web server for many types of clients. It uses Kerberos authentication for a secure single sign-on to all of the resources to which a user is given permissions. It can also use the latest features such as Wired Equivalent Privacy (WEP) for wireless networks and virtual private networking (VPN) for secure access to remote corporate networks. Since it is Unix based, it offers all of the same file and print capabilities and application support as the Unix and Linux servers, such as the latest versions of Samba.

NetWare

NetWare is a server operating system produced by Novell. First introduced in the early 1990s, NetWare has been through many revisions and is now one of the most secure and full-featured operating systems available today. Many administrators feel that NetWare has actually been a more secure and more manageable server product than any other over the years. Many administrators know nothing except NetWare and and therefore will not give it up. Despite this fact, Novell continues to lose market share to the latest Microsoft server operating systems. NetWare servers do, however, make excellent file servers because of the way their NFS file system indexes all of the information on the computer.

There are many ways to connect to a NetWare server. You can do so using a Novell client software installed on the client computer over the operating system of your choice. In addition, Microsoft provides a tool called *Client Services for NetWare (CSNW)*, which allows its clients to connect directly to a NetWare server, and a tool called *Gateway (and client) Services for NetWare (GSNW)*, which allows a client to connect to a Microsoft server that is connected to a NetWare server. When you install these tools, the NWLink protocol that emulates the Novell IPX/SPX protocol is also installed. This allows additional connectivity to the Novell server, although the latest Novell servers use TCP/IP, not IPX/SPX, as their default protocol. You can also use the Telnet protocol to connect to and manage NetWare servers.

Windows

When you just say "Windows" to describe all of the server operating systems that Microsoft has released over the years, that's a little like saying "cars" to describe what has come out of Detroit's assembly lines. In other words, there have been many operating systems and many service packs for each of the operating systems, which, in some cases, dramatically changed the capabilities of the operating system. Rather than discussing all of the details of each of the server operating systems produced by Microsoft, we will instead focus on the commonalities of the server operating systems in regard to the methods that a client can use to connect to the server and use resources contained on the server. All of the newest operating systems (beginning with Windows 95) have Microsoft Client included in the software.

There are many ways in which Microsoft clients can connect to and use resources on a Microsoft server. The following is a list of the most common methods used:

Network Neighborhood/My Network Places This is a server and share location service (shown in Figure 3.1) that provides a GUI-based tool on which users can point and click to connect to resources. The list of resources is frequently updated automatically by the browsing service on the network. These tools can also be located within the Windows Explore and My Computer tools.

FIGURE 3.1 My Network Places

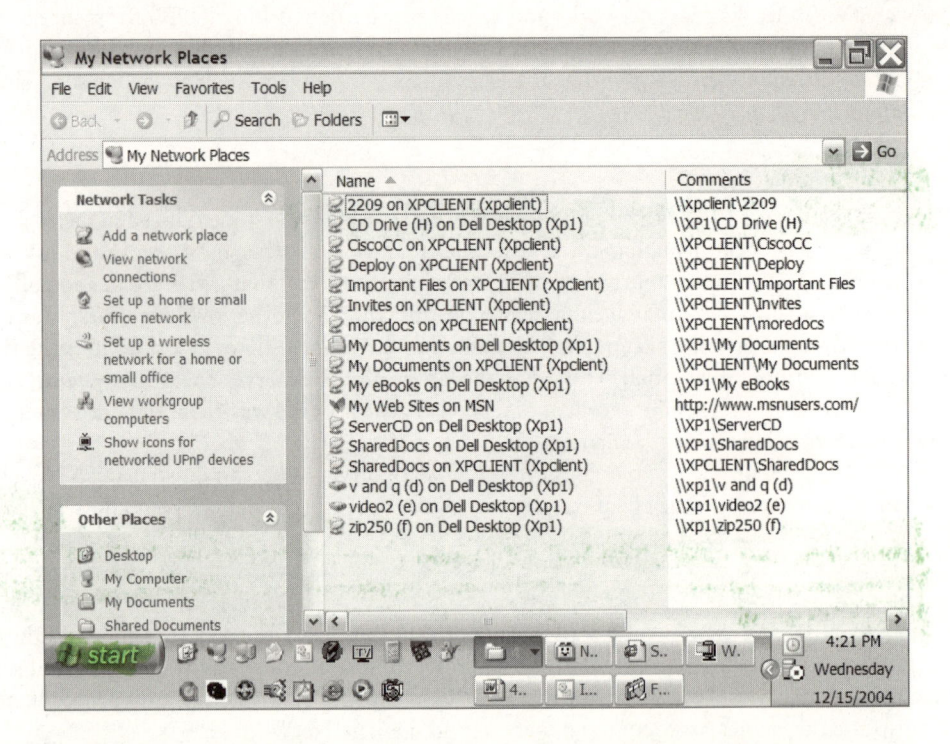

Mapped network drives Users and administrators can use the Windows Explore tool (shown in Figure 3.2) to map a network drive and make it easily accessible in the future.

Universal Naming Convention (UNC) command You can access shared resources on a Microsoft network by typing the UNC command that indicates the server where the resources are stored and the name of the share that identifies the resources. The syntax for the UNC command is \\server\share, where server is the name of the server that contains the resource and share is the name of the shared folder or other resource on the server.

Remote Desktop Connection You can connect to a server remotely from a client or another server, provided that you have the permissions and the server to which you are connecting is configured to accept the connection. Users can also use Remote Desktop Connection to connect to resources and programs on a server. You can configure Remote Desktop Connection to allow a user to connect to a server resource and automatically run a program that provides access to a line-of-business application. In this way, you can enable users to utilize their PCs more like dumb terminals to connect to and use specific resources.

Microsoft also makes sure that their networks are accessible to other clients. Most client operating systems such as Novell, Unix, Macintosh, and Linux have software that allows them to connect to and use resources on a Microsoft network. While they may not have all of the options that the Microsoft clients have, most do have the general capability to connect to the resource.

3.1 Identifying Server Operating System Access to Network Resources 117

FIGURE 3.2 Mapping a network drive

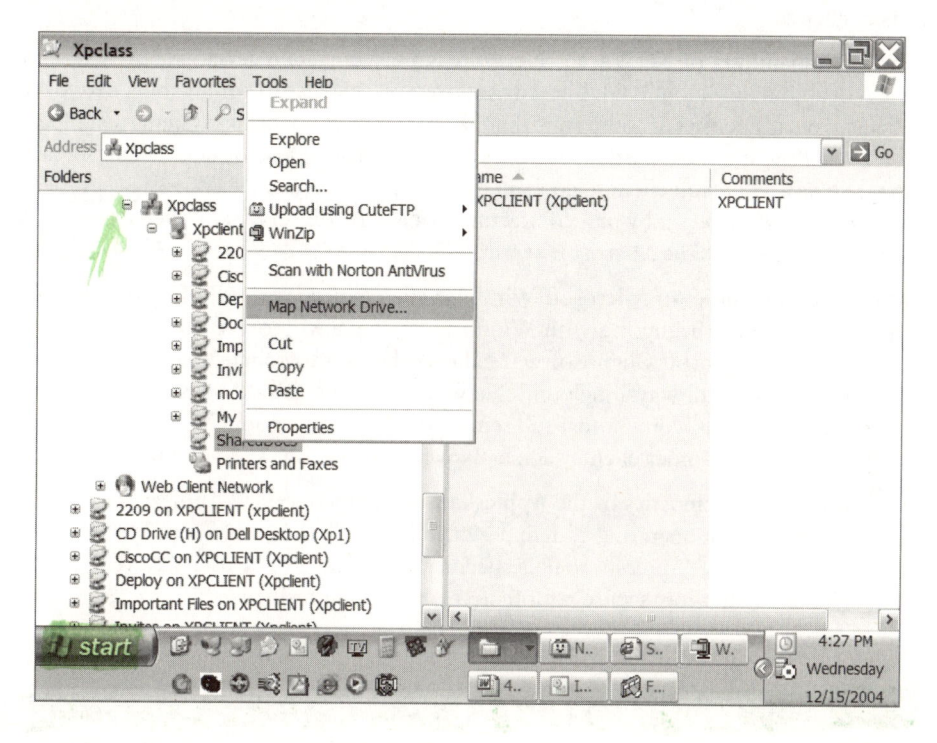

Appleshare IP (Internet Protocol)

Appleshare IP is a service from Apple that is specifically designed to provide secure remote access for Macintosh clients to Mac OS X Servers. We will discuss this service in greater detail later in this chapter in the section on remote access.

Exam Essentials

Describe the capabilities of Unix servers. Unix servers are still in use today largely because of their high degree of flexibility in regard to applications and clients. Most connections to a Unix-based server are made using Telnet or another, more secure remote protocol. Unix is still mostly command line driven and does not offer the GUI tools that other operating systems offer.

Be familiar with the capabilities of Linux. Linux is a spin-off from Unix, but it does provide a GUI. Linux servers can be accessed using Telnet or an array of tools provided by Linux clients. The main distinction of Linux software is its open source architecture, but this distinction is also a disadvantage because of the lack of standardization of the product.

Know the capabilities of Mac OS X Server. Mac OS X Server is a newer product designed to be used with Macintosh clients and other computers. Mac OS X is designed to use TCP/IP instead of the proprietary Apple protocols. Mac OS X Server can make a good web server for many clients.

List the capabilities of NetWare. NetWare is a server system developed by Novell. It offers an array of command-line and GUI-based tools that you can use to administer a network. NetWare clients typically consist of computers that have Microsoft operating systems installed along with the Novell client network and operating system. Microsoft also offers a client operating system that allows a Microsoft client to connect to a NetWare server (CSNW). The clients can also connect to a NetWare server by first connecting to a Microsoft server and then using a gateway connection provided by the Microsoft server (GSNW).

Know the capabilities of Microsoft Windows client software. All of the newest Microsoft operating systems (beginning with Windows 95) have Microsoft Client included in the software. The Microsoft Client software allows the user to connect to a Microsoft network in a number of different ways, including Network Neighborhood/My Network Places, mapped network drives, UNC commands, and remote desktop connection. Microsoft also makes its networks accessible to other clients such as Novell, Macintosh, and Unix clients.

Describe the characteristics of the Appleshare IP protocol. The Appleshare IP protocol is a relatively new client operating system designed by Apple to be used with Macintosh clients and the TCP/IP protocol. Appleshare IP is specifically designed to be used as a remote access server and has tools that allow secure remote access for Macintosh clients.

3.2 Identifying Capabilities Clients Need to Use Network Resources

For two computers to communicate over a network, they must have three components in common. It is essential that you understand the role of these components so you can design, manage, and troubleshoot networks.

Critical Information

A computer connection over a network requires a common media, a common protocol, and a common client or service. In this section, we discuss each of these subjects in detail.

Common Network Media

"Network media" is a loose term for anything that is connecting two computers together to form a network. This can be cables and wires or wireless communication such as Wi-Fi access or even infrared light. The main requirement in order for the network media to be effective is that the computers that are going to communicate share the network media in common. In other words, just because one computer can connect with a cable and another computer can connect with a radio signal does not mean that the two computers can connect to each other. In fact, just because two computers can connect with a wireless connection does not mean that they can connect to each other. However, if two wired computers are connected to a common hub or if two computers are connected with a wireless connection and share the same frequency, then they have a chance at connecting to each other, assuming that all of the other components are present.

Common Protocol

Most computers in use today share the common protocol of TCP/IP. This is because TCP/IP has become the de facto standard protocol for communication on the Internet. Whether TCP/IP is chosen as the common protocol between two computers, or some other protocol, such as IPX/SPX or AppleTalk, is chosen, the main requirement is that both computers share the same protocol and that the protocol be configured properly to allow the computers to communicate with each other. In regard to TCP/IP, this can be accomplished with manual configuration, or special servers and services can automatically configure the protocol address. Other protocols are self-configuring; an example is IPX/SPX, which uses the MAC address of a computer to complete the configuration.

Common Client

The term "client" can sometimes be a confusing one because it's used interchangeably to refer to a client computer, a client operating system, and sometimes even a person (as in "a client of a law firm"). Still another use for the term "client" is the networking software that is used to connect computers. The type of client used will depend completely on the vendor of the operating system software, but it's not quite that simple either.

Vendors such as Microsoft and Novell provide client software that can be used to connect to their servers and use resources. The services called CSNW and GSNW (which we discussed earlier in the chapter) are actually clients that Microsoft provides, which can be added as a second client to the Microsoft Client software included with the Microsoft operating system. Likewise, Novell "clients" are just computers with another type of operating system installed first (Novell does not make an operating system that runs a client PC) and then followed up with an installation of Novell client software.

Exam Essentials

List the requirements for common network media. The media that computers use is not important in regard to their ability to communicate with each other, only the fact that the media must be common between the computers. A common network media is a cabled media or a wireless media. Some computers have multiple connections that allow more than one type of media on the same computer.

Know the requirements for a common network protocol. A protocol is like a language that computers use to communicate within a network. The main requirement of a common network protocol is that the two computers use the same protocol and that the protocol be configured properly for connectivity. The most common protocol used for network connectivity is TCP/IP, but many more protocols are in use today.

Understand the requirements for a common network client. The type of client that you use will largely depend on the vendor of the client operating system that you choose. Microsoft operating systems come installed with a client called Microsoft Client. Some vendors also provide client operating system software that allows their clients to communicate with the servers and clients of other vendors.

3.3 Identifying Tools Used for Wiring

Someone once said "The job is whole lot easier when you use the right tools!" This statement is certainly true in regard to wiring networks. While wiring networks is not "rocket science," it can be tedious and time consuming. Once you understand what goes into wiring a network, you will probably gain a much keener insight into why wireless networks have become so popular.

Critical Information

You should know the general purpose and features of each of the main tools that are used to wire and test a network. Be able to identify the proper tool for a given task.

Wire Crimpers

Typically LANs are wired with category 5, 5e, or 6 cable and RJ-45 connectors. While you can purchase these types of cables with the connectors already installed on them, they are only available in designated lengths. Network engineers often need to customize the cable installation lengths, so they have to cut their own cables from a spool of wire and then attach the RJ-45 connectors to the cable's wires. This requires that they place the wires into the RJ-45 connector with the colors in the correct order. This order varies depending on whether the network engineer intends to make a straight-through, crossover, or rollover cable. Table 3.1 shows the standard order of the colors for each type of cable and gives a brief description of the use of each type of cable.

Actually, you can you use any colors that you want, as long as you are consistent. You can use the wire crimper to strip the outer insulation from the cable to expose the wires so you can insert them into the connector. *Wire crimpers*, shown in Figure 3.3, resemble a pair of special pliers that have the right features to strip the wire as well as to hold the connector in place as you squeeze its teeth into position over the inserted wires. It is not necessary to strip the insulation from each individual wire, because the connector will "bite" through the insulation to make the contact. At first, the process of crimping wires is a tedious one, but with practice you can crimp like the professionals!

TABLE 3.1 Color Schemes for Network Cables

Cable Type	Color Scheme	Intended Use
Straight-through	Same on both sides. Usually as follows (holding the connector upright and looking from left to right): White/Orange; Orange; White/Green; Blue; White/Blue; Green; White/Brown; Brown	Used as patch cables to connect dissimilar equipment, such as connecting a switch to a router.
Crossover	Pins 1 and 3 and pins 2 and 6 are switched. One end is configured as above, but the other end is configured as follows (holding the connector upright and looking from left to right): White/Green; Green; White/Orange; Blue; White/Blue; Orange; White/Brown; Brown	Typically used to connect similar devices, such connecting a hub to a hub or a computer to a computer. May be used to connect two computers so that one can be used to debug the other one.
Rollover	One side is completely opposite of the other side. Typically, one end is configured as a straight-through cable and the other end is configured as follows (holding the connector upright and looking from left to right): Brown; White/Brown; Green; White/Blue; Blue; White/Orange; Orange	Typically used to manage network equipment by plugging a computer's serial port into the console port of the network equipment.

FIGURE 3.3 Wire crimpers

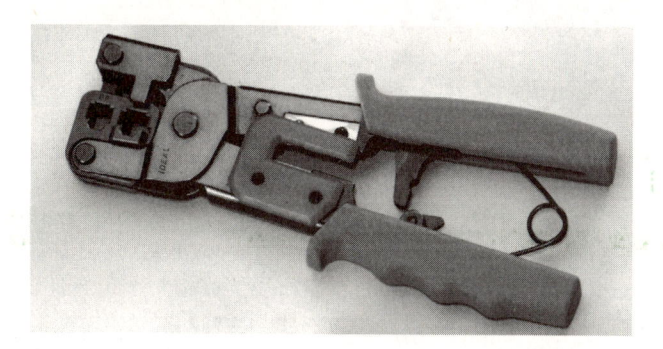

Media Tester

After you have created your new cable, you probably want to test it to make sure that it works properly. If you made only one cable, then you would likely just install it where you had intended to use it and make sure that it works. This is assuming that a network is already in place and that computers are available to test the connection. If this is not the case, or if you are creating many cables as part of a network implementation, then you might want to be able to test the cable without actually installing it in the network. In that case, you could use a media tester.

A *media tester*, shown in Figure 3.4, is a device that sends a current through each wire of a cable to determine whether each wire can carry the current from end to end within the cable. If each wire can perform as expected, then the cable will be able to carry the computer signal from end to end as well. Some media testers indicate that a cable is good or bad with a series of lights, others use sounds, and still others have LED or LCD panels that indicate the test results. These devices can be handy for network design as well as for troubleshooting a connectivity problem in a network.

FIGURE 3.4 A media tester

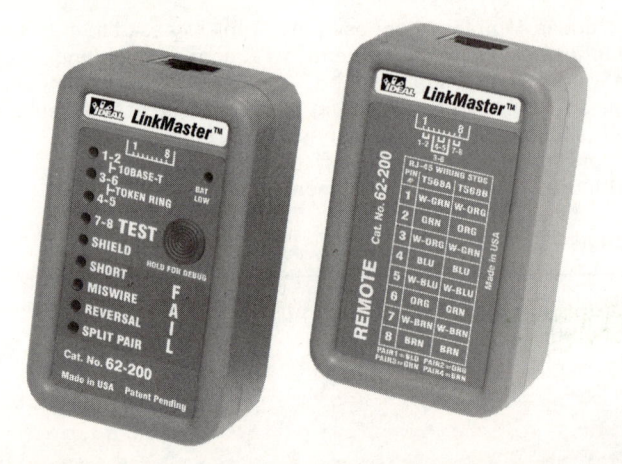

Punch-Down Tool

To increase the flexibility and fault tolerance of a network, most organizations do not use a continuous cable from end to end for each computer connection. Instead, each cable is connected through a series of patch panels. These patch panels provide a method of quickly changing a cable that is part of a computer's connection to the network. Typically, the front side of patch panel has several RJ-45 connector ports, but the back of the panel does not have ports and instead is "hard wired" with the wires from the cables "punched down" into special connectors that hold them securely in place. This is where the *punch-down tool* comes into play.

3.3 Identifying Tools Used for Wiring 123

The process of punching down a wire properly takes a considerable amount of force. You could try to do it without the special tool, but you would probably break the wire or not be able to make the proper connection at all. The punch-down tool, shown in Figure 3.5, assists you in applying the right amount of pressure in the right direction. As you push in with the tool, you load up a spring, which then releases the proper amount of force to press the wire firmly into the connector while stripping the insulation off the side of the wire to ensure a firm connection with the metal connector. With a little practice, you will be able to "punch down" wires with ease.

FIGURE 3.5 A punch-down tool

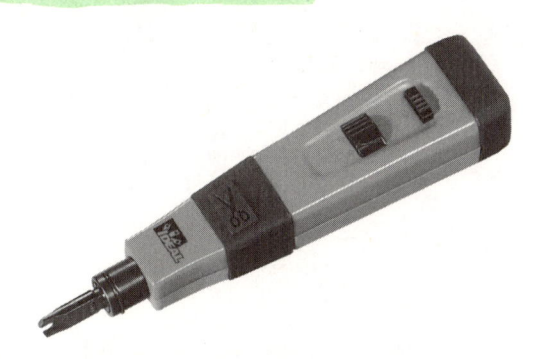

Tone Generator

To test the connectivity of wires that run through walls and other obstructions, it is sometimes necessary to use a tool to produce a signal (or tone) on one end and then determine whether that signal can still be heard on the other end. The device that produces the signal is called the *tone generator*. There is also another device (which is seldom mentioned by its own name) called the tone locator. You can use the tone locator to find the signal in the wire on the other end from the tone generator and thus prove the connectivity of the wire through the obstruction.

The tone generator and the tone locator, shown in Figure 3.6, are sometimes referred to as the "fox and hound." It is not usually necessary to strip any insulation from the wires in order to locate the tone. The tone locator can usually find the tone through the insulation if you place the tone locator close to the wire. The only real disadvantage of a tone generator is that it generally takes two people to use one effectively to test several wires in a cable. Much more sophisticated devices are available, such as time domain reflectors (TDRs), which can be used by one person to determine connectivity and even determine where a break has occurred in a wire.

> **NOTE** You should know that there are also specialized tools that are used to check the continuity of coaxial cable as well as fiber-optic cable.

FIGURE 3.6 A tone generator and tone locator

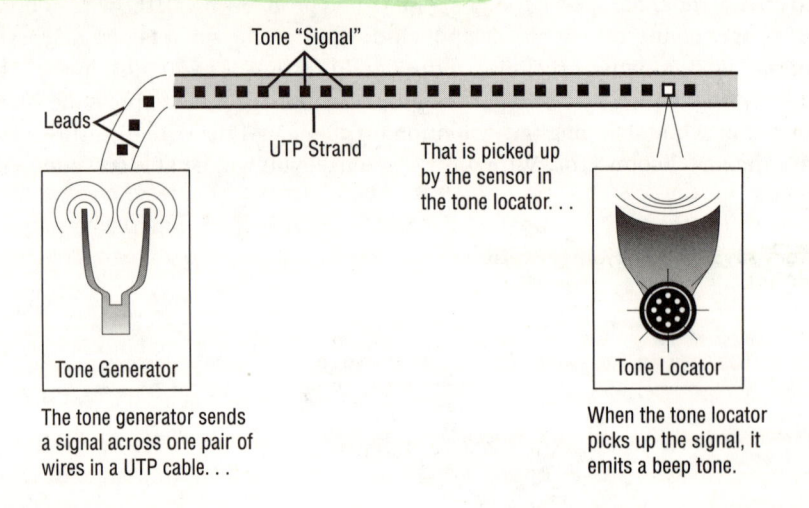

The tone generator sends a signal across one pair of wires in a UTP cable...

When the tone locator picks up the signal, it emits a beep tone.

Exam Essentials

Know how and when to use wire crimpers. Wire crimpers are plier-like tools used to strip the outer insulation from a cable and to compress the RJ-45 connector onto the wires inserted into it. The connector will bite through the insulation of each of the individual wires, creating a solid connection as long as the tool is used properly. Wire crimpers can be used to create straight-through, crossover, and rollover cables depending on the order in which the wires are inserted into the connectors at each end of the cable.

Explain the purpose of media testers. Media testers are specialized devices used to test the continuity of wires within a cable. Most media testers send a current through the wires to determine whether there is continuity through the wire. Media testers come in many versions; some have lights, sounds, or other types of output.

Know the purpose of a punch-down tool. A punch-down tool is used to secure wires to a patch panel. A punch down tool is a very specialized tool that applies just the right amount of force in the right direction to secure the wire. The punch-down tool and connector also cause a portion of the wire's insulation to be stripped off so there is no need to strip the insulation in each wire.

List the characteristics of a tone generator. A tone generator is a device that sends a signal through a wire so that you can verify the continuity of the wire, even if it goes through a wall or other obstruction. The signal that the tone generator produces can be sensed through the insulation of the wire by the tone locator. The tone generator and tone locator pair are sometimes referred to as the "fox and hound."

3.4 Configuring a Remote Connection

Remote connectivity to a network involves connecting to the network through another network or series of networks, such as the Internet. Many organizations allow their employees to connect to their networks from home or on the road from a hotel. When this is allowed, the job of the administrator is to provide a connection that works in roughly the same way for the user but provides security for the organization. One of the main factors with remote connectivity is authentication. You need to make sure that the users who are connecting to your network are really who they say they are. Authentication can be accomplished using many different methods and many different protocols. Basically speaking, users can prove their identity through a network with one of the following three pieces of information:

- Something that they know; for example, a password or a PIN number from a secure ID card
- Something that they have; for example, a smart card or other type of ID card that can be read through a network
- Something that they are; for example, a fingerprint, retina scan, or other type of biometric authentication

In this section, we will examine the remote protocols and authentication mechanisms that are available with each of the main server systems.

Critical Information

You should understand remote connectivity in regard to protocols used and authentication methods available for each of the following operating systems.

Unix/Linux/Mac OS X Server

As we discussed earlier, one of the advantages of Unix is its tremendous flexibility. This being the case, you can use a Unix-based server as a remote access server. In fact, many devices are available that can use the Unix platform and the TCP/IP protocol. You can configure these devices for many authentication protocols and for SSL connections as well. The main disadvantage of using these devices is that you will have to do most, if not all, of the configuring on the command-line interface. You can find more information about available devices by searching the Internet for "Unix remote access."

Access to Linux servers is typically provided through the main console or through a remote access package, such as Telnet. The main problem with Telnet is that the authentication to a Telnet server (entering the username and password) is transmitted in clear text. Since this is not a secure form of communication, we recommend that you use SSH instead of Telnet. SSH operates in a similar manner to Telnet, but the user credentials are automatically encrypted during authentication. You can obtain SSH on the Web at **www.freessh.org**. Linux clients can use the TCP/IP protocol and SSH to gain remote access to Linux servers.

Mac OS X Servers can also use SSH to provide a secure remote connection through the Internet. You can use the TCP/IP protocol with a secure logon provided by SSH to give users access to the servers. You should use the secure protocols that we discussed in Chapter 2, such as SCP or SFTP, to transfer data in encrypted form as opposed to FTP, which transfers the data in clear text.

NetWare

Remote connectivity to NetWare servers can be provided to Novell clients by adding a special *NetWare Loadable Module (NLM)* that provides the remote connectivity to the servers. This product was originally released in 1995 and has been enhanced by Novell over the last few years. NLMs now support all of the latest remote access protocols, such as CHAP. Microsoft clients can also gain remote connectivity to a NetWare server through a Gateway and Client Services for NetWare (GSNW) server installed in a Microsoft network. In addition, clients can access resources on web-based NetWare servers with their browsers.

Microsoft Windows

Microsoft Windows servers provide remote access connections for clients through *Remote Access Server (RAS)* on Windows NT 4.0 and through *Routing and Remote Access Server (RRAS)* on Windows 2000 Server and Windows Server 2003. Microsoft clients can use the New Connection Wizard to quickly configure dial-up and VPN connections to a Microsoft server. Clients can choose from many authentication protocols, as we discussed in Chapter 2. Figure 3.7 shows the New Connection Wizard on a Windows XP Professional client computer.

FIGURE 3.7 The New Connection Wizard

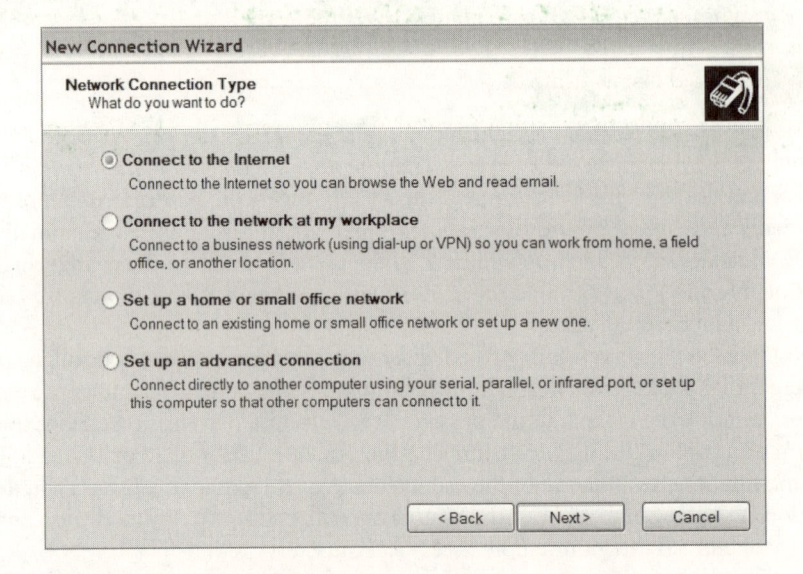

Appleshare IP (Internet Protocol)

Appleshare IP servers have been available from Apple since the mid-1990s. They are specifically developed for secure remote access services for Macintosh clients. They provide secure intranet access as well as secure access from the Internet. Appleshare IP products can also filter IP addresses and provide a proxy service for clients.

> **NOTE** You can find more information about Appleshare IP products by visiting Apple's web pages at www.apple.com

Exam Essentials

Be familiar with remote connectivity recommendations with Unix-based servers. You should know the remote connectivity options with Unix-based servers such as Unix itself, Linux, and Mac OS X server. Unix servers will likely require configuration from a command line, whereas Linux and Mac OS X provide some GUI input. A protocol such as SSH should be used to secure the remote login to the servers; you can obtain SSH on the www.freessh.org website. You should use a secure protocol such as SCP or SFTP to transfer files between servers and clients.

Know how to configure remote connectivity for NetWare servers. Remote connectivity from client computers running Novell Client to servers running NetWare was first established in 1995 with the release of an NLM designed specifically for remote access services. Remote access services to NetWare services have been enhanced over the years, and they now support all of the latest remote access protocols, such as CHAP. Web-based NetWare servers can be accessed and used by all authorized clients using their browsers.

Understand remote connectivity with Microsoft Windows servers. All Microsoft Windows servers, including Windows NT 4.0, provide built-in remote access services. Microsoft clients can be quickly configured for dial-up as well as VPN connections using the New Connection wizard on the client. Microsoft clients can be configured with a large variety of encryption and authentication protocols to meet the needs of your organization.

Understand remote connectivity with Appleshare IP. Appleshare IP is a product of Apple Computer that was developed specifically for remote access and web-based solutions. Appleshare IP server products are built primarily to provide Apple Macintosh clients with secure access to Mac OS X servers. Appleshare IP products include IP filtering services as well as proxy services.

3.5 Identifying the Purpose, Benefits, and Characteristics of Firewalls

Generally speaking, a *firewall* is a hardware/software service that prevents packets from flowing through an interface from one network to another unless they meet the criteria specified by the firewall. In this section, we will discuss the main reasons that you might use a firewall and the benefits that you receive from using firewalls. In addition, we will discuss the characteristics of firewalls and some considerations of which you should be aware.

Critical Information

You should know the purpose of using a firewall. In addition, you should understand the main benefits that an organization obtains by using firewalls. Finally, you should understand the characteristics of a firewall and special factors that an organization may need to consider when incorporating firewalls.

The Purpose of a Firewall

When you think about a firewall in today's environment, you probably think first about a device or a piece of software that is designed to keep the Internet out of your computer or your network. While this is true, it is not the only reason that organizations use firewalls.

An organization might use a firewall to keep valuable information from slipping out of the organization unnoticed. For example, a company might prevent all FTP traffic from leaving the network or leaving specific portions of the network. This would be done to prevent people on the inside from inadvertently or intentionally sending sensitive corporate files to other parties. In addition, an organization might use firewall filters to prevent specific types of traffic from flowing through its own subnets. This might be done to prevent users from playing games on the network or to prevent them from sharing music files, and so on.

Today's firewalls have become very sophisticated. Earlier firewalls worked primarily at layers 3 and 4 (the Network and Transport layers) of the OSI model and could filter traffic by IP address or by port numbers and protocols. Newer firewalls can also work at layer 7 (the Application layer) and can filter traffic based on the content of the message itself. In other words, a layer 7 firewall can be used to prevent documents that contain sensitive or inappropriate information from passing through an interface. This granular capability of filtering can be a great asset to an organization if the firewall is configured properly.

The Benefits of a Firewall

The main benefit of a firewall is that it allows you to control traffic into and out of computers and networks, thus increasing the security of the network and hiding the resources within it. An organization can use a corporate firewall to keep its network separated from other networks and from the Internet. A corporate firewall can provide a barrier that keeps attackers from accessing or changing a company's sensitive data. Users can utilize the *Internet Connection*

3.5 Identifying the Purpose, Benefits, and Characteristics of Firewalls

Firewall (ICF) built into the Windows XP operating system to block unwanted traffic that was not filtered by the corporate firewall. Windows XP is the only client operating system that provides the ICF firewall. The ICF does not filter traffic going out of a Windows XP client computer, only traffic going in. Figure 3.8 shows the ICF settings on a Windows XP computer with Service Pack 2 installed. Using both the corporate firewall and the Internet Connection Firewall provides multiple layers of security.

FIGURE 3.8 The Internet Connection Firewall

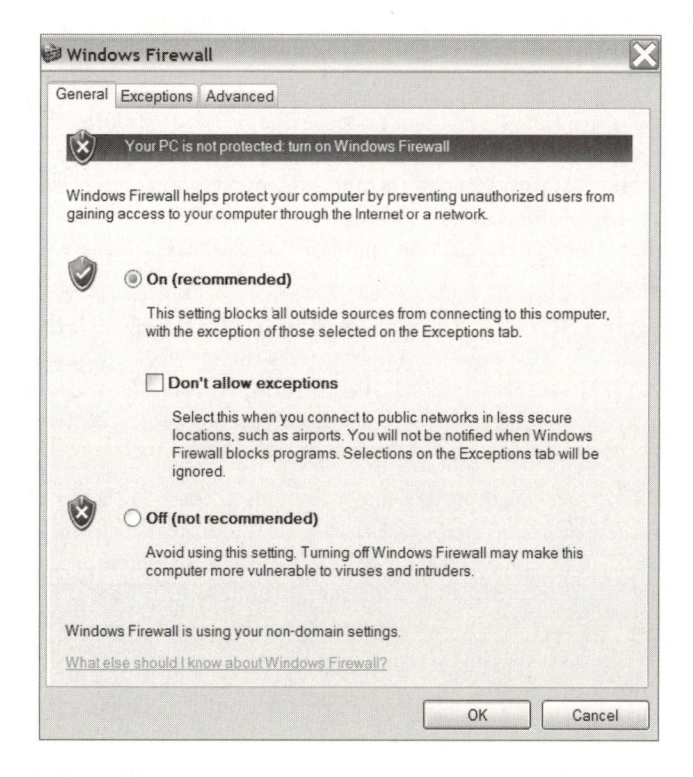

> **NOTE**
> You can obtain free firewall software for most clients on the Web at www.zonelabs.com

Considerations when Using a Firewall

If you decide to use firewalls in your organization, you should be aware that some applications that require specific protocols may be blocked by the firewall. Most corporate firewalls are initially configured to block all traffic except for the specific protocols and IP addresses that are configured on the firewall. This means that if you or your firewall administrator miss a protocol in your configuration, then the application that was supposed to work through the firewall will instead fail. For example, you won't be able to use SSL unless you open port 443.

You should also know that there are many types of firewalls from which to choose. Some firewalls are hardware based, some software based, and some are a combination of the two. If you use multiple firewalls, you should realize that the filtering effect will be cumulative as the traffic flows through each of the firewalls. Using ICF on all of your clients will keep clients from being able to share resources on the client computer unless exceptions are configured in the firewall.

Exam Essentials

Understand the purpose of a firewall. The main purpose of a firewall is to filter traffic to and from a network or a computer. Firewalls can be used to filter traffic based on many different conditions, including IP addresses, protocols, ports, and even the data that the traffic contains. Most firewalls are used to protect a network or a computer from the Internet, but they can also be used to filter traffic going out of a computer or a network or to filter traffic between two subnets in the same organization.

Describe the benefits of using a firewall. The main benefit of using a firewall is that it allows you to filter traffic into and out of a network. This protects the network from attacks from the inside as well as from outside of the network. In addition, you should understand that multiple firewalls can provide a layered security that further enhances the effectiveness of firewall filtering.

Know the characteristics and considerations of using a firewall. There are many choices in regard to hardware- and software-based corporate firewalls. Windows XP clients include an Internet Connection Firewall (ICF) that can filter traffic going into a client computer. These firewall filters may keep some applications from functioning if the specific protocol for the application has not been allowed through the firewall. Using the ICF on all of your Windows XP clients will prevent the clients from sharing resources on their own computers unless special exceptions are configured in the firewall.

3.6 Identifying the Purpose, Benefits, and Characteristics of Using a Proxy Service

The term "proxy" is defined as the function or authority of acting for another. It can be used in legal settings, where a person is given the authority to be the proxy for another person and to therefore act on that person's behalf. In computer terminology, a *proxy service* is a service that makes a connection to the Internet on behalf of a user. The proxy service provides many benefits to an organization by making the Internet connection instead of letting each client make its own connections.

Critical Information

You should understand the purpose of a proxy service. In addition, you should understand the main benefits that a proxy service provides an organization. Finally, you should understand what is involved in using a proxy service and the special configuration that will be required for clients to use the proxy service.

The Purpose of a Proxy Service

The main purpose of a proxy service is to make Internet connections on behalf of the clients in a network. It is positioned between the clients and the Internet, and it intercepts the client's Internet requests and makes the request on behalf of the client. Clients are configured to use the proxy service to make the connection instead of making the connection on their own. We will discuss this configuration in greater depth later in this section.

The Benefits of a Proxy Service

Since the proxy service is in between the Internet and clients, it can provide many benefits to the organization as a whole. The main benefits that the proxy service provides are as follows:

Improved performance   Since the proxy service caches all of the requests that go through it, it can often quickly resolve an IP address from a hostname without any DNS servers. If many clients in the network tend to use the same pages, these pages are often already in the cache when the clients requests them.

Improved control   Since the proxy service makes the request on behalf of the client, it can be configured to only make specific requests for specific clients at specified times. For example, an organization could use a proxy service to keep specified groups of users from browsing the Internet from 9:00 a.m. to 4:00 p.m. but allow it at all other times. Likewise, all clients could be prevented from browsing specified sites on the Internet if those sites are deemed inappropriate.

Reporting   Since the proxy service makes the requests on behalf of the client, it can also keep a detailed record of all of the requests that it makes. This record can contain such information as the name of the client, the requested site, and the time that the request was made. The report can include information about requests that were granted as well as those that were not granted. This type of information can be helpful to the Human Resources department of an organization if they are building a case against someone who is using the Internet in an inappropriate manner.

Considerations when Using a Proxy Service

If a proxy service is used in a network, the clients will need to be configured to use the proxy service. The exact configuration of the clients will depend on what client is used, but it will likely be found in the browser settings on the client. In Windows XP Professional, for example, you can find the configuration settings for using a proxy service in the Local Area Network (LAN) Settings screen in Internet Explorer (see Figure 3.9). (To open this screen, choose Internet Options from the Tools menu, select the Connections tab, and click the LAN Settings button.)

You can configure the client computers to automatically detect a proxy server, or you can manually configure the address and port of the proxy server. You should also check the option Bypass Proxy Server for Local Addresses if your clients will also be using sites within your own intranet.

FIGURE 3.9 The LAN Settings screen in Internet Explorer

> **NOTE** You can also use the Internet Explorer Administration Kit to configure multiple clients with the address of the proxy server as well as other Internet Explorer settings.

Exam Essentials

Describe the purpose of a proxy service. The main purpose of a proxy service is to make Internet requests on behalf of a client.

List the benefits of a proxy service. A proxy service provides many benefits for a client, including improved performance and detailed reporting. The proxy service can provide these benefits because it caches client requests when it receives them. The proxy service can provide improved control and can prevent groups of clients from accessing specified sites or from browsing the Web at specified times.

Know how to use a proxy service. Clients must be configured to use a proxy service. This configuration will likely be part of the client's browser configuration settings. Clients can usually be configured to automatically detect a proxy server, or they can be manually configured with the address and port of the server.

3.7 Determining the Impact of Network Configurations

The connectivity of a network is both physical and logical. In order to have a functioning network, all of the components of both physical and logical connectivity must be configured properly. In this section, we focus on the logical configuration of the network, such as ports, authentication protocols, and encryption protocols. These must all be configured properly between computers in order for the network to operate effectively.

If 99 percent of the logical configuration is correct but only one part is misconfigured, the result will often be the same as if 100 percent of the network were misconfigured: no connectivity. Because of this fact, it is very important that you understand all of the components involved in the configuration. Once you do, you will be able to determine the potential impact if one of the components is misconfigured.

Critical Information

You should understand the impact of a misconfiguration in regard to the main logical components in a network configuration. Be able to determine the impact on network functionality of each of the logical components both when they are configured properly and when they are misconfigured.

Port Blocking

As we discussed in Chapter 2, ports are logical locations in the computer at which a particular application is received. If a specific port is blocked by a firewall configuration or other type of filtering software or device, then the application that corresponds to the blocked port will not function. You might well be able to determine that a port must be blocked because of the fact that all other applications function normally. For example, if a firewall blocks port 80, you will not be able to use the connection to browse the Web but, as long as ports 20 and 21 are not blocked, you will be able to use FTP on the same connection. You can obtain a short list of port numbers from Chapter 2 of this book. A more complete list is also available on the Web at http://www.iana.org/assignments/port-numbers.

Authentication Protocols

A variety of authentication protocols can be used to prove a computer's and/or a user's identity over a network. As we discussed in Chapter 2, these protocols have evolved over the years and have become increasingly sophisticated. It is important that the protocols be configured the same on both (or all) of the computers that will need to authenticate to each other. You can configure most servers to accept multiple protocols of varying sophistication so that each client can then be configured with the most secure protocols that it can handle. For example, since Windows 2000 and Windows XP clients can use MS-CHAP v2 but Windows NT Workstation cannot, you should configure the server with MS-CHAP v2 as well as MS-CHAP, but you should configure the Windows 2000 and Windows XP clients with only MS-CHAP v2 and the

Windows NT Workstation clients with only MS-CHAP. In this way, each client will use its strongest available authentication protocol. The only exception to this rule will be in the case that other servers in your network cannot use MS-CHAP v2. In that case, you should configure both protocols on the clients as well.

If authentication protocols are configured properly on both sides of a connection, then the computers will reach an agreement on how to authenticate to each other and authentication will take place. This process will take some time. Often the amount of time that authentication requires is not of great concern, but you should know that the connection will take longer to establish than if the authentication did not have to be performed. Some software indicates to the user that the connecting computers are currently authenticating and asks the user to wait.

If authentication protocols are not configured the same on both sides of a connection, such that the computers can reach some common agreement in regard to authentication, then the connection will fail and the error will likely indicate that the computers could not authenticate. This message is usually different from an "Access Denied" message or a message that indicates that the computers could not connect. This is because the computers actually did connect with each other and they had a short conversation, but either they could not agree on an authentication protocol that both could use or the authentication failed.

Encryption Protocols

Whereas authentication is proving one's identity, encryption is scrambling up messages so that they can be read only by the sender and the intended recipient(s). Encryption protocols must also be configured the same on both sides of a connection in order for communication to occur normally. The difference is that an errant encryption protocol could very possibly look like a lack of any connection at all, since the computers might not be able to see each other. Actually, there are two instances in which encryption protocols are used: first they are used to secure the logon and authentication of a connection, and then they are used to scramble the data that is being sent over the connection. The types of encryption protocols that you use will depend on the type of client that you are using and the type of application that is being used. For example, encryption protocols such as Secure Hash Algorithm (SHA) or Data Encryption Standard (DES) might be used to encrypt authentication and/or data during a session.

Exam Essentials

Know how port blocking can affect network functionality. Each port is very specific to an application. If a port is blocked, the application associated with it will not be able to operate through the connection. The best indicator that a port may be blocked will be that other applications will function through the same connection.

Understand how authentication protocols can affect network functionality. The key to authentication is that both of the computers in the communication must be able to use the same authentication protocol to authenticate. You can configure computers with multiple authentication protocols, and this is typically done with servers rather than with clients; however, clients that might connect to multiple servers could also benefit from being configured with multiple authentication protocols. Authentication-related errors will most likely be indicated by a clear message from the software.

Explain how encryption protocols affect network functionality. Encryption protocols are used when computers are authenticating as well as when data is being transferred between the computers. A failure in regard to an encryption protocol that would be used to authenticate could manifest itself as a failure to connect at all. The specific type of encryption protocols used will depend on the client and the applications used.

3.8 Identifying the Main Characteristics of VLANs

Virtual local area networks (VLANs) are logical subnets that are formed using switches. One of the advantages of VLANs is that they do not have to conform to the physical characteristics of a building but instead can be set up in any manner that the administrator chooses. Another advantage is that VLANs can be formed without the use of routers. For example, suppose you have a four-story building that has sales personnel on all four floors of the building mixed in with other departments. Now, suppose you have a switch located on each of the floors. Without VLANs, your sales people's computers would have to be attached to the switch that eventually connects to the router that created the subnet. In other words, because of the physical location of your sales people's computers, they would be in the same subnet as the other computers on that floor, even if that may not be the best way of controlling the network traffic.

With VLANs, the traffic that is designated for a particular VLAN will only be sent to the ports are assigned to that VLAN. This allows you to control traffic with much greater flexibility and makes the location of the user's computer much less important in regard to controlling traffic. When a VLAN spans more than one switch, the connections that carry all of the VLAN traffic are referred to as *trunks*. Of course, you can still use a router to connect all of the VLANs, just as you would any other type of subnets.

Critical Information

You should understand how VLANs work, including the advantages of using VLANs and how VLANs are created on a switch.

The Advantages of VLANs

How you build VLANs will vary with the type of hardware that you use, but the IEEE has developed a standard called 802.1q that ensures the interoperability of VLAN technologies developed by all of today's vendors of switches. Developing this standard was an important step because VLANs offer many advantages to an organization, including the following:

Increased security When you create virtual (logical) boundaries, network segments are isolated. You can then join them again using a router and apply *access lists*, which filter traffic by IP addresses and/or protocols, to the router for increased security.

Increased performance Because VLANs create separate subnets, they reduce the effect of broadcasts across the entire network. In essence, they divide the network into smaller segments and each segment controls its own traffic.

Organization Network users are linked to the other users that they communicate with most often. Also, the users are linked more closely to the network resources that they use most often.

Simplified administration Adds, moves, and changes become much simpler when VLANs are used. VLANs give the network administrator and the network design team more flexibility in regard to traffic control.

How VLANs Are Formed

So now you are probably wondering how the switches determine which ports are for which VLAN. Well, there are two basic methods that are used to assign VLANs to a port: port based and MAC based. In the paragraphs that follow, we discuss each of these methods.

Port-Based VLANs

With port-based VLANs, each port is assigned to a specific VLAN. A port can only be assigned to one VLAN. This port assignment is often referred to as a *VLAN membership*. For example, suppose a switch has 24 ports but only ports 1–6 are assigned to the sales department. In this case, traffic that was received on port 1 would be sent only to ports 2–6. In other words, all of the other ports on the switch would be isolated from that traffic. The precise configuration of VLAN membership varies from vendor to vendor and sometimes even from product to product within the same vendor, but in all cases a port can be assigned to only one VLAN.

MAC Address–Based VLANs

MAC address–based VLANs assign each computer a VLAN based on the MAC address on the NIC of the computer. This is a completely different type of assignment that in effect makes the computer a member of the VLAN instead of a port. The advantage of this type of VLAN assignment is that the computer can be moved anywhere in the network where the VLAN exists and it will still be recognized and automatically given the correct configuration routes. The main disadvantage of this type of VLAN is that the MAC address must be constantly maintained in order for the VLAN to perform correctly. If the NIC of a computer fails, then the new MAC address will need to be updated on the switch.

Exam Essentials

List the main advantages of VLANs. VLANS provide increased security by creating logical segments in a network. VLANs increase performance in a network by reducing or eliminating the effect of broadcasts throughout the network. They improve the organization of a network by closely connecting the computers and the resources that work together. VLANs simplify ongoing network administration, allowing the network administrator or network designer much more flexibility in regard to network design.

Explain how VLANs are created on a switch. There are two main methods of creating VLANs on a switch: port based and MAC based. Port-based VLANs require that each port be assigned to one and only one VLAN. This assignment is called a membership. MAC-based VLANs are assigned based on the MAC address on the NIC of the computer. This means that the computer can be moved to anywhere in the organization where the VLAN exists and it will still get the same assignment.

3.9 Identifying Characteristics and Purposes of Extranets and Intranets

Just as the technologies of networking have evolved, so has terminology that we use to talk about networks. Before the Internet was popular, there was no need to talk about other types of networks because all networks were just...well, networks. Now that the Internet is commonplace, we also need to define the types of networks that are not connected to or not included in the Internet. In this section, we will discuss the two other types of networks that are commonplace in today's business environment: *extranets* and *intranets*.

Critical Information

Many organizations have both extranets and intranets, which they use on a daily basis. Although both extranets and intranets are used primarily for business reasons, they are very different in their design and in their purpose. You should be able to recognize the differences between an extranet and an intranet. You should be able to identify the main characteristics and purposes of extranets and intranets.

Extranets

Your organization may want to give employees of another organization access to some parts of your network. You may want to provide this access because you are working closely with the other organization. Perhaps the employees need access to your inventory or to your pricing on specific items so that they can correctly price and promise delivery on a product for which your organization supplies parts. Perhaps you are a delivery company that gives access to your computers so that your customers will know where their package is in your system and therefore will trust you more in regard to a delivery date. These are just a couple of reasons that a business might use an extranet.

The main goal of an extranet is to provide a vendor or a partner with a value-added resource in the form of access to your network. When you provide an extranet you must keep in mind the security risks. There are two main security considerations in regard to extranets. You should be familiar with these security risks and the tools that you can use to mitigate them.

First, there's the concern of authentication to your network. If you want to give someone access to your network, then you need to make sure that the entity that you're giving access to is actually the one that was intended. Information that is of a benign nature to your vendor or partner may be sensitive information if it were to fall into the hands of your competitor. For example, the knowledge that you plan to build a certain number of units of a given product might be of great interest to a company that builds a competitive product. Second, there is a concern of permission and authorization to resources. Just because you want to give a vendor access to your inventory reports does not mean that you want them to have access to your executive payroll reports as well. If anyone is accidentally given access to this type of information, it becomes very hard to undo the damage that has already been done. You can't just erase the memory from the user's head!

To combat the problems regarding authentication, strong authentication protocols such as certificate-based IPSec should be used. This will ensure that you're communicating with the vendor or the partner that you intended. To address the issue of permissions and authorization to resources, carefully configure NTFS and share permissions for the users who will be accessing your resources. Some organizations create a new user account for each of the employees of the other organization. They then map the user's certificates to the new account for the purposes of authentication and authorization to resources. Server operating systems such as Windows 2000 and Windows Server 2003 provide the capability to map certificates to user accounts.

Intranets

As you know, some resources in an organization are only useful and appropriate to the employees of that organization. Suppose your organization wants to share these files and folders with all of the employees who need them. You could share them in the file and folder structure of the network so that users could access them with My Computer or Windows Explorer, but another method of sharing these resources is to place them on a web server so that the users can access the resources from any browser. If the pages on the web server are accessible only from within your own network, then you have truly created an intranet. If the pages can also be accessed by the users from outside the organization, then you have created a secure web page from the outside and an intranet on the inside of your network.

The main purpose of an intranet is to share information within an organization and allow users to access that information with their browsers. Security concerns are the same as with any other information in the network, but permissions can be controlled with web-based permissions as well as NTFS and share permissions. Authentication is typically provided as a pass-through from a user's logon credentials. In other words, the user who is already logged on to the network will typically not have to authenticate again to access an intranet page.

Exam Essentials

Know the purpose and characteristics of an extranet. The main purpose of an extranet is to provide a value-added resource to a vendor, supplier, or partner of an organization. An extranet creates concerns in regard to authentication and authorization, and should be protected using strong authentication protocols, certificates, and closely monitored NTFS and share permissions.

Understand the purpose and characteristics of an intranet. The main purpose of an intranet is to provide users with access to files and folders through their browsers. True intranet resources are not available on the Internet. Authentication and authorization of intranet resources is really no different than that of other resources and in fact is often a pass-through from the user's normal logon credentials.

3.10 Using Antivirus Software

There are over 60,000 known viruses today. In addition, more viruses and worms are created on a daily basis. While most viruses are simply a nuisance, some can be very dangerous to your system. Because of this, you should have an antivirus program installed on every server and client computer within your organization. The only real protection is complete protection. In this section, we discuss the importance of antivirus software.

Critical Information

You should know the purpose of *antivirus software*. In addition, you should know the benefits gained by installing antivirus software on all of the computers in your organization. Finally, you should be able to list the characteristics of antivirus software so that you can get the most from your software.

The Purpose of Antivirus Software

The main purpose of antivirus software is to protect your computer by detecting and eradicating viruses before they have a chance to damage your computer or the data contained within it. In order for antivirus software to be effective, it must be continually updated with the latest virus definitions. Most antivirus software vendors offer an automatic update of virus definitions through their websites. To prevent viruses from slipping through, you should ensure that the antivirus software installed on your servers and clients is updated regularly. There are many antivirus software vendors from which you can choose, but the most well known are Symantec's Norton AntiVirus and McAfee Antivirus. Both Norton and McAfee offer automatic updates through the Web.

The Benefits of Using Antivirus Software

To realize the greatest benefit of using antivirus software, make sure that you have it installed and enabled on all of the servers and clients in your organization. The greatest benefit of using antivirus software is that you don't have to hassle with viruses on a daily basis. This is especially true if all of the computers in your organization are equipped with the software. If any computer does not have antivirus software, it can become infected with a virus and thereby spread the infection to other computers that also do not have antivirus software. In addition, computers that are equipped with antivirus software will be forced to take measures against the virus; often resulting in warning messages on the user's monitor.

As we said earlier, most viruses are just a nuisance but some can be very dangerous to your computers and especially the data contained in them. The time lost in reinstalling computer systems and applications is a business cost that is not necessary and often cannot be justified. In fact, the total economic impact of damage caused by viruses and worms is measured in billions of dollars per year. You can save your organization more than just headaches and hassles by implementing an antivirus program; you can save your organization money.

Considerations When Using Antivirus Software

Most of the considerations in regard to using antivirus software fall into the advantages column. This is especially true if the antivirus software is installed on all computers and maintained using automatic updates. There are, however, a couple of disadvantages. You should be aware of these disadvantages and the methods you can employ to overcome them.

The first is in regard to the overall performance of the computer. Since the antivirus software requires processor and memory resources, it can potentially slow down the performance of a computer. You can overcome this problem by ensuring that the computer has more than the required resources, such as processor and memory. The second involves the installation of applications. Because the antivirus software protects against changing the critical files in your computer, any application that requires a change in these files in order to be installed properly will have to fight with the antivirus software to install itself into your computer. Overcoming this problem is accomplished by simply disabling the antivirus software prior to performing an installation of other software. Most antivirus software can be quickly disabled simply by right-clicking on its icon and selecting the Disable option. You should, of course, reenable the antivirus software as soon as you finish installing the new application.

Exam Essentials

Describe the purpose of antivirus software. The main purpose of antivirus software is to protect a computer from becoming infected by viruses that can damage it and the data on it. Antivirus software works best when it is installed on every computer within your organization.

Understand the benefits of antivirus software. The greatest benefit of antivirus software is not having to hassle with viruses on a daily basis. Although most viruses are just a nuisance, some viruses can cause tremendous harm to your computers and the data they contain. The damage caused by viruses and the time required to repair the damage can equate to large sums of money in even a small organization; therefore, antivirus software can save an organization a tremendous amount of money.

3.11 Identifying the Purpose and Characteristics of Fault Tolerance

Fault tolerance can be defined as the ability to lose a network component without losing data or functionality in the network. There are many different types of fault tolerance in a typical network, including fault tolerance for power, communication links, storage devices, and network services. In this section, we will discuss the various forms of fault tolerance for a network.

Critical Information

You should know the purpose and characteristics of fault tolerance in a computer network. More specifically, you should know the purpose and characteristics of fault tolerance in regard to power, communication links, storage devices, and network services.

Fault-Tolerant Power

Fault-tolerant power usually comes in the form of an *uninterrupted power supply (UPS)*. A UPS is essentially a battery backup that provides power to the computer in the event that the power from the power company fails. Typically a UPS is used as a temporary solution to allow servers and sometimes clients to be shut down in an orderly manner, to prevent data loss. A UPS is typically a device that contains a battery and a power conditioner. It is plugged into the power outlet so that the computers and other essential hardware can then be plugged into it. Typically, less essential devices that pull a great amount of current, such as laser printers, are not plugged into the UPS. In very large organizations that must continue to operate, a bank of batteries is used and a generator is also provided in the circuit to continually charge the battery so that the computer systems can continue to operate.

Fault-Tolerant Communication Links

The main purpose of a network is to provide a way that computers can share resources, such as files, folders, and printers. Once a network is established, people begin to rely on the network being in place and operational. For this reason, many organizations provide multiple communication links between users and essential resources. Some organizations use multiple links that are of the same bandwidth to provide traffic load balancing as well as fault tolerance. Other organizations simply provide a less expensive backup link that can be used if the primary link should fail. For example, an organization might use a T1 communications link as its primary link but have an Integrated Systems Digital Network (ISDN) link as a backup. The main purpose of providing fault-tolerant communications links is to ensure that network users can remain productive even if one of the links fails. This is especially important in organizations that absolutely must be able to communicate, such as law enforcement agencies and hospitals.

Fault-Tolerant Storage

Fault-tolerant storage on a network is typically accomplished by having multiple physical drives. This is usually done on servers rather than clients. While there are many different forms of fault tolerance in regard to hard drive configurations, the general term used to describe all types of fault tolerance obtained by multiple physical drives is *redundant arrays of inexpensive disks (RAID)*. Many forms of RAID exist, but we will focus only on the most common forms of RAID that you might encounter and those that are likely to be on the test. The most common forms of RAID configurations are RAID 0, RAID 1, and RAID 5. In the paragraphs that follow, we will discuss each of these RAID configurations.

RAID 0

Actually, it's not even appropriate for us to be discussing *RAID 0* under the context of fault-tolerant solutions, since it provides no fault tolerance. In fact, the only reason that we're discussing RAID 0 at all is to provide a contrast between it and the other most common forms of RAID, which do provide fault tolerance. RAID 0 works by spreading data over multiple disks. The only real advantage of this configuration is that it provides increased input performance over that of a single disk. This is especially evident when multiple controllers are also used. The disadvantage of RAID 0 is that it not only does not provide fault tolerance but it actually increases the risk to data contained on the disks, since a failure in any one of the disks will result in a loss of all of the data on all of the disks. Typically, RAID 0 is used in temporary situations when it is necessary to move large amounts of data as quickly as possible and where other data-recovery solutions, such as backups, can be performed in tandem with moving the data.

RAID 1

RAID 1 is a fault-tolerant disk configuration that writes the same data to more than one hard disk. The data is written to both hard disks so that even if one disk fails the other disk will still contain the data. If the disks both use the same controller card, then the configuration is referred to as *disk mirroring*. If each disk has its own controller card, then the configuration can also be referred to as *disk duplexing*. The advantages of RAID 1 are that it provides fault tolerance and it can be used on all partitions, including those that contain the system and boot files. The main disadvantage of RAID 1 is that it is only 50 percent efficient in regard to data storage. For example, if you want to store 40GB worth of data in a mirrored configuration, you will require a total of 80GB worth of free disk space. RAID 1 configurations are therefore mostly used to provide fault tolerance to the partitions that contain the system and/or boot files on a server and other more efficient methods, such as RAID 5, are used to store large amounts of data.

RAID 5

RAID 5 is a fault-tolerant disk configuration that provides an efficient method of storing large amounts of data. In a RAID 5 configuration, data is striped across multiple physical disks arranged in an array while at the same time an additional copy of the data is distributed across all of the disks in the array. The additional data is called parity data. It can be used to rebuild the entire array if any one disk should fail. This parity data is distributed across the disks in such a way that if any one disk fails the parity data on all of the other disks replaces the data lost on the failed disk.

3.11 Identifying the Purpose and Characteristics of Fault Tolerance

The main advantage of RAID 5 is that it provides a much more efficient method of storing large amounts of data. In most systems, you can use as few as 3 physical disks and as many as 32 physical disks. Typically, the number of physical disks used in RAID 5 does not even begin to approach the number 32. This is due to the fact that the more disks that are in the configuration, the greater the chance of losing not just one disk but two disks at the same time. If this should happen, then all of the data on all of the disks would be lost. For this reason, most RAID 5 configurations contain between 5 and 10 physical disks.

The efficiency of data storage, however, increases with a number of physical disks. For example a RAID 5 array that contains 4 100GB disks could store 300GB worth of data, because 100GB will be used for parity data. This is an efficiency ratio of 75 percent. On the other hand, a RAID 5 array with ten 100GB physical disks could store 900GB worth of data, because still only 100GB will be used for parity data. This is an efficiency ratio of 90 percent. Typically, an organization chooses a balance between an acceptable efficiency ratio and an acceptable risk in regard to the number of physical disks in the array.

Fault-Tolerant Network Services

Most networks rely on specific services in order for the network to function properly. Services such as IP address assignment and name resolution are absolutely essential in order for users to remain productive in a network. Because of this fact, most network designers build fault tolerance into their network designs in regard to these services. You can have multiple DHCP servers as long as they don't give out the same IP addresses. For name resolution, you can have multiple DNS servers and multiple WINS servers. You can configure each client with the IP addresses of multiple DNS and WINS servers. In fact, you can even combine the use of network services and allow the DHCP server to configure multiple WINS and DNS addresses on each client.

In addition, it is possible to provide fault tolerance for an entire server. This is accomplished by grouping it with another computer or even several other computers so that each computer has a connection to the centralized data between all of the computers. This type of configuration is referred to as a *cluster*. The main advantage of *clustering* is that it provides tremendous fault tolerance and therefore tremendous availability of the clustered resources. The main disadvantage of clustering is that it is very expensive to implement and maintain. Because of this, clustering is primarily used only by very large organizations or by organizations that absolutely must have their data, such as law enforcement agencies and hospitals.

Exam Essentials

Know the purpose and characteristics of fault-tolerant power. Fault-tolerant power usually comes in the form of a UPS. Most UPSs consist of a power conditioner and a battery. The UPS is generally plugged into a power outlet and charges a battery that is used to power a client or server so that the server will continue to run off the battery for a small amount of time in the event of a power failure. The main purpose of the UPS is to provide temporary power and allow the computer to be shut down in an orderly manner to prevent the loss of data.

Describe the characteristics of fault-tolerant communication links. Fault-tolerant communication links are often used in organizations to ensure that clients can continue to have access to resources if one link fails. Some organizations also use these multiple links for load balancing of traffic, and other organizations simply provide a standby or backup link. Redundant communication links are most important when the organization absolutely must have a communication link even in the event that their primary link fails.

List the characteristics of fault-tolerant storage. Fault-tolerant storage is usually accomplished using multiple physical disks in RAID arrays. Three main levels of RAID are typically used in today's networks: RAID 0, RAID 1, and RAID 5. RAID 0 actually provides no fault tolerance.

Know the characteristics of RAID 1. RAID 1 refers to disk mirroring or disk duplexing, depending on whether you are using one controller card or two. The main advantages of RAID 1 are that it provides fault tolerance and that it can be used on all partitions, including the partitions that contain the system and boot files. The main disadvantage of RAID 1 is that it is only 50 percent efficient in regard to data storage.

List the characteristics of RAID 5. RAID 5 is a fault-tolerant solution that stripes data onto multiple disks along with parity data that is distributed throughout all of the disks. The parity data is distributed in such a way that the loss of any one disk can be replaced by the parity data distributed across all of the other disks. A loss of two disks at the same time would result in a loss of all of the data on all of the disks. Most organizations prefer RAID 5 over RAID 1 for storing large amounts of data because it is much more efficient than RAID 1.

Know the characteristics of fault-tolerant network services. It is possible to provide fault tolerance on all of the most essential network services, such as DHCP servers, WINS servers, and DNS servers. Network clients can be configured for multiple network services so that they are provided with fault tolerance in the event that one machine fails. Most network servers can also be clustered so as to provide fault tolerance for the entire machine. The main advantage of clustering is a high degree of reliability and availability, but clustering is often cost prohibitive to an organization.

3.12 Identifying the Purpose and Characteristics of Disaster Recovery

Whereas fault tolerance can be defined as the capability of losing a network component without losing data and or functionality, *disaster recovery* is the process of rebuilding the network after having lost functionality or data. In fact, the definition of "disaster" to a network administrator is any event that could cause a loss of data or functionality in the network. A disaster could therefore be a natural disaster such as a tornado or an earthquake, or it could be simply a mistake that causes a loss of functionality or data. In this section, we discuss the elements involved in disaster recovery.

Critical Information

You should be able to identify the purpose and characteristics of disaster recovery. More specifically, you should be able to identify the purpose and characteristics of disaster recovery in regard to backup and recovery, offsite storage, hot and cold spares, and hot, warm, and cold sites.

Backup and Recovery

Even if you use RAID you should still implement and maintain a backup and recovery strategy. You can choose among many different types of backups, but your choice will largely depend on the amount of time that you have to back up data and the amount of time that you will allow to restore data. A backup type is not defined by the media on which it is recorded, but rather is defined by the elements that are backed up. In the paragraphs that follow, we discuss the main types of backups and compare and contrast these types. You should know the advantages and disadvantages of each type of backup.

Full Backups

In many organizations today only a *full backup* is used. A full backup simply makes a backup of all selected files and folders. These files and folders can be selected using backup tools provided with the server software. The advantage of a full backup is that all of the data can be restored in one session. In other words, if you performed a backup to tape, it would take only one tape to fully restore the data. The main disadvantage of a full backup is that it takes the longest amount of time to create; therefore, some organizations simply don't have time to create a full backup every day. Because of this fact, many organizations use a full backup at the beginning of the week combined with another type of backup during the week.

Incremental Backups

An *incremental backup* takes much less time because only the files and folders that have changed since the last full or incremental backup are included in it. In order for the system to know what to back up, the incremental backup uses a special bit called an *archive bit*, which identifies all of the files that have changed since the last backup. An incremental backup uses the archive bit and then clears the archive bit when it has finished copying the file. The system then begins again, adding archive bits to files and folders that have changed after the last backup.

In an organization with a relatively normal schedule, an incremental backup will take about the same amount of time every day (or night). The obvious advantage of an incremental backup is that there will be enough time to create the backup while users are not on the system or while the traffic is relatively light. The main disadvantage of an incremental backup is that a full restore will require the last full backup plus all of the incremental backups to be run in the same sequence that they were backed up. This means that a restore from a combination of full and incremental backups will take much longer than a restore from a single full backup. If users are waiting for the restore, the restore time might seem even longer. For example, suppose an organization uses a backup schedule that requires a full backup on Monday and an incremental backup on Tuesday through Friday. If the system should crash at the start of Friday morning, a restore would require running Monday's full backup and then running Tuesday's, Wednesday's, and Thursday's incremental backups in succession. This could be a time-consuming process while users are waiting to get to their data.

Differential Backups

A *differential backup* is a backup that includes all of the files and folders that have changed since the last full backup. This becomes very different than an incremental backup as we progress through a week. A differential backup is created by using the archive bit in a different manner. To understand the difference in the way that a differential backup uses the archive bit, you have to walk yourself through a standard week of differential backups.

Suppose an organization requires a backup schedule that includes a full backup on Monday and a differential backup on Tuesday through Friday. After the full backup on Monday, the system will begin placing archive bits on the files and folders that have changed since the last full backup. The differential backup on Tuesday will use the archive bits to determine what to back up, but it will not clear the archive bits after it uses them. This means that on Wednesday the differential backup will include all of the files that have changed since the last full backup on Monday. Likewise, on Thursday the differential backup will include all of the files that have changed since the last full backup on Monday. As you can see, the backup will take longer to perform on each day because it replaces the backup from the previous day and then adds to it.

Because of this fact, if the system were to crash at the start of Friday morning, then only the last full backup and the last differential backup will need to be restored in order to complete a full restoration. Since only two restores must take place, the restoration will be faster than it would have been if they had used incremental backups. It should be noted that this system will still be slower than if a full backup had been performed every day.

A Comparison of Backup Methods

You may have noticed that we have combined full and incremental backups as well as full and differential backups but we have not combined incremental and differential backups. This is because incremental and differential backups should not be combined in a backup schedule. Table 3.2 illustrates the differences between full, incremental, and differential backups.

Offsite Storage

In the event of a physical or environmental disaster such as a tornado, earthquake, or fire, the data on your servers as well as the data on any locally stored backups could be destroyed. For this reason, many organizations use an *offsite storage* facility for their backups. Typically, the offsite backup is a copy of a locally stored backup. Using this method, the organization maintains the ability to quickly restore data with the local copy while at the same time ensuring that the data is safe in the event of disaster. Many companies specialize in storing data offsite for organizations. You should, however, realize that your backup tapes have a tremendous amount of sensitive information regarding your organization, so you should choose only a most trusted organization to store a copy of that data. Some organizations with multiple locations simply store a copy of each location's backup at their other location.

3.12 Identifying the Purpose and Characteristics of Disaster Recovery

TABLE 3.2 Comparing Backup Methods

Method	What Is Backed Up	Restore Procedure	Archive Bit
Full	All data	Restores all data with a single backup	Does not use the archive bit
Incremental	All data that has changed since the last full or incremental backup	Requires the last full backup plus all of the incremental backups since the last full backup to be restored in the order that they were backed up	Uses the archive bit and clears it after the file is backed up
Differential	All data that has changed since the last full backup	Requires only the last full backup and the last differential backup	Uses the archive bit, but does not clear it

Hot and Cold Spares

Depending on the type of hardware that you are using and the sophistication of its components, you may be able to use both hot and cold spares. A *hot spare* is typically a device, such as a hard drive or a network interface card, that is already in place and powered up, ready to be used in the event that the primary device fails. Typically, hot spares require no intervention by the network administrator in order to replace the failed device.

A *cold spare*, on the other hand, is simply a device that is suitable to replace the primary device and is stored in a convenient location so as to be easily installed by the network administrator in the event that the primary device fails. While a cold spare solution is typically much less expensive than a hot spare solution, it does require intervention by the network administrator. For example, if a company operates 24 hours a day and a NIC on a server that is protected by a hot spare fails in the middle of the night, anyone who needs connectivity to the server will still be provided connectivity through the hot spare and the network administrator will not have to fix the problem during the night.

Hot, Warm, and Cold Sites

In the event of a natural disaster, the main goal of the network administrator is to get the network back up and running as soon as possible. As we discussed earlier, a significant part of bringing the network back up is the ability to replace the data from the backups. This is why offsite storage is highly recommended for most organizations.

Just the ability to replace the data, however, may not be enough to get the network back up and running if the hardware has also been damaged or destroyed. For this reason, many organizations have an alternate site to be used in the event of a natural disaster. Depending on the degree of planning and preparation, these alternate sites can be divided into three categories: hot sites, warm sites, and cold sites. You should be able to compare and contrast the different types of alternate sites. In addition, you should know the advantages and disadvantages of each type. In the paragraphs that follow, we discuss each type of alternate site.

Hot Sites

A *hot site* is an alternate site that is completely equipped to handle all computer needs for an organization. Hot sites have servers, client computers, printers, and network equipment installed and ready for use. Everything is powered up and has been recently tested to ensure that it can meet the computer needs of the organization in the event of a disaster.

As you can imagine, hot sites are very expensive to implement and maintain and are therefore very rarely used. In fact, hot sites are typically used only when lives or national security would be at risk. Most organizations choose a less expensive option for their alternate sites.

Warm Sites

Warm sites are alternate sites that provide an environment including power and connectivity that can be used as a place to move computer equipment in the event of a disaster. Typically, there is no computer equipment or a very small amount of computer equipment in a warm site. Because of this fact, warm sites cannot actually be tested and therefore are not as complete an alternative site as hot sites. Also, since all of the computer equipment must be moved in the event of a disaster, warm sites do not provide as immediate disaster recovery as hot sites provide. The main advantage of warm sites over hot sites is that they are much less expensive to implement and maintain. Consequently, most organizations choose the warm site approach for their alternate sites.

Cold Sites

A *cold site* is simply a location agreed upon in advance that can be used in the event of a natural disaster. It does not contain any computer equipment and may not even be specifically configured in regard to power or connectivity. In other words, it's just a building or a portion of a building that computer equipment could be moved to in the event of a disaster. The only advantage offered by a cold site is that it is very inexpensive. In fact, some organizations simply make an agreement with another organization that each could use a portion of their building in the event of a disaster. In this case, the cold site costs the company absolutely nothing; which coincidentally is about what it's worth!

Location of Alternate Sites

You should understand that any alternate site would only be effective if it is not also damaged by the natural disaster. For this reason, an alternate site should typically be balanced in regard to its geographical location. It must be close enough so that computer equipment and users can be moved to it rather easily, but at the same time it must be far enough away from the primary site so as not to be affected by the same natural disaster. For example, if the primary site is located close to the coast of Florida and therefore in the path of potential hurricanes, an alternate site should be chosen that is not likely to be affected by hurricanes.

Review Questions

1. Which type of server is primarily controlled using a command-line interface?
   A. Linux
   B. Unix
   C. Windows
   D. Mac OS X Server

2. Which of the following are the most basic components required for connectivity in a network? (Choose three.)
   A. A common client
   B. A common operating system
   C. A common protocol
   D. Network media

3. Which device is used to receive a signal that establishes continuity of the wires within a cable, even when the cable is installed in a wall or another obstruction?
   A. A tone generator
   B. A media tester
   C. A punch-down tool
   D. A tone locator

4. Which secure protocol should be used for remote administration of Mac OS X Servers because it encrypts the user's credentials during authentication?
   A. Telnet
   B. SSL
   C. SSH
   D. MS-CHAP

5. Which of the following Microsoft client operating systems have a built-in firewall? (Choose all that apply.)
   A. Windows 2000 Professional
   B. Windows 98
   C. Windows NT Workstation
   D. Windows XP Professional

6. Which of the following are benefits of using a proxy service? (Choose all that apply.)
   A. Improved performance
   B. More available RAM
   C. Reporting
   D. Access to secure sites

7. Which of the following are true of VLANs? (Choose all that apply.)
   A. VLANs are logical subnets.
   B. VLANs can communicate with other VLANs without using a router.
   C. VLANs can be created using a hub or a switch.
   D. VLANs provide simplified administration in a network.

8. Which of the following are true in regard to an extranet? (Choose all that apply.)
   A. Extranets are additional subnets that are not used on a network.
   B. Extranets provide a value-added resource for a partner or vendor.
   C. Extranets increase the security of a network.
   D. Extranets require additional security measures in regard to authentication and authorization.

9. Which of the following are true in regard to antivirus software? (Choose all that apply.)
   A. Antivirus software requires regular updates in order to be effective.
   B. Antivirus software is designed for clients and not for servers.
   C. Antivirus software is designed to keep viruses from damaging your computers and data.
   D. Most companies cannot afford to install antivirus software on all of their computers.

10. Which type of fault-tolerant storage can be used to provide fault tolerance for the drive that contains the system files on a server?
    A. RAID 0
    B. RAID 1
    C. RAID 5
    D. None of the above

11. How would the physical and logical topology of an IBM Token Ring network best be described?
    A. A physical ring and a logical star
    B. A physical mesh and a logical star
    C. A physical star and a logical ring
    D. A physical bus and a logical star

12. At which of the following speeds is 802.11b capable of communicating? (Choose two.)
   A. 11Mbps
   B. 54Mbps
   C. 3Mbps
   D. 20Mbps

13. Which of the following devices might cause interference to an 802.11g network? (Choose two.)
   A. A 900MHz wireless phone
   B. A Bluetooth keyboard and mouse
   C. An FM radio
   D. A 2.4GHz wireless phone

14. Which of following network cables should be used to connect two similar devices, such as a hub to a hub or a computer to a computer? (Choose all that apply.)
   A. Straight-through cable
   B. Rollover cable
   C. Crossover cable
   D. Coaxial cable

15. Which of the following benefits does a firewall provide? (Choose two.)
   A. Filters packets by, application, port number, IP address
   B. Filters packets into and out of a network
   C. Assigns a temporary IP address to all computers on the network
   D. Resolves hostnames to IP addresses for use on the Internet

Answers to Review Questions

1. **B.** The advantage of a Unix server is that it is very flexible in regard to the type of clients that can be used on it. The biggest disadvantage is that Unix servers are primarily configured and controlled using the command line.

2. **A, C, D.** The most basic components required for connectivity in a network are a common client, a common protocol, and network media. Many dissimilar operating systems can be connected through a network. Networks only require routers if they are intended to connect to other networks or to the Internet.

3. **D.** A tone locator is used to receive the signal produced by a tone generator. The ability to receive the signal proves the continuity of the wires within the cable. Neither a media tester nor a punch-down tool is used for this purpose.

4. **C.** SSH is a remote administration and remote control protocol similar to Telnet. The biggest difference between SSH and Telnet is that SSH encrypts a user's credentials while the user is authenticating and then maintains a secure environment throughout the session. This results in a much more secure method of remote administration. SSL is used to secure communication on the Internet for banking and e-commerce. MS-CHAP is a remote access authentication protocol used only by Microsoft clients.

5. **D.** The only Microsoft Windows client operating system that includes a built-in firewall is Windows XP. The built-in firewall is referred to as the Internet Connection Firewall (ICF). It controls traffic going into, but not out of, the computer.

6. **A, C.** The main benefits of using a proxy service are improved performance, improved control, and reporting. A proxy service does not provide more available RAM. A proxy service does not provide a user with access to any sites to which he would not otherwise have access.

7. **A, D.** Virtual local area networks (VLANs) are logical subnets that are created using a switch, not a hub. VLANs cannot communicate with other VLANs without using a router. VLANs provide simplified administration, through greater flexibility in network design.

8. **B, D.** Extranets are formed when an organization decides to give employees of another organization restricted access to its network. Extranets provide a value-added resource for a vendor or partner of a company. Extranets do not increase security in a network and in fact might actually pose a security risk unless they are configured properly. Extranets require additional security measures in regard to authentication and authorization.

9. **A, C.** Antivirus software is designed to keep viruses from damaging or computers and data, but it requires regular updates of virus definitions in order to remain effective. Antivirus software is designed for clients as well as servers. It should be installed on all of the computers in an organization. Not only is it affordable, but actually an organization can't afford to do without it.

10. **B.** RAID 1 can be used to provide fault-tolerant storage for the drive that contains the system files on a server. RAID 0 does not provide fault tolerance. RAID 5 cannot be used on the drive that contains the system files.

11. C. The IBM Token Ring network uses multistation access units (MSAUs) instead of normal hubs. The MSAUs contain the ring; therefore the IBM Token Ring network is a physical star and a logical ring.

12. A, C. The 802.11b wireless protocol is capable of communicating at a maximum of 11 Mbps. It can also communicate at a considerably lower speed depending on the device and the conditions of the environment. It cannot communicate faster than 11Mbps.

13. B, D. The and 802.11b and 802.11g network uses the 2.4GHz radio band. A 2.4GHz wireless phone, or a Bluetooth device (which also uses the 2.4GHz radio band) can interfere with this type of network. An FM radio and a 900MHz wireless phone are not likely to interfere with this type of network.

14. C, D. In a network using twisted-pair wire, a crossover cable should be used to connect similar devices. In a network using coaxial cable, the coaxial cable can be used as long as it is terminated on both ends. You should not use a straight-through cable or a rollover cable to connect similar network devices.

15. A, B. A firewall is a hardware device and/or software program that filters packets into and out of a network. Firewalls can filter packets by application, port number, IP address, and more. Firewalls do not assign temporary IP addresses or resolve hostnames to IP addresses.

Chapter 4

Domain 4 Network Support

COMPTIA NETWORK+ EXAM OBJECTIVES COVERED IN THIS CHAPTER:

- ✓ **4.1 Given a troubleshooting scenario, select the appropriate network utility from the following:**
  - ping
  - tracert / traceroute
  - arp
  - netstat
  - nbtstat
  - ipconfig / ifconfig
  - winipcfg
  - nslookup / dig
- ✓ **4.2 Given output from a network diagnostic utility, identify the utility and interpret the output.**
- ✓ **4.3 Given a network scenario, interpret visual indicators (For example: link LEDs (Light Emitting Diode) and collision LEDs (Light Emitting Diode)) to determine the nature of a stated problem.**
- ✓ **4.4 Given a troubleshooting scenario involving a client accessing remote network services, identify the cause of the problem (For example: file services, print services, authentication failure, protocol configuration, physical connectivity and SOHO (Small Office / Home Office) router).**

✓ **4.5 Given a troubleshooting scenario between a client and the following server environments, identify the cause of a stated problem:**
- UNIX / Linux / Mac OS X Server
- NetWare
- Windows
- Appleshare IP (Internet Protocol)

✓ **4.6 Given a scenario, determine the impact of modifying, adding or removing network services (For example: DHCP (Dynamic Host Configuration Protocol), DNS (Domain Name Service) and WINS (Windows Internet Name Server)) for network resources and users.**

✓ **4.7 Given a troubleshooting scenario involving a network with a particular physical topology (For example: bus, star, mesh or ring) and including a network diagram, identify the network area affected and the cause of the stated failure.**

✓ **4.8 Given a network troubleshooting scenario involving an infrastructure (For example: wired or wireless) problem, identify the cause of a stated problem (For example: bad media, interference, network hardware or environment).**

✓ **4.9 Given a network problem scenario, select an appropriate course of action based on a logical troubleshooting strategy. This strategy can include the following steps:**

✓ **1. Identify the symptoms and potential causes**

✓ **2. Identify the affected area**

✓ **3. Establish what has changed**

✓ **4. Select the most probable cause**

✓ **5. Implement an action plan and solution including potential effects**

✓ **6. Test the result**

✓ **7. Identify the results and effects of the solution**

✓ **8. Document the solution and process**

To be an effective network administrator, you have to know more than just how to implement a network; you have to know how to keep it running efficiently. This means that you have to be able to troubleshoot the network to quickly determine the nature of a problem and devise a solution. Depending on the operating systems that you use, there are many tools that you can utilize to assist you in troubleshooting network problems. In this chapter, we will focus on how to use these tools to troubleshoot the most common network problems. In addition, we will discuss a general troubleshooting strategy that you can use to keep a network running efficiently.

4.1 Troubleshooting Using the Appropriate Network Utility

There are many troubleshooting utilities built into the most common operating systems. Most of these utilities are based on the command line and are not obvious to the common user. As a network administrator, your knowledge of the existence and the proper use of these tools will set you apart from your competition. In this section, we will discuss and illustrate the proper use of the most common troubleshooting utilities.

Critical Information

Given a troubleshooting scenario, you should be able to select the appropriate network utility. This means that you should know the function and most common use of each of the main network utilities. In this section, we discuss each of these networking tools in detail.

ping

The *ping* tool is one of the most common utilities used by network administrators. It is primarily used to establish general network connectivity, but it can also be used to test name resolution in a network. The ping tool includes switches that allow you to customize your test. You should know how the ping tool operates and its most common uses in network troubleshooting.

You initiate a ping request by simply typing the word ping at a command prompt followed by a space and then the IP address or hostname of the host to which you would like to test connectivity. You can also use many options in ping to make a request more specific, as shown in Figure 4.1.

FIGURE 4.1 The ping tool

```
C:\Documents and Settings\Bill Ferguson.XP1>ping /?

Usage: ping [-t] [-a] [-n count] [-l size] [-f] [-i TTL] [-v TOS]
            [-r count] [-s count] [[-j host-list] | [-k host-list]]
            [-w timeout] target_name

Options:
    -t              Ping the specified host until stopped.
                    To see statistics and continue - type Control-Break;
                    To stop - type Control-C.
    -a              Resolve addresses to hostnames.
    -n count        Number of echo requests to send.
    -l size         Send buffer size.
    -f              Set Don't Fragment flag in packet.
    -i TTL          Time To Live.
    -v TOS          Type Of Service.
    -r count        Record route for count hops.
    -s count        Timestamp for count hops.
    -j host-list    Loose source route along host-list.
    -k host-list    Strict source route along host-list.
    -w timeout      Timeout in milliseconds to wait for each reply.

C:\Documents and Settings\Bill Ferguson.XP1>
```

For example, to ping a host with the IP address of 192.168.1.105, type the following at the command prompt:

ping 192.168.1.105

Similarly, to ping a host with the hostname of xpclient, type the following at the command prompt:

ping xpclient

When you ping a host from a system using a Microsoft client, four packets are transmitted onto the wire with the destination address that you specified. These are referred to as *echo request packets*. When the host identified by the destination address receives the packets, it will reply with special packets called *echo reply packets*. When the computer from which you are initiating the ping request receives the echo reply packets, this establishes the fact that there is general network connectivity between the two computers. An error message such as *destination host unreachable* or *request timed out* indicates that there is no connectivity between your computer and the other computer.

If you only want to establish general network connectivity, then you should ping the IP address of the host on the network. To take the ping tool a step further, you can also ping the hostname of the client instead of just the IP address. In order for a ping request with a hostname to be interpreted by the network, the hostname must be resolved to an IP address by a name resolution mechanism such as DNS or WINS (discussed in Chapter 2). After the hostname is resolved to an IP address, then the packets can be delivered to the computer with that IP address. In this way, pinging the hostname of a computer on the network will test both your name resolution systems as well as the general connectivity of the computer to the network.

Now let's put this into practice. Suppose that you have a troubleshooting scenario whereby a client cannot connect to a server using a specific application, for instance an e-mail application such as Microsoft Outlook. Since the essence of all troubleshooting is isolation, you might first want to make sure the client has general connectivity to the server. By successfully pinging the IP address of the server from the client that is having the problem, you can eliminate the options that the problem is of a physical nature, such as wiring, cable connections, and so on. You will also eliminate the option that the IP address of the client is not configured properly. On the other hand, if you do not get a reply, then you will know that the problem is either of a physical nature or due to an improper configuration, and therefore probably has little to do with Outlook.

To take the test a little further, you could also ping the hostname of the server from the client that is having the problem. If you received a reply when you pinged the IP address but you do not receive a reply when you ping the hostname, then the problem is likely related to name resolution. This test does not completely solve your problem, but it's a first step that does make sure that you are setting off in the right direction to solve it. To customize your ping request, you can use the switches provided with the tool. The switches give you the option to send a set number of packets, a continuous ping, and so on. To see a list of the all of the switches, type the following at the command prompt:

ping /?

tracert/traceroute

Suppose that you use the ping tool and find that you have a problem with connectivity in your network. Now let's suppose that your network is a complex configuration of hubs, switches, and routers that carry information to all of the hosts within it. Furthermore, suppose that the computer that you are pinging is located on the other side of your network and that you have to transmit through multiple routers to get to the subnet of the destination computer. If you simply did not get a reply, then how could you possibly know where the communication broke down? The answer is, you couldn't—at least not with the ping tool.

The *tracert* tool (also called the *traceroute* tool) is a network utility that uses the same technologies as the ping tool, but takes them a step further. Using the tracert tool, you can determine not only that the connection cannot be made to a computer, but also which router could not forward the packet to the next subnet. In other words, you can isolate a network failure to a specific location in your network.

> **NOTE** The terms "tracert" and "traceroute" are sometimes used interchangeably, but they are not actually the same; *traceroute* is the generic term for this type of tool, which can be used by Novell, Cisco, and other types of TCP/IP hosts, while *tracert* is specific to Microsoft clients and servers in a TCP/IP network.

The traceroute tool works in much the same way as the ping tool in that it sends echo request packets through the network. The difference is that the tracert tool uses the *time to live (TTL)* mechanism built into each packet to determine where the communication failure exists. You should know how the tracert tool operates and the most common uses of the tool.

You initiate the tracert tool on a Microsoft client by typing **tracert** followed by a space and then the IP address or hostname of the computer to which you want to test connectivity. You can find a complete list of tracert commands by typing **tracert /?** as shown in Figure 4.2.

FIGURE 4.2 The tracert tool

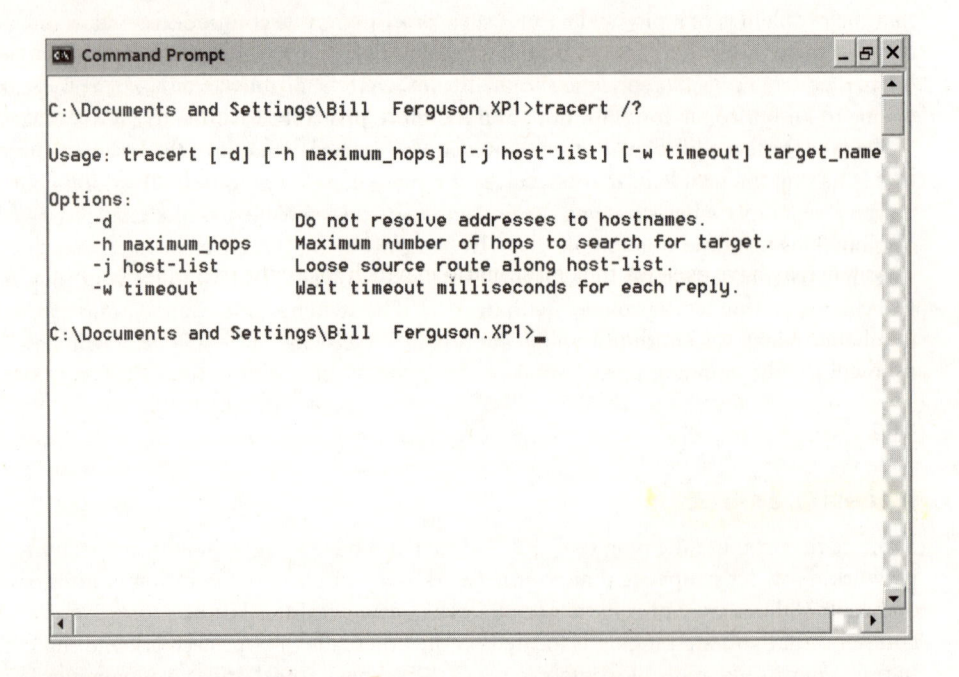

```
C:\Documents and Settings\Bill Ferguson.XP1>tracert /?

Usage: tracert [-d] [-h maximum_hops] [-j host-list] [-w timeout] target_name

Options:
    -d                 Do not resolve addresses to hostnames.
    -h maximum_hops    Maximum number of hops to search for target.
    -j host-list       Loose source route along host-list.
    -w timeout         Wait timeout milliseconds for each reply.

C:\Documents and Settings\Bill Ferguson.XP1>
```

For example, if you wanted to perform a tracert to **mct.billfergusonv.net**, you could type the following at the command prompt:

tracert mct.billfergusonv.net

The tracert tool sends echo request packets just as the ping tool does, but it makes a very important change in each of the packets. This change affects the TTL of the packet, which is the number of hops that it can take through a network without being delivered before it is discarded by a network device.

In a normal ping request from a Microsoft client, each echo request packet has a TTL of 128. This means that it can bounce around a network until it has gone through 128 router interfaces (sometimes through the same interfaces many times) before it will be discarded. The reason that packets have a TTL is so that they can be discarded by the network in the event that they cannot be delivered. Each router decrements the TTL as it forwards the packet. If the result of decrementing the TTL is that the TTL will be reduced to a value of 0, then the router is responsible for discarding the packet and sending a message back to the network identifying itself by its IP address and noting that it has discarded the packet. The tracert tool uses this fact to gather information about the route the packets are taking through the network.

When you initiate the tracert request, an echo request packet is first sent out with a TTL value of 1. This means that the first router that it encounters will discard it and send a message back through the network indicating that it has done so. The message that the router sends back is recorded as the first hop that the packet has to take through the network. The time (in milliseconds) that elapses between the sending of the packets and the return of the message is also recorded. After this is done, the tracert tool automatically sends out a new packet with the TTL value of 2. The first router simply processes the packet normally, decrementing the TTL to 1 and forwarding it to the next router. The second router, however, discards the packet and sends a message back through the network identifying itself by its IP address. This becomes the second hop on the tracert report. This process continues until all of the hops between the local computer and the destination host are listed or one of the routers fails to reply. If a router fails to reply, then you have isolated the source of your problem.

As you may have guessed, the best scenario in which to use the traceroute utility is when you are troubleshooting a connectivity problem that must communicate through multiple routers. You would likely use the ping tool first to establish connectivity, or in this case the lack of it, and then use the traceroute tool to isolate the problem. In addition, since the traceroute tool records statistics regarding the time that routers take to forward packets, it can also assist you in discovering network weaknesses before they become a large problem. In other words, if the times seem unusually high, then you might want to take a closer look at the routers or the interfaces with higher times.

arp

As we discussed in Chapter 2, arp is a service that works in the background and resolves IP addresses to MAC addresses so that packets can be delivered to their destination. As you may recall, each computer keeps an *arp cache* of entries that have been recently resolved (within the last 10 minutes). The computer checks the arp cache first, and then, if the entry is not in the cache, arp will be used to broadcast into the local network and request that the computer with a specific IP address respond with its MAC address so that the packet can be addressed and delivered.

Since the packets cannot be delivered until the MAC address is discovered, arp is a crucial component in the system. Because of this fact, you should know how to identify problems that might be caused by an errant arp cache. In addition, you should know how to troubleshoot the arp cache when necessary.

You can access the arp tool and the syntax for its use by typing the following at a command prompt:

arp /?

The two general types of entries found in an arp cache are dynamic and static, as shown in Figure 4.3. Your knowledge of both types of entries is essential to understanding how arp operates and therefore how to troubleshoot it. You should be able to distinguish between dynamic and static entries in an arp cache. Static entries are indicated with an "s" whereas dynamic entries are indicated with a "d".

FIGURE 4.3 The arp tool

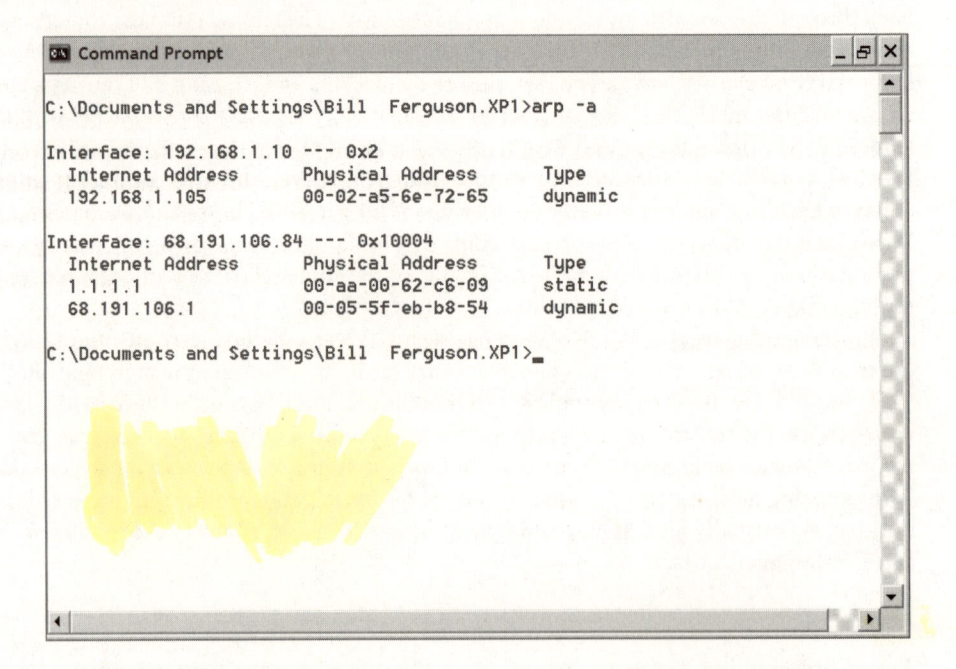

```
Command Prompt

C:\Documents and Settings\Bill Ferguson.XP1>arp -a

Interface: 192.168.1.10 --- 0x2
  Internet Address      Physical Address       Type
  192.168.1.105         00-02-a5-6e-72-65      dynamic

Interface: 68.191.106.84 --- 0x10004
  Internet Address      Physical Address       Type
  1.1.1.1               00-aa-00-62-c6-09      static
  68.191.106.1          00-05-5f-eb-b8-54      dynamic

C:\Documents and Settings\Bill Ferguson.XP1>
```

Dynamic entries are automatically added to the cache when arp is used to resolve an IP address to a MAC address. The lifetime of these entries varies between operating systems but is generally no more than about 10 minutes, unless they are used within the 10 minutes, in which case the clock starts again. Dynamic entries typically do not cause problems. They are clearly marked as **dynamic**.

Static entries, on the other hand, are very different from dynamic entries. Static entries must be added by an administrator and, once added, become a permanent entry in the cache unless they are deleted. For example, if you wanted to add a static entry to an arp cache for a computer with of an IP address of 192.168.1.10 and a MAC address of 00-aa-00-62-c6-09, you would type the following at the command prompt:

arp -s 192.168.1.10   00-aa-00-62-c6-09

Now, before you start adding static entries to all of your computers, let's discuss the advantages and disadvantages of static entries. There is only one reason to add a static entry to an arp cache: faster IP-to-MAC address resolution between two computers on the same network. Adding a static entry might increase performance, but this is very doubtful on today's modern networks. In addition, adding a static entry to resolve an IP address to a MAC address does not affect the name resolution time to resolve the hostname to an IP address, which usually must occur first.

While the advantages of adding a static entry are ambiguous, the disadvantages are very real. Adding a static entry to an arp cache ties a specific MAC address to a specific IP address. This might be fine as long as you don't change the NIC on the computer identifying the entry. If the NIC should fail and be replaced by another NIC, the static entry for the IP address will override the dynamic entry that would otherwise be created in the cache. In other words, since the IP address of the computer will already be listed in the static entry, another IP address and MAC address (the dynamic entry) will not be added. Of course, the new NIC would have a different MAC address, so the arp cache would be incorrect. Consequently, computers with the static entry would not be able to communicate with the computer containing the new NIC.

To troubleshoot the problem, you should remove the static entry from the arp cache. You can remove the static entry for the previous example by typing the following at a command prompt:

arp -d 192.168.1.10   00-aa-00-62-c6-09

> **NOTE:** You can also use a wildcard (*) in place of the IP address and MAC address to delete all hosts from the arp cache.

netstat

Suppose that you are troubleshooting an application for a user and you know the application uses a specific protocol and therefore a specific port or ports, for example, FTP and ports 20 and 21. If the user's computer is having a problem running the application, you might want to make sure that computer is active and listening on the appropriate ports. This is the type of scenario that might require your use of the *netstat* tool.

You can use the netstat tool to display protocol statistics and current TCP/IP connections, as shown in Figure 4.4. The netstat tool has many switches, or options, that you can use to customize the output for your situation. Table 4.1 lists the options available in netstat and the general function of each option. You can list the syntax and all of the options by typing the following at the command prompt:

netstat /?

When you use it with no options, netstat simply displays active TCP/IP connections.

FIGURE 4.4 The netstat tool

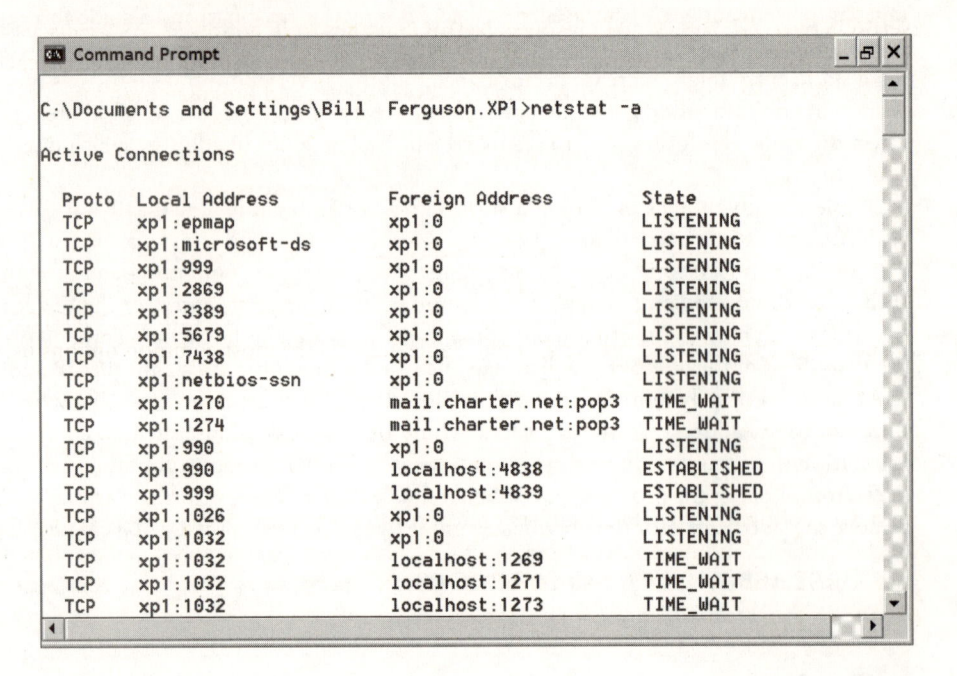

```
Command Prompt

C:\Documents and Settings\Bill Ferguson.XP1>netstat -a

Active Connections

  Proto  Local Address          Foreign Address        State
  TCP    xp1:epmap              xp1:0                  LISTENING
  TCP    xp1:microsoft-ds       xp1:0                  LISTENING
  TCP    xp1:999                xp1:0                  LISTENING
  TCP    xp1:2869               xp1:0                  LISTENING
  TCP    xp1:3389               xp1:0                  LISTENING
  TCP    xp1:5679               xp1:0                  LISTENING
  TCP    xp1:7438               xp1:0                  LISTENING
  TCP    xp1:netbios-ssn        xp1:0                  LISTENING
  TCP    xp1:1270               mail.charter.net:pop3  TIME_WAIT
  TCP    xp1:1274               mail.charter.net:pop3  TIME_WAIT
  TCP    xp1:990                xp1:0                  LISTENING
  TCP    xp1:990                localhost:4838         ESTABLISHED
  TCP    xp1:999                localhost:4839         ESTABLISHED
  TCP    xp1:1026               xp1:0                  LISTENING
  TCP    xp1:1032               xp1:0                  LISTENING
  TCP    xp1:1032               localhost:1269         TIME_WAIT
  TCP    xp1:1032               localhost:1271         TIME_WAIT
  TCP    xp1:1032               localhost:1273         TIME_WAIT
```

TABLE 4.1 Common netstat Options

netstat Option	Display
netstat -a	Displays all connections.
netstat -r	Creates a routing table of computer and all active connections.
netstat -o	Processes IDs so you can view the owner of the port for each connection.
netstat -e	Displays Ethernet statistics, such as packet discards and errors.
netstat -s	Displays per-protocol statistics, such as detailed TCP and UDP statistics.
netstat -n	Does not convert addresses and port numbers to names but instead shows them as IP addresses.

nbtstat

NetBIOS over TCP/IP (NetBT) resolves NetBIOS names to IP addresses. As we discussed in Chapter 2, TCP/IP provides many options for NetBIOS name resolution, including cache lookup, WINS server query, broadcast, DNS server query, and Lmhosts and Hosts file lookup. Since name resolution can become very complex, you need a tool that can assist you in sorting out what is working and what is not working. The nbtstat utility lets you troubleshoot name resolution problems. In addition, you can use this tool to remove or correct a preloaded entry in the NetBIOS name cache.

The nbtstat utility has a fairly complex syntax, which allows you to customize a query. You can also keep it simple and just use the beginning of the syntax to obtain a broader range of output. You can view the syntax of nbtstat and the options available by simply typing **nbtstat** at a command prompt and pressing Enter. Table 4.2 lists the most common options used with nbtstat.

ipconfig/ifconfig

The *ipconfig* command is a tool that displays network configuration values and refreshes addresses configured by DHCP servers on Microsoft computers. It can also be used for a wide range of other troubleshooting scenarios. The *ifconfig* command is the same sort of command that is used by Unix and Linux systems. You should know the purpose and main functionality of both of these commands.

TABLE 4.2 Common nbtstat Options

nbtstat Option	Display
nbtstat -n	Displays names registered locally by the system.
nbtstat -c	Displays NetBIOS name cache entries.
nbtstat -R	Purges the NetBIOS name cache and reloads it from the Lmhosts file.
nbtstat -RR	Releases NetBIOS names registered with the WINS server and then renews their registration.
nbtstat - a name	Performs a NetBIOS adapter status command against the computer specified by name Displays the local NetBIOS name table for the computer and the MAC address of the computer.
nbtstat -S	Lists the current NetBIOS sessions and their status, including statistics.

ipconfig

The **ipconfig** command used without any switches, or options, displays the IP address, subnet mask, and default gateway of all of the network adapters on a computer. It can be used as a very quick method of verifying a basic IP configuration. By adding switches to the **ipconfig** command, you can get much more information about the configuration, and you can control other network parameters such as the DNS resolver cache on a computer. In addition, you can release and renew IP addresses that are assigned by a DHCP server, provided that the computer is configured to obtain an IP address automatically. Table 4.3 shows the additional switches or parameters available with the **ipconfig** command and what each one enables you to do.

ifconfig

The **ifconfig** command is used in Unix and Linux operating systems to configure interfaces and view information about configured interfaces. The syntax of **ifconfig** is very different from that of **ipconfig**. You will be glad to know that you will not have to memorize the syntax of the **ifconfig** command, but you should know the general uses of the command as we discussed. You can, however, find information about the entire syntax and use of the **ifconfig** command on the Web at www.linux.com.

TABLE 4.3 Common *ipconfig* Commands

ipconfig Command	Purpose
ipconfig /all	Displays the full TCP/IP configuration for all adapters. (Adapters include physical interfaces as well as dial-up connections.)
ipconfig /renew	Releases and renews the IP address on an adapter. (Computer must be configured to obtain an IP address automatically.)
ipconfig /release	Releases an IP address that was obtained automatically but does not renew an address. This is a useful tool when moving a computer from one subnet to another.
ipconfig /flushdns	Flushes the DNS client resolver cache. This can be a useful tool when you're troubleshooting name resolution problems.
ipconfig /displaydns	Displays the contents of the DNS client resolver cache. Includes entries that are preloaded from the Hosts file as well as recently obtained resource records.
ipconfig /registerdns	Initiates manual dynamic registration for the DNS names and IP addresses that are configured on a computer. Especially useful when troubleshooting DNS name resolution problems.

4.1 Troubleshooting Using the Appropriate Network Utility

TABLE 4.3 Common *ipconfig* Commands *(continued)*

ipconfig Command	Purpose
ipconfig /showclassid	Shows special DHCP server configuration options on the client when it is configured. This tells the DHCP server to give the client a different set of options based on its class.
ipconfig /setclassid	Used to configure the class of a client so as to match the configured classes in a DHCP server. Ensures that the client will receive the appropriate options from the DHCP server based on its class.
ipconfig /?	Displays help and syntax for the command.

winipcfg

A GUI-based tool, *winipcfg* can be used to view IP configuration and to release and renew IP addresses. It is rarely used in today's networks because it is only available on Windows 9*x* systems, such as Windows 95, Windows 98, and Windows Me. In fact, Windows 98 and Windows Me have both winipcfg and ipconfig.

You initiate winipcfg on a Windows 9*x* computer by clicking Start ➢ Run and typing **winipcfg** . This opens a GUI tool, as shown in Figure 4.5. You can view the MAC address and assigned IP address of each of the adapters on the computer. You can also release and renew the IP addresses. While this GUI tool does provide some convenience, it does not offer the capability that the new **ipconfig** command provides.

FIGURE 4.5 The winipcfg tool

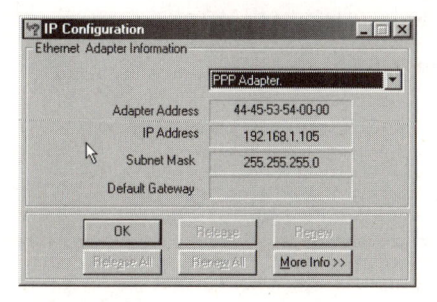

nslookup

As we have discussed many times, DNS is an essential component in most networks. This is especially true if you are using Windows 2000 Server or Windows Server 2003 with Active Directory. The *nslookup* utility allows you to troubleshoot problems related to DNS. You can use nslookup to research information about a DNS server or to set a DNS configuration on server. You can use nslookup in either noninteractive or interactive mode. You should know the difference between these two methods of use.

To use nslookup in noninteractive mode, simply type the command that you want to initiate. At the command prompt, you can enter interactive mode to determine what to type. To do this, type **nslookup**, press Enter, and then type **?** to see a list of all of the commands that you can execute. Determine the command that you want to use and then type **exit** to get out of interactive mode. There are many commands that you can use with nslookup. It's not necessary that you know all of them (thank goodness!), but you should know that they all relate to hostname resolution in one way or another and that the tool is generally used on large domain-based networks.

To use nslookup in interactive mode, type **nslookup** and then press Enter. You can then execute multiple nslookup queries and commands from within the nslookup utility. To exit the utility, simply type **exit**. The commands in interactive mode are the same as those in noninteractive mode, except that you don't have to type **nslookup** before each command. Figure 4.6 shows the nslookup tool in interactive mode.

FIGURE 4.6 The nslookup tool in interactive mode

```
Command Prompt - nslookup

C:\Documents and Settings\Bill Ferguson.XP1>nslookup
Default Server:  dns.a1.charter.com
Address:  24.196.17.8

> ?
Commands:   (identifiers are shown in uppercase, [] means optional)
NAME            - print info about the host/domain NAME using default server
NAME1 NAME2     - as above, but use NAME2 as server
help or ?       - print info on common commands
set OPTION      - set an option
    all                 - print options, current server and host
    [no]debug           - print debugging information
    [no]d2              - print exhaustive debugging information
    [no]defname         - append domain name to each query
    [no]recurse         - ask for recursive answer to query
    [no]search          - use domain search list
    [no]vc              - always use a virtual circuit
    domain=NAME         - set default domain name to NAME
    srchlist=N1[/N2/.../N6] - set domain to N1 and search list to N1,N2, etc.
    root=NAME           - set root server to NAME
    retry=X             - set number of retries to X
    timeout=X           - set initial time-out interval to X seconds
    type=X              - set query type (ex. A,ANY,CNAME,MX,NS,PTR,SOA,SRV)
```

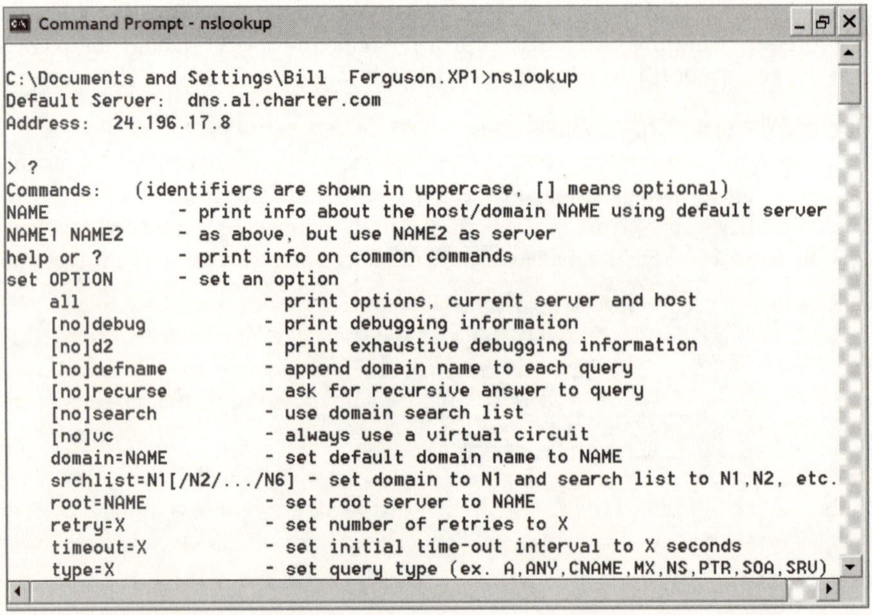

Exam Essentials

Know when to use the ping utility. The ping utility is one of the most commonly used of all network tools. It is typically used to verify physical network connectivity between computers but can also be used to test name resolution by pinging the hostname of a computer instead of the IP address.

Know when to use the tracert (traceroute) utility. The tracert (also referred to as traceroute) utility is typically used to determine more information about a network problem after a ping was unsuccessful. This utility manipulates the TTL of the packets that it sends onto the network so as to force each of the routers to send its identity when it discards the packet. The tracert utility can be used to isolate a network failure to a specific interface on a router.

Know when to use the arp utility. The arp utility is primarily used to modify the arp cache, which is used to resolve IP addresses to MAC address. There are two types of arp entries: dynamic and static. Dynamic entries are much less likely to cause a problem than static entries. Changing a NIC on a computer for which other computers have a static arp entry can cause the computer to be unavailable on the network.

Know when to use the netstat utility. The netstat utility displays protocol statistics for active and listening ports. It can be used to determine whether an application is failing because the ports that it requires are not functional. The netstat utility has many options or switches that enable you to customize a query.

Know when to use the nbtstat utility. The nbtstat utility displays information about the NetBIOS name cache, which is a factor in NetBIOS name resolution. The nbtstat tool can be used to troubleshoot name resolution problems by displaying information as well as by clearing invalid information from the cache. You should be able to list the most common options or switches for the `nbtstat` command.

Know when to use ipconfig/ifconfig. The `ipconfig` and `ifconfig` commands enable you to view information about interfaces and to configure interfaces. The `ipconfig` command is used on Microsoft systems, whereas the `ifconfig` command is used on Unix and Linux systems. Be familiar with the most common options or switches used with these commands.

Know when to use the winipcfg utility. The winipcfg utility is a GUI-based tool that is only available on Windows 95, Windows 98, and Windows Me. This utility enables you to view configuration information and to release and renew IP addresses for computers that are configured to obtain an IP address automatically, but it does not have the flexibility of the command line–based ipconfig utility.

Know when to use the nslookup utility. The nslookup utility is a tool that you can use to troubleshoot hostname resolution. You can use this utility in either noninteractive or interactive mode. The nslookup tool would most likely be used to troubleshoot name resolution in a large domain-based network.

4.2 Identifying Network Utilities and Their Output

Now that we have discussed the general function and use of each of the most common network utilities, you may be wondering what you should be looking for when you use each of the utilities. Each utility has a specific purpose and an expected output of which you should be aware. In other words, if you know what you are looking for in the output, then you can spot a detail that doesn't seem to fit and that could indicate a problem.

Critical Information

You should be able to identify the output from each of the main network utilities as having originated from that utility. In addition, you should be able to interpret the output of the most common network utilities and spot inconsistencies that may signal a problem. In this section, we will discuss each network utility's expected output and possible inconsistencies in detail.

ping

When you ping a network host from a Microsoft computer, four echo request packets are sent with the destination address of the host. If the ping is completely successful, all four packets will receive a reply and the packet percentage loss will be 0 percent, as shown in Figure 4.7.

FIGURE 4.7 A completely successful ping

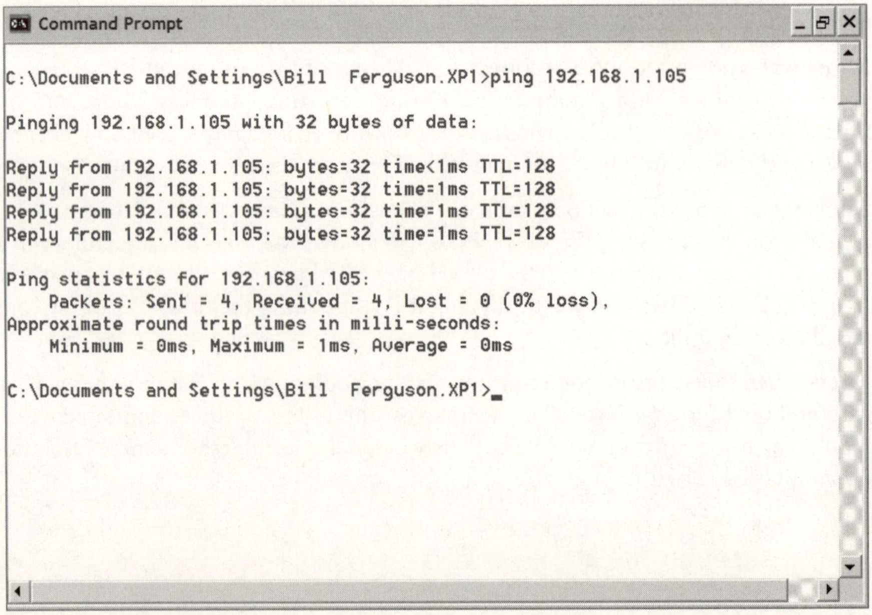

```
Command Prompt

C:\Documents and Settings\Bill Ferguson.XP1>ping 192.168.1.105

Pinging 192.168.1.105 with 32 bytes of data:

Reply from 192.168.1.105: bytes=32 time<1ms TTL=128
Reply from 192.168.1.105: bytes=32 time=1ms TTL=128
Reply from 192.168.1.105: bytes=32 time=1ms TTL=128
Reply from 192.168.1.105: bytes=32 time=1ms TTL=128

Ping statistics for 192.168.1.105:
    Packets: Sent = 4, Received = 4, Lost = 0 (0% loss),
Approximate round trip times in milli-seconds:
    Minimum = 0ms, Maximum = 1ms, Average = 0ms

C:\Documents and Settings\Bill Ferguson.XP1>_
```

If the ping is not completely successful, some of the packets may be replied to while others are not. This would most likely indicate a failing NIC or a *flapping connection*. Still another possibility is that the ping is not replied to at all. If you pinged the IP address, no reply would indicate that there is no physical connectivity between the two computers, but the output could come back in a few different forms such as a *request timed out* message or a *destination host unreachable* message. A request timed out message usually indicates that no other entity replied to the packets at all, whereas a destination host unreachable message is a message from a router indicating that the host is recognized on the network but that it cannot be contacted at this time. In either case, your next step should be to attempt to isolate the problem further by using another tool such as tracert.

tracert/traceroute

As we mentioned before, the main purpose of the tracert (traceroute) utility is to isolate a network issue to a specific interface on a specific router. The expected output of the utility is a list of the routers that the packets are encountering as they traverse the network to their destination. The time (in milliseconds) should also be relatively even between each router interface, as shown in Figure 4.8. If the trace does not complete, then the last router that is listed is the best place to start troubleshooting the problem; the problem will likely be the next router in the path. The error could be due to an improper configuration or to filtering, such as a firewall or an access list. In addition, if any of the hops seem to take a significantly longer period of time, this may indicate a problem with a device or a problem regarding too much traffic in a network segment.

FIGURE 4.8 A healthy trace

```
Command Prompt - tracert mct.billfergusonv.net

C:\Documents and Settings\Bill Ferguson.XP1>tracert mct.billfergusonv.net

Tracing route to mct.billfergusonv.net [216.21.229.196]
over a maximum of 30 hops:

  1     9 ms    14 ms     9 ms  10.106.32.1
  2     9 ms     9 ms    13 ms  er1ge2-0ldsal.lds.al.charter.com [24.196.0.1]
  3    14 ms    19 ms    13 ms  65.90.64.17
  4    13 ms    16 ms    13 ms  P5-0.c0.atln.broadwing.net [216.140.12.41]
  5    29 ms    25 ms    38 ms  so7-1-0.C1.wash.broadwing.net [216.140.8.21]
  6    29 ms    33 ms    32 ms  s1-3-0.c1.nwyk.broadwing.net [216.140.16.14]
  7    27 ms    30 ms    29 ms  p6-2.a0.nwyk.broadwing.net [216.140.10.194]
  8    29 ms    29 ms    29 ms  broadwing-gw.n54ny.ip.att.net [192.205.32.105]
  9    29 ms    32 ms    41 ms  tbr1-p012402.n54ny.ip.att.net [12.122.11.213]
```

arp

The arp cache in most computers should contain the dynamic entries that have been added by the system for hosts that have been resolved within the last 10 minutes. In rare cases, the arp cache might also contain static entries added by an administrator, but static entries are usually not recommended and are rarely used on most computers. (Refer to the information about arp in section 4.1 of this chapter.) Since most, if not all, of the entries are dynamic, the arp cache should be expected to change frequently. You can test the arp cache by simply pinging a computer in your network that is not currently listed in the arp cache. After you ping the computer and successfully get a reply, the computer's IP address and MAC address should be listed in your arp cache as a dynamic entry. This entry will also contain the physical (MAC) address of the computer that you pinged.

netstat

Depending on the options or switches that you have chosen, a **netstat** command could have many different looks. The common thread between looks, however, will be that it will focus on ports. Some **netstat** commands display active and listening ports while other commands focus on specifics about the ports, such as the protocols that are being used on them. Figure 4.9 shows a **netstat** command with the -s switch to display per-protocol statistics.

FIGURE 4.9 netstat -s

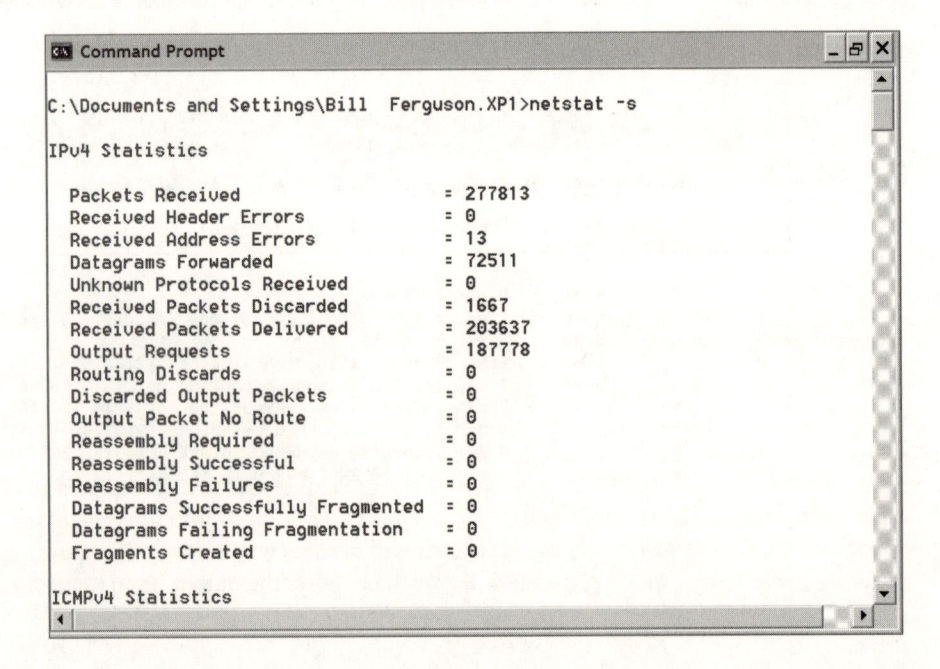

```
C:\Documents and Settings\Bill Ferguson.XP1>netstat -s

IPv4 Statistics

  Packets Received                   = 277813
  Received Header Errors             = 0
  Received Address Errors            = 13
  Datagrams Forwarded                = 72511
  Unknown Protocols Received         = 0
  Received Packets Discarded         = 1667
  Received Packets Delivered         = 203637
  Output Requests                    = 187778
  Routing Discards                   = 0
  Discarded Output Packets           = 0
  Output Packet No Route             = 0
  Reassembly Required                = 0
  Reassembly Successful              = 0
  Reassembly Failures                = 0
  Datagrams Successfully Fragmented  = 0
  Datagrams Failing Fragmentation    = 0
  Fragments Created                  = 0

ICMPv4 Statistics
```

nbtstat

Since nbtstat is a utility that enables you to view and manage the NetBIOS name cache, most nbtstat output will be directly related to NetBIOS over TCP/IP. As with netstat, the output may differ greatly depending on the options or switches that you choose. All of the output, however, will relate to NetBIOS names or statistics. Figure 4.10 shows the **nbtstat -S** command, which displays a list of current NetBIOS sessions and their status.

FIGURE 4.10 nbtstat -S

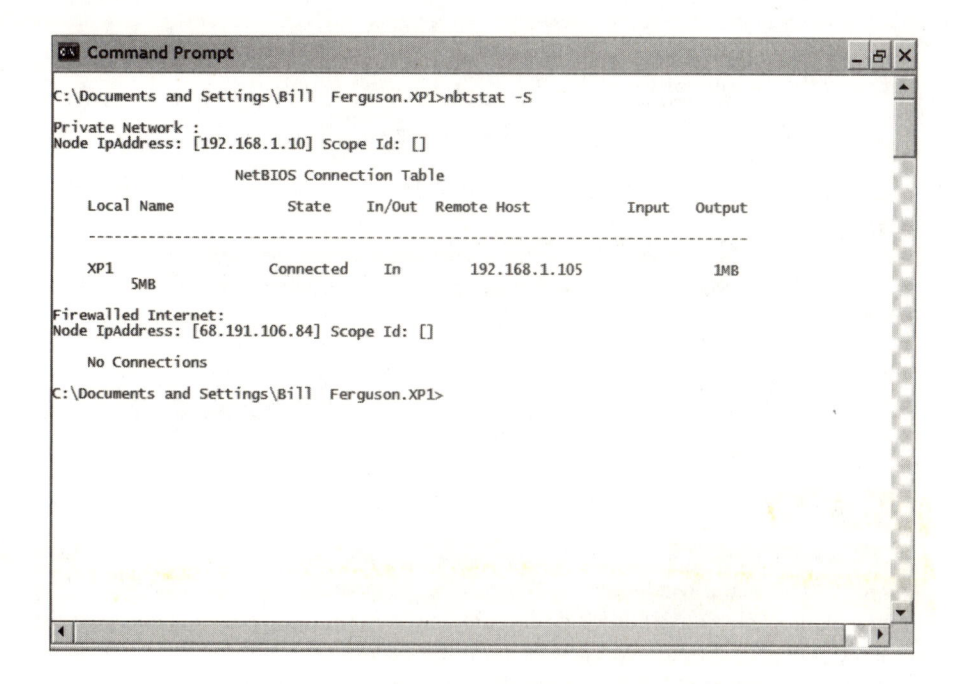

```
C:\Documents and Settings\Bill Ferguson.XP1>nbtstat -S
Private Network :
Node IpAddress: [192.168.1.10] Scope Id: []

                    NetBIOS Connection Table

    Local Name          State       In/Out  Remote Host          Input     Output
    -------------------------------------------------------------------------------
    XP1                 Connected   In      192.168.1.105                  1MB
        SMB

Firewalled Internet:
Node IpAddress: [68.191.106.84] Scope Id: []

    No Connections

C:\Documents and Settings\Bill Ferguson.XP1>
```

ipconfig

As mentioned before, the **ipconfig** command with no switches simply displays the IP address, subnet mask, and default gateway of all of the adapters on the computer. If the computer is configured for IPv6 as well as IPv4, then the **ipconfig** command will display both addresses. When used with switches, the **ipconfig** command is a very flexible tool that can be used to clear the DNS cache, release and renew IP addresses, and so on. The output from this command will be specific to the type of command, but all output will in some way relate to IP address configuration or name resolution configuration. Figure 4.11 shows the output of an **ipconfig /all** command.

FIGURE 4.11 ipconfig /all

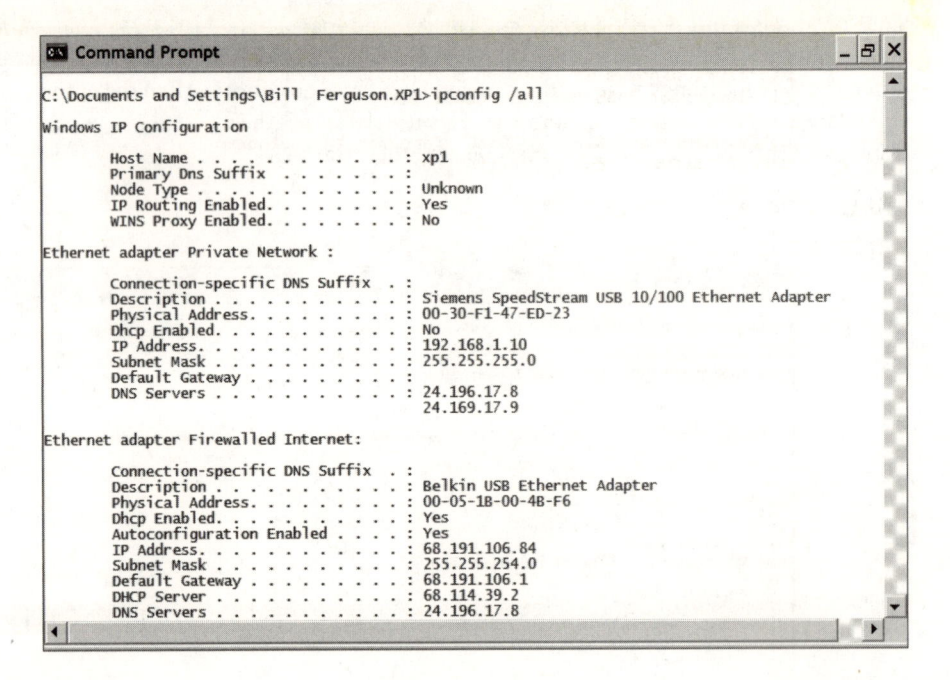

```
C:\Documents and Settings\Bill Ferguson.XP1>ipconfig /all
Windows IP Configuration

        Host Name . . . . . . . . . . . . : xp1
        Primary Dns Suffix  . . . . . . . :
        Node Type . . . . . . . . . . . . : Unknown
        IP Routing Enabled. . . . . . . . : Yes
        WINS Proxy Enabled. . . . . . . . : No

Ethernet adapter Private Network :

        Connection-specific DNS Suffix  . :
        Description . . . . . . . . . . . : Siemens SpeedStream USB 10/100 Ethernet Adapter
        Physical Address. . . . . . . . . : 00-30-F1-47-ED-23
        Dhcp Enabled. . . . . . . . . . . : No
        IP Address. . . . . . . . . . . . : 192.168.1.10
        Subnet Mask . . . . . . . . . . . : 255.255.255.0
        Default Gateway . . . . . . . . . :
        DNS Servers . . . . . . . . . . . : 24.196.17.8
                                            24.169.17.9

Ethernet adapter Firewalled Internet:

        Connection-specific DNS Suffix  . :
        Description . . . . . . . . . . . : Belkin USB Ethernet Adapter
        Physical Address. . . . . . . . . : 00-05-1B-00-4B-F6
        Dhcp Enabled. . . . . . . . . . . : Yes
        Autoconfiguration Enabled . . . . : Yes
        IP Address. . . . . . . . . . . . : 68.191.106.84
        Subnet Mask . . . . . . . . . . . : 255.255.254.0
        Default Gateway . . . . . . . . . : 68.191.106.1
        DHCP Server . . . . . . . . . . . : 68.114.39.2
        DNS Servers . . . . . . . . . . . : 24.196.17.8
```

nslookup

Since the nslookup utility is specifically focused on hostname resolution, all output from the nslookup command will be related to hostname resolution files and/or services. If a computer is a member of an Active Directory domain, and you simply type **nslookup** at the command prompt, then you should expect to see output indicating the authoritative DNS server for that domain. This action will also put you into the interactive mode of nslookup, where you can type ? to determine your other options. Figure 4.12 shows the results of typing **nslookup** on computer that is a member of a domain.

Exam Essentials

Be able to identify and interpret the output of the ping command. Be able to identify the output of a ping command and interpret whether the ping was successful or unsuccessful. If the ping was unsuccessful, then you should be able to interpret whether it was actually received by any other network host. You should also be able to interpret a partially successful ping as related to a failing NIC or a flapping network connection.

FIGURE 4.12 Running nslookup on a domain

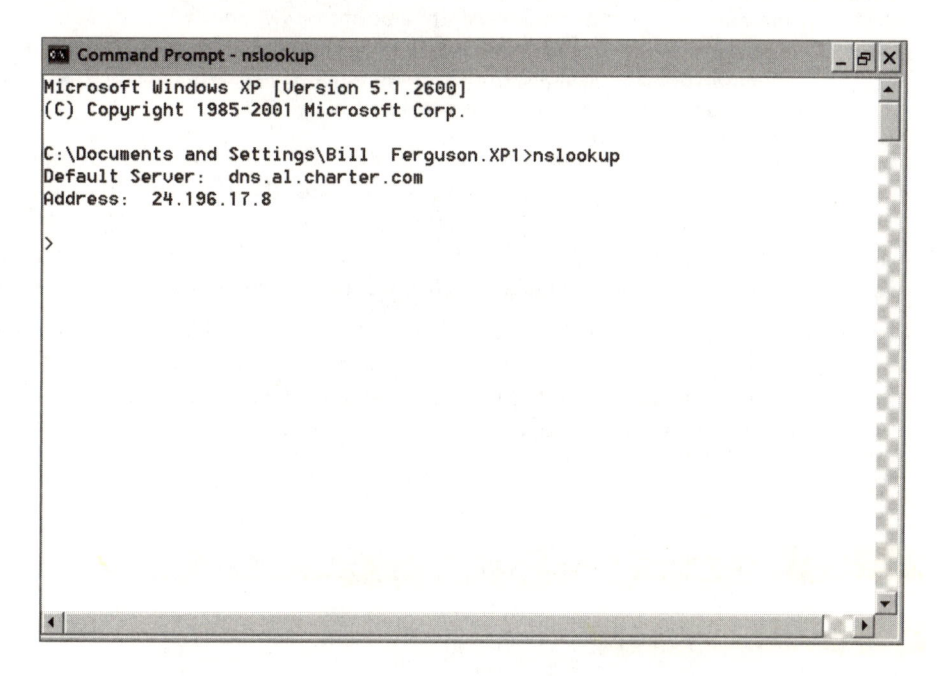

```
Command Prompt - nslookup

Microsoft Windows XP [Version 5.1.2600]
(C) Copyright 1985-2001 Microsoft Corp.

C:\Documents and Settings\Bill Ferguson.XP1>nslookup
Default Server:  dns.al.charter.com
Address:  24.196.17.8

>
```

Be able to identify and interpret the output of the tracert /traceroute command. The expected output of a tracert command is a list of routers that the echo request packets must traverse on their way to their destination. The times at each router should be fairly consistent; an unusually high amount of time might indicate a failing device or too much traffic in that part of the network. A trace that does not complete will generally isolate the network problem as the last router on its list or the next router in the path.

Be able to identify and interpret the output of the arp command. The arp cache in most computers should contain only the dynamic entries that have been added by the system for hosts for which it has resolved a MAC address in the last 10 minutes. It is possible to add a static (permanent) entry to an arp cache, but it's not recommended in most cases. On your computer you can test the arp cache by pinging a computer on the network that is not currently listed and then viewing the arp cache to make sure that the computer's IP address and MAC address are listed.

Be able to identify and interpret the output of the netstat command. A netstat command's output can have many different looks, depending on the options that are chosen with the command. The common thread will be that each relates in some way to ports. The netstat command output may just list the active ports, or it may have very specific statistics about the protocols used on the ports.

Be able to identify and interpret the output of the nbtstat command. The output of the nbtstat command may vary depending on the options or switches selected. The common thread of all output types is that they will relate to NetBIOS over TCP/IP. You can use some nbtstat commands to make changes to the NetBIOS name cache, such as the -R command, which purges the cache.

Be able to identify and interpret the output of the ipconfig command. The output from an ipconfig command with no switches or options shows only the IP address (IP v4 and/or IP v6), subnet mask, and default gateway of each of the adapters in the computer. The ipconfig command switches make it a very flexible tool that you can use to view the entire IP configuration of a computer and even to make changes, such as releasing and renewing dynamic IP addresses.

Be able to identify and interpret the output of the nslookup command. The nslookup command output can take on many looks, depending on the options that you select. The common thread will be that they are related to hostname resolution. The nslookup utility has two basic modes: noninteractive and interactive. You enter the interactive mode simply by typing nslookup at the command prompt.

4.3 Interpreting Visual Indicators in a Network

Sometimes you can solve a problem very quickly, if you just know what to look for on a device. Most devices such as routers, switches, hubs, and even network interface cards (NICs) have *light-emitting diodes (LEDs)* that can tell you quite a lot if you are "listening." In this section, we discuss the most common of these types of LEDs and what you can interpret from them.

Critical Information

You should know how to interpret the signals given by LEDs on devices in your network. We will focus on the most common types of LEDs: *link LEDs* and *collision LEDs*.

Link LEDs

You are not always in front of a computer when you are connecting network devices. Sometimes a computer is connected through a series of devices and you may be in a network closet out of sight of the computers that you are connecting. When this is case, you can have some reasonable assurance that a device is properly connected if you see that a link LED, also called a link light, is lit when you plug the cable into the device. Typically a lit link light indicates that the computer is properly connected and that it is powered up. The reason that we say "typically" is because it is possible that an improperly made cable that cannot actually transmit signal can still result in a lit link light. This is because the power and ground wires within the cable are separate from the wires that actually send the data. Although this is an unusual situation, you should be aware that it can occur.

Now, let's discuss what a lit link light means and what it does not mean. A lit link light typically means that the computer (or other network device) has a physical connection to the network device. A lit link light on a hub or a switch will generally be accompanied by the link light on the NIC in the computer. What the lit link light does not mean is that the computer is configured properly to send data. In other words, you will still see a link light on the computers and the switch even if all of the computers are configured for IP addresses that won't actually communicate with each other. Therefore, the real benefit of having the link light comes when you don't see it lit. If the link lights are not lit, then it doesn't matter how correct the address configurations are; the computers still can't talk. Now, you may be wondering, "What if the light is burned out?" Well, LEDs use very little power and therefore create very little heat. As a result, they don't burn out very frequently at all. In fact, it's a very rare occurrence to have a burned-out LED.

Collision LEDs

Some devices, such as hubs and switches, have a special LED that indicates that collisions are occurring in the network. Network *collisions* occur when two devices attempt to send a signal on the same channel at the same time. They generally occur on a network that is improperly configured or has too much traffic in the network segment. Collisions decrease the performance of the network segment because damaged packets must be resent by the devices. Collision LEDs don't tell you the cause of the collision, but they do alert you to the fact that collisions are occurring.

Exam Essentials

Know how to interpret link LEDs. Link LEDs typically indicate that two network devices are physically connected to each other. However this is not always the case, because it is still possible that a cable could be improperly designed for network signals. A connection indicated by the link LED does not in any way indicate that the computers are logically configured properly to communicate with each other.

Be able to interpret collision LEDs. Collision LEDs are typically found on network devices such as hubs and switches. Collisions are undesirable network behavior because they decrease the performance of the network segment, since damaged packets must be resent. Collision LEDs do not necessarily indicate the cause of collisions, but simply indicate that they are occurring.

4.4 Troubleshooting Client Access to Remote Services in a Network

The greatest benefit of creating a network is the ability to share resources between the computers within the network. This benefit can only be realized if all of the components of the network are configured properly to allow the client to access the resources. Basically, there is no "in between" or "almost able to connect"; either all of the factors that affect network communication are configured properly or the network will not function properly for the user. Because of this, it is important that you understand all of the factors that can be involved in network communication and how to troubleshoot any problems that crop up related to these factors. In this section, we discuss each of these factors in detail.

Critical Information

You should understand and be able to troubleshoot all of the factors involved in a client connecting to remote resources on a network. These include:

- File services
- Print services
- Authentication
- Protocol configuration
- Physical connectivity
- Small office/home office (SOHO) router

File Services

File services are protocols or services that enable computers to communicate with one another on a network for the purpose of sharing information. In other words, they enable the process of sharing files and folders on a network. Depending on the type of computers on your network, you might use many different types of file services. In this section, we discuss the most common file services used in today's networks: SMB, NetWare, and NFS.

Server Message Block (SMB)

Server message block (SMB) is a protocol used for sharing files, folders, and printers. It was first developed by IBM in the early 1980s, but it has since been enhanced and refined by Microsoft and other companies. SMB works as a client server, request response mechanism in many clients and servers, including all Microsoft clients and servers. Clients typically connect to the servers using the NetBIOS over TCP/IP protocol, but other protocols can also be used, such as IPX/SPX. Responding to the need for higher security, the latest Microsoft operating systems use SMB signing, which forces servers to identify themselves with a digital certificate instead of just a NetBIOS name. The newest versions of SMB that support signing are also being referred to as *Common Internet File System (CIFS)*.

Typically, SMB works with few errors, but if you decide to use SMB signing with the newer operating systems, you should ensure that all clients and servers are capable of providing the service. Windows 2000 and later clients and servers provide this capability through Group Policy. Windows NT Service Pack 3 and higher can also be modified to provide SMB signing capability. There are two main levels of security with SMB:

Share level Protection is applied at the share on the server. Each share can have its own password. This would most likely be used in a workgroup environment, rather than in a domain environment.

User level Access to files and folders is based on user rights. A user must either log into the server itself or log into the domain of which the server is a member. This is the most common type of SMB file service.

NetWare File Services

NetWare file services work in roughly the same way as SMB: they provide access to files and folders through a network. NetWare file services, however, are proprietary to NetWare servers and clients. The most common troubleshooting that you might encounter would involve permissions for network shares. NetWare has a complex and sophisticated system of permissions for users and groups. This can be an advantage if you are familiar with the system—or a disadvantage if you are not.

NFS/Samba

NFS is the original file-sharing system used by Linux clients and servers. NFS allows a type of "drive mapping" that enables a disk on the server to be shared for the client so that the user can utilize the remote disk in the same way as the local disks on his computer. *Samba* is an extension of NFS which makes a type of SMB functionality available so the client can access specific files and folders on a disk. In addition, Samba makes shares available to Windows clients as well as Linux clients.

Print Services

Just as file services allow access to shared files and folders in a network, print services allow users to utilize shared printers. It's easier to understand printing terminology if you remember that *printers* are actually software and not hardware. Now, before you think I'm joking or just plain crazy, let me explain that a little further.

Printers are the software installed in an operating system that allows client computers to access and print to the *print devices* on a network. This may, at first, seem like just a distinction in terminology, but it's actually a very important fact. It's important because once you understand that printers are software, then print permissions, printer priorities, and printer pools become much easier to understand as well. Depending on the operating system you are using, the file systems that we discussed earlier can all provide print services, including permissions, printer priorities, and printer pools. In the paragraphs that follow, we will discuss each of these concepts in detail.

Printer Permissions

The exact terminology of printer permissions varies with the file and print service that you use, but all printer permissions offer approximately the same levels of permissions. We will use Microsoft printer permissions as an example, since they are the most common. Microsoft printer permissions are as follows:

Print Allows a user to print to a printer and therefore receive output from the print device. A user can also manage his own document in the printer's queue, but cannot manage documents of other users.

Manage Documents Allows a user to manage the print queue in regard to all of the documents. The user can also pause printing and stop and restart the spooler. A user with only Manage Documents permissions cannot print to the printer.

Manage Printer Allows a user to print, to manage the queue and all of the print device operations, and to manage the printer and change its properties and the permissions of all users assigned to the printer.

Printer Priorities

When more than one user or group of users is utilizing the same print device, you can use *printer priorities* to determine whose documents will be given priority in the print queue. With printer priorities, multiple printers are used for the same print device, with different priorities assigned to each of the printers. Permissions are then used to ensure that only the groups that should have the higher-priority printer are able to access it. The result of sending a print job with a higher-priority printer is that the print job with higher priority will "jump" over all of the lower-priority print jobs in the queue and be printed as soon as the current document finishes printing. Figure 4.13 shows the Priority setting on the Advanced tab of a printer's properties dialog box.

FIGURE 4.13 The Priority setting for a printer

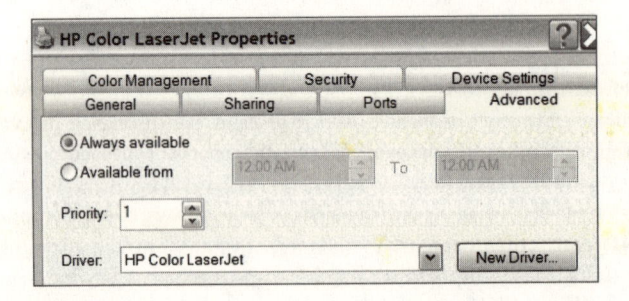

Printer Pools

Printer pools are logically the opposite of printer priorities. Whereas printer priorities involve multiple printers with only one print device, printer pools involve multiple print devices that all use the same printer. When a user sends a print job to a printer that controls a printer pool, the printer sends the print job to the first available print device. Printer pools are useful when a large clerical staff sends a great number of documents to the printer and that one device cannot possibly keep up with the demand on an ongoing basis. Some third-party services, such as HP Jetdirect, inform a user about the print device to which the document was sent; most operating system file and print services do not. For this reason, all of the print devices should be located in the same physical area to make finding the printed document easier for the user. Also, all of the print devices in a printer pool should ideally be identical, since they will all use exactly the same printer. Figure 4.14 shows the port settings on a printer with a printer pool.

FIGURE 4.14 Printer pool settings on a printer

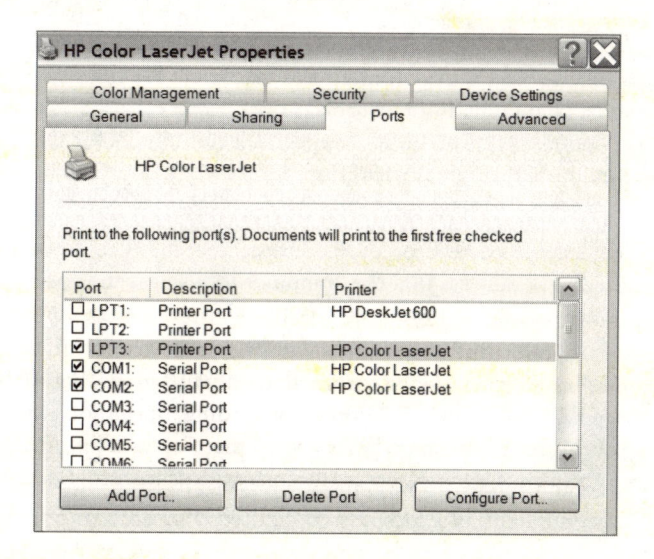

Authentication

As we discussed earlier, authentication is the process of proving the identity of a user or a computer. Many types of authentication protocols are in use today, and they continue to evolve with the need for increased security in today's networks. In Chapter 2, we discussed the various authentication protocols that can be used between clients and servers in a remote connection. We also discussed the local authentication protocols that can be used within a network, such as Kerberos.

The main factor of which you should be aware in regard to authentication is the fact that two computers that are attempting to communicate must share an authentication protocol in order for communication to be successful. In fact, the best way to understand authentication is to think about it in regard to only two computers at a time. In other words, the client may be able to authenticate to many servers using several different methods, but the main factor that we are concerned with is "Can it authenticate with a specific server with a method that the server understands?" If it can, then the other methods that it might also be able to use are of little of no consequence for this specific connection. If it cannot, then we should make sure that the client and the server have at least one configured authentication mechanism in common.

Protocol Configuration

In Chapter 2 we discussed the major protocols (or rules of behavior) that computers use to communicate with one another in a network. We also stated that TCP/IP was by far the most common protocol used in today's networks. In this section, we briefly discuss the most common TCP/IP configuration errors that affect *remote connections*.

It should be understood that we are defining "remote connections" as any connection to a resource or service outside of the computer. This means that remote connections could be connections to a resource on your own LAN or they could be a connection through the Internet. With this in mind, the major factors that might affect TCP/IP protocol configuration and therefore require troubleshooting are as follows:

IP address   The IP address configured for a computer must be correct for the subnet in which the computer exists and it must be unique. If the address is not correct for the subnet, then the computer will not be able to communicate at all. If the address is not unique for the subnet, an error will result and the computer that originally had the address will be notified with an error as well.

Subnet mask   If a subnet mask is not correct for an IP address, then the IP address really isn't correct either. This is because the IP address that the computer looks at is the computer's IP address "anded" with its subnet mask. *Anding* is a binary calculation that the computer uses with all IP addresses and subnet masks to determine the *network ID* and *host ID* of the address. If the subnet mask is not correct, you should change the subnet mask to match that of the other computers in the same subnet that are able to communicate.

Default gateway   A default gateway is the address that the computer uses to communicate outside of its own network. The default gateway for a computer is typically the router interface that is within its own subnet. If a computer has a correctly configured IP address and subnet mask but does not have a correctly configured default gateway, then the computer will be able to communicate within its own subnet but will not be able to communicate outside of its own subnet, or to the Internet. If a computer has these symptoms, you should configure its default gateway the same as the other computers within its subnet that can communicate with computers outside of their own subnet.

DNS address   The DNS address is the main name resolution address that computers use in today's networks. Computers use the DNS servers in their network and outside of their network to resolve hostnames to IP addresses. If the DNS address is not correct, the computer will usually have a very slow and unreliable connection to resources in your network. This is because the computer is actually using other backup methods of name resolution, as we discussed in Chapter 2.

WINS address   The WINS address is a name resolution address used primarily by Microsoft client and server computers earlier than Windows 2000. Legacy computers and applications use NetBIOS names, rather than hostnames, to refer to computers on the network. WINS, as discussed in Chapter 2, is a dynamic database that resolves NetBIOS names to IP addresses.

Physical Connectivity

Verifying physical connectivity on a network involves your sense of sight as well as your understanding of network tools. You have to pay attention to all of the elements that tell you whether you have physical connectivity. We have discussed some of these elements in previous sections, but the following is a summary that you can use as a checklist:

Cable connections   Cables connectors must be securely plugged into the computer or network device to ensure physical connectivity.

Link lights   Link lights (or link LEDs) are included with most NICs and network devices. You should make sure the link light is lit as part of verifying network connectivity. (As mentioned earlier, this is still no guarantee because the cable could be improperly configured.)

Indicators on the desktop, notification area, or other software tools   Most operating systems have a method of indicating whether a connection on a computer is properly connected to another computer. On Windows XP, for example, this is revealed in the notification area of the Taskbar.

Ping   Use the ping tool on a command prompt to verify physical connectivity. If you get a reply from the computer that you pinged, the physical connectivity (as well as proper IP configuration) is assured.

Small Office/Home Office (SOHO) Routers

Not long ago, a router was a network device that was configured only by a trained network professional. Today many individuals are setting up home networks or small office networks that do not require a network administrator. This development has opened the door for a new type of router called a *Small Office/Home Office (SOHO) router*. These routers are typically inexpensive compared with the larger routers used in most networks. They are available from Cisco, Linksys, Belkin, and other vendors who usually provide not only the device but also the software that walks you through installing the router. Many of these SOHO routers also offer such services as automatic address assignment and firewalls. You should refer to the vendor's website for details on configuring and troubleshooting these products.

Exam Essentials

Know how to troubleshoot file services.   File services enable communication between computers in a network. Each network operating system vendor provides its own file services for network communication and to share files and folders. Microsoft uses Server Message Block (SMB) and it has very few problems, except with the newest operating systems that use SMB digital signing to enhance security. SMB signing for the newest clients and servers (Windows 2000, Windows XP, and Windows Server 2003) can be controlled through group policy; Windows NT with SP3 can also be modified for SMB signing.

Be able to troubleshoot print services.   Print services are included with file services on the offerings of network operating system vendors. Print services might include printer permissions, printer priorities, and printer pooling. Be familiar with the permissions assigned to printers on a Microsoft network. You should know the difference between printer priorities and printer pooling and therefore how to get started troubleshooting each of these services.

Know how to troubleshoot authentication. Be familiar with the specific authentication protocols used for LANs as well as remote access networks, as discussed in Chapter 2. Troubleshooting authentication on a network should be accomplished by focusing on two computers at a time and determining the authentication protocols that each of them has in common. Servers and clients can be assigned multiple authentication protocols so that clients can use different protocols to communicate with various servers on a network.

Be able to troubleshoot protocol configuration. TCP/IP is by far the most prevalent protocol in use today. There are many elements involved in TCP/IP configuration, including (but not limited to) IP address, subnet mask, default gateway, DNS address, and WINS address. You should be able to recognize the likely symptoms of an improper configuration of each of these elements.

Know how to troubleshoot physical connectivity. Troubleshooting physical connectivity is accomplished by being observant of all aspects of your network. There are many indicators that assist you in troubleshooting physical connectivity, such as link lights and desktop notifications. A successful ping indicates proper physical connectivity and a proper (or at least functional) IP address.

Be able to troubleshoot SOHO routers. The SOHO router is a relatively new network component that has come into existence because of the large number of small office networks and home office networks. SOHO routers and the software that accompany them are designed to be installed by an individual who is not a networking professional. SOHO routers often have features such as automatic address assignment and firewalls; the best reference is the vendor's instructional information or the vendor website.

4.5 Identifying Common Network Problems

A client server environment cannot be all things to all people; each type of client server environment has its strengths and its weaknesses. It's important that you understand what to look for when troubleshooting the most common client server environments. This will help you identify and fix problems more accurately and therefore more quickly, enabling a user to remain productive.

Critical Information

Given a troubleshooting scenario between a client and the following server environments, you should be able to identify the cause of a stated problem.

Unix/Linux/Mac OS X Server

As we discussed in Chapter 3, Unix is a flexible operating system that is mostly command line driven. Linux is a spin-off from Unix that provides some GUI capability. Mac OS X Server is a product from Apple that can be used as a server in multiple types of network settings, including with Linux. In the following paragraphs, we will discuss the relative merits and potential problems when you use each of these systems in your network.

Unix

Unix is a command line–based operating system that is still used in many organizations today. Often, the Unix server provides some type of line-of-business application that has been used by the organization for many years and would therefore be more trouble to move than the change would be worth. Unix servers can communicate with other servers and clients, but you sometimes must install additional software to make them effective. For example, Microsoft clients can access Unix web servers with their browsers and no additional software, but access to a Unix file and print server requires that *Services for Unix* be installed on the client. Also, Unix servers cannot dynamically register their address with a WINS server, so you would need to add a static entry for the Unix server on the WINS server if you have legacy clients that use NetBIOS name resolution to find servers.

Linux

Linux is a Unix-like operating system that has some GUI capability. It is offered free to the public, and its code is open source and can be changed. Because there are so many versions of Linux, its tough to make a blanket statement about issues that you might encounter with Linux servers or clients. Some distributions of Linux are Red Hat, SuSE, Debian, and Caldera. The following are key features of the Linux operating system:

Multitasking   Linux supports multitasking, which is the ability to run several programs simultaneously.

Multiplatform   Linux is able to operate on various platforms, not just on Intel machines.

Multiprocessor support   Linux recognizes multiple processors on a single system.

Development   The source code is available in all noncommercial programs for Linux.

Virtual consoles   Linux supports virtual consoles, which are essentially independent logon sessions.

File system support   The native file system for Linux is EXT2, but Linux also supports FAT, HFS (for Macintosh), VFAT, and CDFS (for CD-ROMs).

Network support   Linux can connect to various network environments. It can support protocols such as TCP/IP, AppleTalk, and IPX/SPX.

With all of the features that Linux has, you might wonder where the problems could be. Well, typically the problems are not with the operating system itself, but rather with the user's ability to work with the system. People who are used to working with a Windows-based system will discover quickly that Linux is a very different environment. In addition, with so many distributions of Linux on the market, not all commands will work the same on all Linux servers and clients. If you decide to incorporate Linux into your network environment, you should standardize on a single distribution as much as possible and provide training for your users.

Mac OS X Server

Mac OS X Server is a product from Apple that combines the most popular technologies of the open source community with the latest version of Unix software. Mac OS X Server can be used with many different operating systems as a powerful web server and Internet server. All of this may sound fantastic, but it is not without its own challenges. The earlier versions of Mac OS X Server contained many bugs that prevented them from being able to communicate effectively with some Microsoft clients and some applications. Later versions have addressed most of these bugs and added new features to enhance compatibility. You should consult the latest information regarding compatibility issues with Mac OS X Server as part of incorporating it into your network. You can find this information on the vendor's website.

NetWare

NetWare is a full-featured operating system that offers all the functions required by an organization, such as file and print services, DNS, DHCP, FTP, and web servers, just to name a few. NetWare was once the server of choice for most organizations, but its popularity has declined sharply with the introduction of the newest Microsoft servers. NetWare is, however, still used in many organizations.

The biggest problems associated with NetWare will likely relate to making Microsoft clients and servers and Novell clients and servers talk to each other. In that regard, you should understand that both Novell and Microsoft have developed software products to provide common ground between Novell and Microsoft products. We discussed some of these products in Chapter 3; the following is a summary of the most common:

Client Services for NetWare (CSNW)   CSNW is a service that can be installed on Microsoft clients (along with the *NWLink* protocol) that allows them to connect directly to NetWare servers provided they have permissions to do so.

Gateway (and Client) Services for NetWare (GSNW)   GSNW is a service that can be installed on Microsoft servers that allows the server to become a gateway to a NetWare server for all of the clients that connect to the server. Installing GSNW installs the NWLink protocol as well.

File and Print Services for NetWare (FPNW)   FPNW is a service that can be installed on Novell clients (which are typically Microsoft operating systems with Novell client installed on them) to allow the Novell client to access a Microsoft server, provided that it has permissions to do so.

Directory Service Manager for Netware (DSMN)   DSMN is a service that can be installed on Microsoft servers that allows them to see Novell NDS (Novell Directory Service) servers as they see Microsoft domain controllers. This service can be used to manage environments that include NDS and Active Directory.

As you can see, if you intend to combine Microsoft systems with Novell systems, then you have a few choices to make. These choices will also relate to the types of applications, protocols, and permission settings that you wish to use in your network.

Windows

Windows is by far the most popular operating system in use today. Windows offers many different types of clients and servers that have evolved over last 20 years. The latest Windows operating systems offer tremendous advantages over the earlier systems in regard to features, functionality, and especially security.

Since there have been so many different Windows clients and servers over the last 20 years, the challenge for many organizations is one of making all of the older servers and clients continue to communicate with the newer servers and clients. To understand this challenge more completely, you must also realize that the newer servers and clients are fundamentally different in their operation than the older (legacy) servers and clients. The following is a list of servers and clients offered by Microsoft Windows and the changes at each level of server or client:

Windows 3.1   This was the first Windows implementation. It was based on the DOS operating system but offered a basic GUI interface and multitasking capability. It did not offer networking.

Windows 3.11   This version of Windows contained all of the same features as Windows 3.1, but also offered the ability to network to other computers. It featured an early version of Microsoft Client.

Windows 95   This was the first 32-bit "operating system" from Microsoft. The reason that "operating system" is in quotes is that the true operating system was still DOS. In other words, Windows 95 was based on the DOS operating system.

Windows NT Workstation   This was the first Windows operating system that was not based on DOS but rather on the NT Kernel. Several versions of this operating system were released during the 1990s. The NT Kernel offered greater stability and reliability than previous operating systems. This Windows operating system offered some GUI capability, but not to the degree of Windows 95. One of the challenges with Windows NT Workstation was that the hardware list that was compatible with it was a much shorter list than that of Windows 95.

Windows 98   This was an enhanced version of Windows 95 that offered even greater GUI capabilities and enhanced support for applications and networking. It was still based on the DOS operating system.

Windows Me (Millennium Edition)   This was the last operating system in the family of Windows 9*x* clients. It was supposed to offer greater functionality and stability, but it was released too soon and contained many bugs. Because of this, Windows Me never picked up much of a following and therefore does not generally have a good reputation with network professionals.

Windows 2000 Professional   This system combined the stability of being built on the NT Kernel with the GUI capability like that of Windows 98. In addition, it offered more security options such as IPSec, Kerberos authentication, and MS-CHAP v2, just to name a few.

Windows XP This is the latest and most full-featured client operating system. Also built on the NT Kernel, it combines stability with GUI features just like Windows 2000 Professional, but it also offers enhanced capabilities in regard to networking, fault tolerance, and security (especially after the latest Service Packs are installed).

Windows NT Server This was the first Microsoft server. Built on the NT Kernel, it offered some stability and reliability, although not to the degree of Microsoft's latest offerings. Windows NT Server can be used as a domain controller. In addition, multiple domain controllers can be used in the same domain. When this is done, one of the domain controllers must be the Primary Domain Controller (PDC) and the other domain controllers are the Backup Domain Controllers (BDCs). All changes to the domain are then first made on the PDC and then replicated to all of the BDCs. This is referred to as *single master replication*. When you use newer Windows servers with Windows NT servers, you must take into account that the newer domains do not use this model of replication.

Windows 2000 Server This version of Windows servers totally changed everything in regard to the methods that domain controllers use to replicate information as well as the security platforms that are used. It introduced Group Policies, which can be used to control user behavior and other security features. There are too many changes to list here. The main thing you should know is that there were so many changes that you can no longer assume that the new operating system will work seamlessly with all of the legacy clients and servers. The more new features you decide to use, such as Group Policies, Certificates, MS-CHAP v2, IPSec, and so on, the more you will have to make special provisions for any legacy clients, servers, or applications. The only way to avoid all of this is to upgrade everything.

Windows Server 2003 As of this writing, this is the latest Windows server offering from Microsoft. It enhances security by requiring a greater amount of configuration for clients to communicate and use resources. In other words, by default Windows Server 2003 is a more secure server than Windows 2000 Server. Windows Server 2003 offers all of the features, stability, and reliability of Windows 2000 Server, and then some. Windows Server 2003 configuration problems often stem from a lack of training or knowledge of the many configuration settings on the product. This can be addressed by requiring that your network professionals receive formal training specific to Windows Server 2003 products.

Appleshare IP

Appleshare IP is a server system that supports Macintosh clients using the Apple Filing Protocol (AFP). It also supports Windows clients using a system that emulates the SMB (CIFS) protocol. While Appleshare IP works rather seamlessly with Macintosh clients, there have been a large number of bugs in regard to its support of Microsoft clients. Newer versions of Appleshare IP have addressed many of these bugs. If you decide to implement an Appleshare IP server in your network, you should obtain the latest information about compatibility with all of the clients, servers, and applications that you intend to use.

Exam Essentials

Understand the basics of compatibility with Unix. Most clients can connect to Unix web servers with their browsers and no other special software. Microsoft clients can also use Services for Unix to connect to and use Unix file and print servers. You might need to include a static entry for a Unix server in dynamic name resolution databases such as WINS.

List the main advantages and disadvantages of Linux. Linux is a full-featured, GUI-based operating system with many variations, called distributions. The open source architecture of Linux software can sometimes make it more difficult to troubleshoot because not all commands work on all distributions. You should provide training for users and administrators who will use Linux in your network.

Describe the main advantages and disadvantages of Mac OS X Server. Mac OS X Server is a product from Apple that combines open source system flexibility with the latest version of Unix software. Mac OS X Server can be used with many different types of operating systems as a powerful web server and Internet server. Earlier versions of Mac OS X Server had many bugs in regard to communication with Microsoft clients, but most of these bugs have been fixed in the later versions. You can obtain the latest information about these bugs and fixes from the vendor's website.

Know how to combine NetWare with Microsoft servers and clients. The most likely problem that you will encounter with NetWare is its compatibility with other clients and servers. You have many options when connecting Microsoft clients to NetWare servers and connecting NetWare clients to Microsoft servers. You should know the differences between CSNW, GSNW, FPNW, and DSMN.

Describe how Microsoft Windows products have changed over time. There have been many versions of Microsoft Windows clients and servers over the last 20 years. The latest versions have featured major changes in operating systems and security requirements. All of these changes may cause previous operating systems not to work seamlessly with the newer servers and clients. The more new features of the latest clients and servers that you use, the greater the chance of having an issue regarding compatibility with legacy clients.

Know the basics of networking with Appleshare IP. Appleshare IP is a server system that supports Macintosh clients using the Apple Filing System and a TCP/IP protocol. Appleshare IP also supports Windows clients by using a version the SMB (CIFS) protocol. Earlier versions of Appleshare IP had many bugs in regard to communicating with Windows clients, but later versions have worked out most of the bugs.

4.6 Determining the Impact of Modifying, Adding, or Removing Network Services

As we discussed in Chapter 2, there are many network services in a typical network, without which the network would not function well or may not function at all. Depending on the type of service and the type of network, removing, adding, or modifying a service could have a huge impact or none at all. You should understand the purpose of most common network services and thereby understand the impact of a change in that service.

Critical Information

Given a scenario, you should be able to determine the impact of modifying, adding, or removing a network service such as DHCP, DNS, or WINS. In this section, we discuss the influence that each of these services has on a network.

Dynamic Host Configuration Protocol (DHCP)

Dynamic Host Configuration Protocol (DHCP) is a service that assigns TCP/IP clients an IP address and other essential addresses when they are started on the network. Clients that are configured to obtain an address from a DHCP server will automatically broadcast a request for an IP address. All DHCP servers that hear the request will make an offer of an address to the client. Typically, the address is considered valid for a specified amount of time, referred to as a *lease*. Clients will attempt to renew their lease before it expires by contacting the DHCP server that gave them the address. Microsoft clients, for example, renew their leases after 50 percent of the lease time has expired. DHCP servers assign and renew these addresses based on a list of available IP addresses, referred to as a *scope*.

If the only DHCP server on a network is removed, the impact of the removal will be on the clients that are trying to obtain a lease from the DHCP server or trying to renew their leases. The clients that already have an IP address that is not up for renewal will not be affected at all. Likewise, clients that are set with a static address will not be affected. The clients that cannot obtain an IP address will no longer be able to communicate on the network.

If another DHCP server is available and can receive the broadcasts from the clients, it will assign the clients an IP address. Typically, broadcasts do not pass through routers, but it is possible, as defined in RFC 1542, to let DHCP server broadcasts pass through most modern routers if they are configured properly.

If a DHCP server is modified or if another DHCP server is added to a network, it is very important to ensure that the IP addresses that it is configured to assign are unique. The addresses should not duplicate any addresses on any other DHCP servers in the network or on any of the devices that are assigned static addresses. If the DHCP server duplicates address assignments, the result will be multiple IP addressing errors on the computers that have the new duplicate address and on the computers that originally had a proper IP address in the network.

Windows 2000 and Windows Server 2003 networks offer extra protection to prevent the error of duplicating addresses. Once a DHCP server is configured for a domain, any additional DHCP servers must be approved by a member of the *Enterprise Admins* group. The process of approving the DHCP server and allowing it to issue IP addresses on the same domain is referred to as *authorization*. Typically, an Enterprise Admin will not authorize a new DHCP server without ensuring that no duplicate address assignments exist.

Domain Name Systems (DNS)

As its name implies Domain Name System (DNS) provides name resolution on a network. Specifically, DNS provides hostname-to-IP address resolution, and vice versa. Queries that are used to resolve a hostname to an IP address are referred to as *forward lookup queries*. Queries that are used to resolve a known IP address to a hostname are referred to as *reverse lookup queries*. Often a DNS server does not work alone but instead refers queries to other DNS servers, a process called *forwarding*. Also, many networks have multiple DNS servers that share the same databases used to resolve queries. These shared databases are referred to as *zone database files*. These can be shared by DNS servers through a process called *zone transfer* or by attaching the information to other transfers, such as Active Directory with Windows 2000 and Windows Server 2003 servers.

If a DNS server is removed, added, or modified, the impact of the change will be completely determined by the other DNS servers that are available in the network and the configuration of the clients that use them. Zone transfers provide not only load balancing of client queries but also fault tolerance if a DNS server were to fail, or in this case be removed. Likewise, clients can be configured with multiple DNS server addresses so that if one DNS server is no longer available, they can quickly query another server. Because of these factors, the removal, addition, or modification of a DNS server could have a major impact or no impact at all on a network and its clients. On the other hand, the removal of the entire DNS service would have an impact on clients because they either would not be able to resolve hostnames to IP addresses or the process would take much longer. In addition, Windows 2000 and Windows Server 2003 domains (which use Active Directory) require the presence of a DNS server.

Windows Internet Name Services (WINS)

Windows Internet Name Services (WINS) is a name-resolution service that provides NetBIOS name-to-IP address resolution on a local area network. Clients that are configured with a WINS server address (either manually or by a DHCP server) will register their NetBIOS name and their IP address with the WINS server when they come onto the network. Clients that need to resolve a NetBIOS name to an IP address can use the WINS server they are configured to use. In addition, clients can be configured to use multiple WINS servers.

> **Note:** In Windows 2000 and Windows Server 2003 networks, clients can be configured to use up to 12 WINS servers.

When a network uses multiple WINS servers, it's important that the WINS servers share the information about the clients that they have registered on the network. This sharing process is referred to as *replication*. Administrators can configure WINS servers to replicate at set times, after a set number of changes, or both.

When we take all of these factors into consideration, it's easier to understand that the addition, removal, or modification of a single WINS server may or may not have a tremendous impact on the network. On the other hand, the removal of the entire WINS service will have an impact on legacy clients and legacy applications that use NetBIOS name resolution. These clients may not be able to communicate effectively with the servers that would otherwise provide resources for them.

Exam Essentials

Explain the impact of modifying, adding, or removing a DHCP server. DHCP servers assign IP addresses and other essential network information, such as name resolution server addresses. The modification, addition, or removal of a DHCP server on a network may not have an immediate impact if clients have already obtained an IP address lease, but that it will have an impact when the clients attempt to renew their leases. Multiple DHCP servers can be installed in a network, as long as the address assignments in their scopes are unique.

Describe the impact of modifying, adding, or removing DNS services. DNS servers provide hostname-to-IP address resolution, and vice versa, on a network. DNS servers rarely work alone, but instead work together with other DNS servers to resolve queries. Clients can be configured with the addresses of multiple DNS servers for fault tolerance in regard to hostname resolution. The removal of DNS services from a network would cause a serious problem in resolving hostnames to IP addresses quickly. In fact, newer networks such as Windows 2000 and Windows Server 2003 require DNS in order for Active Directory to operate at all. The removal, addition, or modification of one DNS server (of many) may have no impact on the network.

Know the impact of modifying, adding, or removing WINS. WINS resolves NetBIOS names to IP addresses. Microsoft clients can be configured with the addresses of up to 12 WINS servers for WINS fault tolerance. Modifying, adding, or removing one WINS server might have little impact on the network, but removing the entire WINS service from the network would affect primarily legacy clients and legacy applications that use NetBIOS names.

4.7 Troubleshooting Various Network Topologies

Depending on the type of network topology that you are using, you might experience a network failure that is specific to that topology. It's important that you understand the basics of each topology so that you can troubleshoot any type of network topology. In this section, we discuss each of the four main network topologies: bus, star, mesh, and ring.

Critical Information

Given a troubleshooting scenario involving a network with a particular network topology, you should be able to identify the network area affected and the cause of the stated failure. You should be familiar with these concepts for the four main network topologies: bus, star, ring, and mesh.

Bus

As we discussed in Chapter 1, the bus topology using coaxial cable became very popular in networks in the late 1980s and early 1990s, before the more sophisticated star topology began to emerge. It used an Ethernet baseband technology and was often referred to as 10BASE 2 or thinnet when thin coaxial cable was used, and as 10BASE 5 or thicknet when thicker coaxial cable was used. The main advantage of the bus topology was that relatively small amounts of coaxial cable could be used to connect computers. The bus topology uses T connectors to connect a signal to a computer and let it run through the T connection at the same time. These T connectors enable the network to continue to function even if one of the computers in the bus should fail or shut down.

The main disadvantage of bus networks was that they were not very fast, only 10Mbps, and they were not very reliable. The chief reason that bus networks are not reliable is that they require a terminator (or resistor) at each end of a segment, which absorbs signal and prevents signal bounce. This means that if the coaxial cable develops a break anywhere in a segment, then essentially two networks are created, neither of which has the required terminators on each end; therefore, all communication in the entire segment will fail. For these reasons, the bus topology has been replaced by the star topology in most networks.

Star

As we discussed in Chapter 1, the star topology is the most common network topology in use today. With the star topology, each computer has its own cable, which is connected to a central hub or switch. This means that a failure in a single computer or even in a single computer's cable will not affect the rest of the network segment. A failure in the hub or switch, however, will affect all of the computers that are connected to it. For this reason, most companies use multiple hubs and switches in a network design to provide alternate paths for client server communication. Also, many companies keep replacement hubs and/or switches standing by in case the primary one should fail.

Mesh

A mesh topology is probably the easiest topology to troubleshoot, because a failure of one connection still leaves other connections available to be used for troubleshooting the failure. As we discussed in Chapter 1, a full mesh provides a connection from every component in the mesh to every other component in the mesh. This creates a tremendous degree of fault tolerance.

Typically a mesh topology is not used to connect individual computers, but instead to connect networks with redundant connections. If two servers in a full mesh cannot communicate, the failure is more than likely with the one of the servers rather than with the connection, since there are multiple connections on which to communicate.

Ring

Ring topologies are not used very often today, because they have been replaced by more reliable and faster star topologies with Ethernet switches. Though they are not common, you still might need to troubleshoot a ring topology network and you might very well be asked about one on the test.

As we discussed in Chapter 1, computers are logically arranged in a circle (or ring) and a special signal called a token is circulated around the ring. When a computer wants to communicate on the ring, it must take possession of the token and attach its message. In IBM Token Ring networks, the token must stay attached the message until the message is delivered and acknowledged. In FDDI networks, the message can be sent and the token can move down the ring and be used by another computer.

In an IBM token ring network a break in the ring will result in all computers not being able to communicate. On the other hand, FDDI networks offer fault tolerance in the form of a dual-ring design consisting of a primary ring and a secondary ring. Ring topology networks also have special packets that detect a slow or failing network. In some ring networks a process called *beaconing* is automatically used by the system to determine where the break occurred.

Exam Essentials

Describe troubleshooting basics of the bus topology. The bus topology is a coaxial cable–based network topology that is not used very often today. The main disadvantage of the bus topology is that, since it requires terminator at each end of a segment, a break anywhere in network segment will cause all communication among all computers in the segment to fail. Because of the use of T connectors, a failed or shut-down computer in a segment will not affect communication of the other computers in the segment.

Know troubleshooting basics for the star topology. The star topology provides a separate network cable for each computer in the network. All of the computers are connected to a central hub or switch. A failure of a computer or even a break in a single network cable will not have an effect on all of the other computers in the network segment. However, a failure of the central hub or switch will have an affect on communication of all computers in the network segment.

List troubleshooting basics of the mesh topology. A mesh topology provides the greatest amount of fault tolerance of any network topology. A mesh topology is typically used between networks and not between individual computers. A full-mesh topology provides a separate connection for every component in a mesh to every other component in the mesh. If a server in a full mesh cannot communicate with another server in the same full mesh, the fault most likely lies with the servers and not with the connections.

Describe troubleshooting basics of the ring topology. A ring topology consists of computers that are logically arranged in a ring. A special packet called a token is circulated around the ring and the computers must have the token in order to communicate on the network. There are two main types of rings: IBM Token Ring and FDDI. IBM Token Rings typically do not offer fault tolerance, so a break in the ring will stop all communication. In contrast, FDDI networks are built on a dual-ring topology with a secondary ring that is used to provide fault tolerance should the primary ring fail.

4.8 Troubleshooting Various Network Infrastructures

While there are many ways to build a network, there are really only two main types of network infrastructure in today's networks: wired and wireless. Based on this infrastructure decision, a network administrator or network designer inherits all of the advantages and disadvantages of that type of network. Typically, wireless networks are not completely wireless but actually a wireless infrastructure connected to a wired infrastructure. This means that the network will benefit from all of the advantages of both but will also suffer from all of the disadvantages of both. In this section, we discuss each of these types of network infrastructures and the potential network problems related to each of them.

Critical Information

Given a network troubleshooting scenario involving an infrastructure problem, you should be able to identify the cause of the problem. This requires that you understand the basic design of the two types of network infrastructure: wired and wireless.

Wired Infrastructure

As we discussed earlier, most of today's networks are designed in a star topology and a *wired infrastructure*. This means that each computer has its own network cable that is connected to a central hub or switch. In a large network, that represents a lot of cable. Whether the cable is made of copper or fiber, there is always the possibility that it can become damaged, by being cut or broken. Copper cable can also suffer from electromagnetic interference (EMI) if the cable runs past an electric motor, fluorescent light fixture, or other high-voltage device. These factors can cause communication to fail intermittently or to fail completely, depending on the severity of the problem. Cable lengths that exceed the maximum recommended without the use of a repeater (or hub) can also affect the reliability of computer communication in a network.

Every component in a network including a NIC, hub, switch, router, etc., has a usable "lifetime" before it fails. In addition, every component will most likely fail at some point because it will be used until it fails. Accordingly, most organizations design and manage networks with fault tolerance and redundant components in mind. Their main goal is that if and when a component fails, it can be quickly replaced by a good component and the users can remain productive.

Wireless Infrastructure

As we explained earlier, typically a *wireless infrastructure* is not completely wireless. Most wireless infrastructures are additions to a wired infrastructure and therefore can have the same potential problems as a wired infrastructure. In addition, wireless networks can also suffer from interference from other devices and other radio signals. As we discussed in Chapter 2, most wireless networks use the 2.4GHz wireless radio band. This means that other devices such as wireless telephone, wireless mice, and wireless keyboards can potentially interfere with the communication on these networks. In addition, the structure of the building in which wireless networks are used can affect the reliability of the signal between the computers on the network. As we discussed in Chapter 2, you can use a "trial and error" method to design a functioning wireless network, or you can purchase special programs that determine where signal is traveling throughout your network and at what signal strength.

Exam Essentials

Understand the basic challenges and potential problems with a wired infrastructure, Today's star topology networks use relatively large amounts of cable, since each computer has its own network cable. Copper cables as well as fiber-optic cables can suffer from breaks or cuts. Copper cable connections can suffer from EMI if they are run close to a high-voltage source, such as an electric motor or a fluorescent light. The many components that connect a star topology (hubs, switches, and routers) have a usable lifetime, which will probably be exceeded before they are taken out of service completely. Therefore, it's not a matter of whether these devices will fail as much as a matter of when they will fail.

Know the basic challenges and potential problems with a wireless infrastructure. Most "wireless" networks are not completely wireless, but instead are a wireless addition to a wired network. Because of this fact, wireless networks can suffer from all of the same problems as wired networks, and then some. You should also understand that wireless networks can suffer from interference due to other devices on the same (or close to the same) frequency. The structure of a building can affect the communication of computers in a wireless network.

4.9 A Troubleshooting Strategy for Network Problems

What seems like common sense in regard to troubleshooting is not as commonly applied as you might imagine. Often network professionals address problems in an unorganized manner. First, they try to determine everything that could possibly be wrong with the network, then they make every change that they assume is warranted, and finally they test the results. This approach leads at best to a solution that cannot be defined or documented, and at worst leads to endless frustration over continually fixing and then rebreaking the network. There is, however, a much better method of troubleshooting a network problem. In this section, we discuss the steps involved in this method and how they can be applied to correct a network problem.

Critical Information

Given a network problem scenario, you should be able to select an appropriate course of action based on a logical troubleshooting strategy. We will discuss the details of the logical troubleshooting strategy that you should know.

Troubleshooting Strategy

An effective network troubleshooting strategy should do more than fix a network problem; it should define the cause of the problem and document the solution to the problem. For this to be possible, you must know what action fixed the problem when you are done. This means that you have to isolate a potential cause, make a change, and test repeatedly until the problem no longer exists. To be more specific, let's say that a user cannot connect to the Internet. You want to start troubleshooting the problem to help the user get connected. You should proceed through the following steps:

1. Identify the symptoms and potential causes. In this case, the symptom seems simple: the user cannot access the Internet. Potential causes could be a problem regarding the user's browser, IP address, subnet mask, default gateway, DNS address, and so on. It could also be a problem with the ISP.

2. Identify the affected area. In other words, which other users also cannot access the Internet? Can this user access internal websites with his browser? Can this user ping the address of other clients and servers in the network?

3. Establish what has changed. In this case, there are many questions that you could ask. Has there been a recent change in ISPs? Has anyone else used the user's computer in the recent past? Has anyone added or deleted any software from the computer between the time that the user could access the Internet and now? For that matter, could this computer ever access the Internet?

4. **Select the most probable cause.** Suppose that you determine that some other users also cannot access the Internet, but not all users. Furthermore, this user can access the internal websites with his browser. Also, this user can ping other clients in the network by their IP address as well as their hostname.

    If this were the case, then it would seem that a DNS address for the servers that lead to the Internet might be at fault. Next, you determine that the ISP the company uses has changed very recently. Could it be possible that the DHCP servers are still configured to assign the old DNS address to clients?

5. **Implement an action plan and solution, including potential affects.** You decide to check the scope options of the DHCP server to determine the DNS address that the DHCP servers are assigning. If the DHCP servers are assigning the old address, this could be the problem. You find that the new DNS address is in the scope, so this is probably not the problem. Next, you check to make sure that the clients that cannot access the Internet have renewed their addresses with the DHCP server since the date of the ISP change, and you find that they have not.

    Your action plan, therefore, is to release and renew the IP addresses of the clients that cannot access the Internet. If they are configured with an invalid DNS server address, this should fix the problem and allow them to connect.

6. **Test the result.** You release and renew the addresses on the clients and then attempt to access a website on their browser. The attempt is successful and the client is restored access to the Internet.

7. **Identify the results and effects of the solution.** In this case, the solution is a permanent one for the clients that were affected (at least until the ISP changes again). You may also want to make sure that all of the other clients have renewed their address, and force a renewal on any clients that haven't, before they find that they can't access the Internet either.

8. **Document the solution and process.** Now that you have solved the problem, you should take a moment to document the entire sequence of events, including the symptoms of the problem, what you did to fix it, and what could be done in the future to prevent it from occurring again. This information might be very useful in the future for you or another network professional.

Exam Essentials

Know how to perform logical troubleshooting. An effective network troubleshooting strategy not only fixes the problem but also identifies its true source and documents the results. You should be able to apply the eight steps of troubleshooting strategy to a network troubleshooting strategy.

Review Questions

1. Which utility can be used to isolate a network problem to a specific router?
   A. ping
   B. tracert
   C. netstat
   D. nbtstat

2. Which network tool has two modes, interactive and noninteractive?
   A. nslookup
   B. ping
   C. tracert
   D. netstat

3. Which of the following does a lit link LED typically indicate? (Choose all that apply.)
   A. The device is physically connected to another device in the network.
   B. The IP addresses are configured properly between the two devices.
   C. The cable connecting the devices is faulty.
   D. The cable connecting the devices is configured properly on at least the power and ground wires.

4. Which type of file service do Windows clients use?
   A. FAT
   B. NTFS
   C. SMB
   D. NFS

5. Which of the following are characteristics of a printer pool? (Choose two.)
   A. Multiple printers
   B. Single print device
   C. Multiple print devices
   D. Single printer

6. Which of the following statements are true? (Choose two.)
   A. FPNW is software that enables Microsoft clients to connect to NetWare servers.
   B. CSNW is software the enables Microsoft clients to connect to NetWare servers.
   C. DSMN is software that allows Microsoft servers to see NDS servers as they do Active Directory domain controllers.
   D. GSNW is software that is installed on Microsoft clients to allow them to connect to NetWare servers.

7. Which services provide name resolution for a network? (Choose all that apply.)
   A. DNS
   B. DHCP
   C. WINS
   D. Firewalls

8. Which types of networks use terminators to prevent signal bounce? (Choose all that apply.)
   A. Bus
   B. Ring
   C. Star
   D. Mesh

9. A wireless infrastructure typically does not have the potential problems of a wired infrastructure.
   A. True
   B. False

10. Which of the following are steps in an effective troubleshooting strategy? (Choose two.)
   A. Repair multiple potential problems, then test.
   B. Establish what has changed.
   C. Identify the affected area.
   D. Restart the affected computer.

11. Which of the following is the most common tool used to confirm connectivity between two hosts on a TCP/IP network?
   A. ipconfig
   B. nslookup
   C. ping
   D. netstat

12. After a successful ping, which tool can be used to determine the physical address of a remote host?
   A. arp
   B. nslookup
   C. tracert
   D. netstat

13. Which tool is used by Unix and Linux operating systems to configure interfaces and to view information about configured interfaces?

    A. ipconfig

    B. winipcfg

    C. nbtstat

    D. ifconfig

14. The newest versions of SMB for Microsoft clients supports digital signing and are also referred to as Common Internet File System (CIFS).

    A. True

    B. False

15. The service that gives an SMB functionality to Linux clients and makes Windows shares available to Linux clients is referred to as what?

    A. Samba

    B. NTFS

    C. Active Directory

    D. NFS

Answers to Review Questions

1. **B.** The tracert tool is used on Microsoft networks to isolate a network problem to a specific router. The ping utility is used to establish connectivity, but it does not isolate the problem. Both netstat and nbtstat are used to control network caches and gather information and statistics about the network.

2. **A.** The nslookup tool can be used in interactive and noninteractive mode. The other network tools do not have two modes of operation.

3. **A, D.** A lit link LED on a device is an indicator that the device is physically connected to another device through the network. It also indicates that the cable being used is configured properly for at least the power and ground wires. This usually, but not always, means that the cable is properly made to transmit data. A lit link LED does not indicate that IP addresses are properly configured between the two computers.

4. **C.** Server Message Block (SMB) is the file service that Windows clients use. FAT and NTFS are filesystems, not file services. NFS is the file service used by Novell for NetWare services and Novell clients.

5. **C, D.** A printer pool is made up of a single printer connected to multiple print devices. The printer sends the print job to the first available print device. The print devices should at least use the same driver and, when possible, they should be identical.

6. **B, C.** Client Services for NetWare (CSNW) enables Microsoft clients to connect to NetWare servers. It is installed with the NWLink protocol. Directory Services Manager for NetWare (DSMN) enables Microsoft servers to see NDS servers as they do Active Directory domain controllers. File and Print Services for NetWare (FPNW) allows Novell clients to connect to Microsoft servers. Gateway (and Client) Services for NetWare (GSNW) is installed on Microsoft servers to provide a connection through the Microsoft server to the NetWare servers for all clients who have been given permission.

7. **A, C.** DNS and WINS provide name resolution for a network. To be specific, DNS resolves hostnames to IP addresses whereas WINS resolves NetBIOS names to IP addresses. DHCP services assign IP addresses and other server addresses, but they do not provide name resolution. Firewalls filter traffic between networks, but they do not provide name resolution.

8. **A.** A bus topology uses terminators to prevent signal bounce. Terminators are not used in the other network topologies.

9. **B.** A wireless infrastructure is typically connected to a wired infrastructure at some point and therefore has all of the same potential problems as a wired infrastructure, and then some.

10. B, C.   The steps in an effective troubleshooting policy are designed to isolate a specific problem, provide a solution, and then document the solution. They are as follows:

1. Identify the symptoms and potential causes.
2. Identify the affected area.
3. Establish what has changed.
4. Select the most probable cause.
5. Implement an action plan and solution, including potential effects.
6. Test the result.
7. Identify the results and effects of the solution.
8. Document the solution and process.

Although restarting the affected computer might prove useful at times, it is not always a step in the troubleshooting strategy.

11. C.   The ping tool is most commonly used to confirm connectivity between two devices on a TCP/IP network. The ipconfig tool is used to determine the IP address and other IP information about a local host. The nslookup tool is used to test and confirm hostname resolution between clients and servers. The netstat tool is used to view active and listening ports on a local host.

12. A.   After a successful ping, you can use the arp-a command at the command prompt to view the physical (MAC) address of the remote host. The nslookup tool is used to test and confirm hostname resolution between clients and servers. The tracert utility is used to view the hops that a packet takes between the source and the destination address. The netstat tool is used to view the active and listening ports of a local host computer.

13. D.   The ifconfig command-line tool can be used on Unix and Linux systems to configure interfaces and to view information about configured interfaces. The ipconfig command-line tool is used with the latest Microsoft operating systems. The winipcfg GUI tool is used with Windows 9*x* clients. The nbtstat tool is used to view NetBIOS over TCP/IP statistics for Microsoft clients.

14. A.   The newest versions of Server Message Block (SMB) that support digital signing between computers, instead of just using a NetBIOS name, are also referred to as Common Internet File System (CIFS).

15. A.   The service that gives an SMB functionality to Linux clients and makes Windows shares to Linux clients is referred to as Samba. NTFS is a secure filesystem used by Windows. Active Directory is the directory information system used by Windows 2000 Server and Windows Server 2003. NFS is the original file-sharing system used by Linux clients and servers.

Index

Note to the reader: Throughout this index **boldfaced** page numbers indicate primary discussions of a topic. *Italicized* page numbers indicate illustrations.

Numbers

10BASE-FL, 13, 15
10BASE-T, 13, 15
10GBASE-ER, 14–15, 16
10GBASE-LR, 14–15, 16
10GBASE-SR, 14–15, 16
100BASE-FX, 14, 15
100BASE-TX, 14, 15
127 network, 60
802 project, 8
802.1q standard, 135
802.1x standard, **99**, **100**
802.2 standard, 9
802.3 standard, 9
802.5 standard, 9
802.11 standard, 9, **31**
802.11a standard, 31, 32
802.11b standard, 11, 31, 32
802.11g standard, 11, 31, 32
1000BASE-CX, 14, 15
1000BASE-LX, 14, 16
1000BASE-SX, 14, 15
1000BASE-TX, 14, 15

A

ACK message, 70
action plan in troubleshooting process, 198
Active Directory, 71
active hub, 26
Address Resolution Protocol (ARP), **74–75**, 79
ADSL (Asymmetric Digital Subscriber Line), 90, 91
Advanced Research Projects Agency (ARPA), 55
AFP (AppleTalk File Protocol), **86**
Alternate Configuration, for IP addresses, 68
alternate sites, location of, **148**
American National Standards Institute (ANSI), 11
American Registry for Internet Numbers (ARIN), 64
anding, 182
antenna, for wireless devices, 33
antivirus software, **139–140**
APIPA (Automatic Private IP Address Assignment), 67, **68**, 69
APNIC (Asia Pacific Network Information Centre), 64
Apple computers. *See* Mac OS X server
AppleShare, 54
Appleshare IP (Internet Protocol), 117, 118, 189
    problem identification, **188**
    for remote connection, **127**
AppleTalk, **54–55**
AppleTalk File Protocol (AFP), **86**
AppleTalk over IP, 54
application installation, antivirus software and, 140
Application layer in OSI model, 48
archive bit, 145
    and differential backup, 146
ARIN (American Registry for Internet Numbers), 64
ARP (Address Resolution Protocol), **74–75**, 79
arp cache, 161
arp utility, **161–163**, *162*, 169, **172**
ARPA (Advanced Research Projects Agency), 55
ARPANET, 55

Asia Pacific Network Information Centre (APNIC), 64
Asymmetric Digital Subscriber Line (ADSL), 90, 91
attenuation, 13
authentication
    for extranets, 138
    protocol configuration, **133–134**
    for remote connection, 125
    by SSL, 98
    time synchronization and, 75
    troubleshooting, **181**, 184
authentication protocols, **100–103**
authorization of DHCP server, 191
Automatic Private IP Address Assignment (APIPA), 67, *68*, 69

B

backup and recovery, **145–146**
    comparison, 147
Backup Domain Controller (BDC), 188
baseband transmission, 14
Basic Rate Interface (BRI), 88
battery, in UPS, 141
beaconing, 194
binary system, 57
    conversion to decimal, 58
Bluetooth, 32
BNC connector, 5
BRI (Basic Rate Interface), 88
bridges, **26–27**, 29
    on Data Link layer, 51
broadband cable, **90**, 91
bus topology, 5, 6, 8
    troubleshooting, **193**, 194

C

cable, **13–16**
    10BASE-FL, 13, 15
    10BASE-T, 13, 15
    10GBASE-ER, 14–15, 16
    10GBASE-LR, 14–15, 16
    10GBASE-SR, 14–15, 16
    100BASE-FX, 14, 15
    100BASE-TX, 14, 15
    1000BASE-CX, 14, 15
    1000BASE-LX, 14, 16
    1000BASE-SX, 14, 15
    1000BASE-TX, 14, 15
    media connectors, **16–21**
        exam essentials, 20–21
        F-type, **17–18**, *18*
        IEEE 1394 (FireWire), *19*, **19–20**
        LC (local connector), *20*, 20
        MTRJ, *20*, 20
        RJ-11, **16–17**, *17*, 20
        RJ-45, **17**, *17*, 20, 120
        SC (standard connector), **19**, *19*
        ST (straight tip), **18**, *18*
    troubleshooting, 195–196
    wire colors, 120–121
cable modem, **90**, 91
    F-type connector for, 17–18, *18*
cache
    arp, 161–162
    on proxy server, 131
Carrier Sense Multiple Access with Collision Avoidance (CSMA/CA), 11, 33
Carrier Sense Multiple Access with Collision Detection (CSMA/CD), 9
Challenge Handshake Authentication Protocol (CHAP), **101**, 102
Channel Service Unit/Data Service Unit (CSU/DSU), **27**, 30
CIFS (Common Internet File System), 114, 178
circuit switching, 87, 89
classful addressing, **59–60**
clear text, passwords in, 100
Client Services for NetWare (CSNW), 115, 186
client software, **119**, 120
clients, troubleshooting remote services access, **178–184**
    authentication, **181**
    file services, **178–179**

physical connectivity, **183**
print services, **179–181**
protocol configuration, **182**
SOHO routers, **183**
clustering, 143
coaxial cable, **23**, *23*, 25
    for Ethernet, 9
    F-type connector for, 17–18, *18*
cold sites, **148**
cold spare, **147**
collision LEDs, **177**
Common Internet File System (CIFS), 114, 178
communication links
    fault tolerance, **141**, 144
    ping utility to test, 157–159
    tracert/traceroute to test, 160–161
Computer Technology Industry Association (CompTIA), xvi
crimpers, **120**, *121*, 124
crossover cable, wire colors, 121
crosstalk, 21–22
CSMA/CA (Carrier Sense Multiple Access with Collision Avoidance), 11, 33
CSMA/see Carrier Sense Multiple Access with Collision Detection (CSMA), 9
CSNW (Client Services for NetWare), 115, 186
CSU/DSU (Channel Service Unit/Data Service Unit), **27**, 30
CuteFTP, 71, 72

D

Data Link layer in OSI model, 49, 51
data storage
    backup and recovery, **145–146**
    fault tolerance, **142–143**, 144
    hot and cold spares, **147**
    offsite, **146**
data verification, by IPSec, 97
default gateway, 58, 65
    troubleshooting, 182
demodulation, 28

Department of Defense, 55
"Destination Host Unreachable" message, 74, *158*, 171
DHCP (Dynamic Host Configuration Protocol), 55
    impact of changes, **190–191**, 192
differential backup, 146, 147
digital certificates, 98
Digital Subscriber Line (xDSL), **90**, 91
direct sequence spread spectrum (DSSS) radio signal, 31
Directory Service Manager for NetWare (DSMN), 186
disaster recovery, **144–148**
disk duplexing, 142
disk mirroring, 142
distance vector protocols, 56
DNS address, 58
    troubleshooting, 182
Domain Name System (DNS), 56, **84–85**
    impact of changes, **191**, 192
    nslookup to troubleshoot, *168*, **168**
    port for, 83
dynamic entries in arp cache, 162
Dynamic Host Configuration Protocol (DHCP), 55
    impact of changes, **190–191**, 192
dynamic IP address configuration, **66–67**, 69
dynamic ports, 82

E

e-mail
    Internet Message Access Protocol version 4 (IMAP4) for, 73
    Post Office Protocol Version 3 (POP3) for, 73
    Simple Mail Transfer Protocol (SMTP) for, 72
EAP (Extensible Authentication Protocol), **102**, 103
EAP Transport Level Security (EAP-TLS), 99
echo reply packets, 158

echo request packets, 158
ELAP. *See also* EtherTalk Link Access
  Protocol (ELAP)
electrical power, uninterrupted power supply
  (UPS), **141**
electromagnetic interference, 22
encryption protocols, 97, **134**, 135
environmental factors, and wireless
  technology, 33–34
Ethernet, 9, 12
  Point-to-Point Protocol over Ethernet
    (PPPoE), **94**, 96
EtherTalk Link Access Protocol (ELAP), 54
exam objectives, xvii–xxii
Extensible Authentication Protocol (EAP),
  102, 103
extranets, **137–138**

F

F-type connector, **17–18**, *18*, 21
fault tolerance, **141–144**
Fiber Distributed Data Interface (FDDI), **11**,
  12, 13, **88**, 89
fiber optic cable, 11, 14
  LC (local connector) for, 20, *20*
  MTRJ connector for, 20, *20*
  SC (standard connector) for, 19, *19*
  ST (straight tip) connector for, 18, *18*
File and Print Services for NetWare
  (FPNW), 186
file services, troubleshooting, **178–179**, 183
File Transfer Protocol (FTP), **71**, 72, 77
  port for, 83
firewalls, 29, 30, **128–130**
  port blocking, 133
FireWire (IEEE 1394) connector, *19*,
  19–20, 21
flapping connection, 171
forward lookup queries, 191
forwarding, 191
"fox and hound," 123

FPNW (File and Print Services for
  NetWare), 186
fragmentation, of IP packets, 70
frequency hopping spread spectrum radio
  (FHSS) signal, 31
FTP. *See* File Transfer Protocol (FTP)
full backup, **145**, 147

G

Gateway Services for NetWare (GSNW),
  115, 186
gateways, 27, 30
Group Policies, 188

H

hexadecimal numbers, for MAC address, 47
hosts, TCP/IP nodes as, 56
hosts.txt file, 56
hot site, **148**
hot spare, **147**
hubs, **26**, 29
  on Physical layer, 50
  in star topology, 5, *5*
  for wireless devices, 28
Hypertext Transfer Protocol (HTTP), **72**, 77
  port for, 83
Hypertext Transfer Protocol Secure
  (HTTPS), **73**, 78
  port for, 83

I

IANA (Internet Assigned Numbers
  Authority), 64
IBM Token Ring technology, 7, **10**, 12,
  194, 195
ICMP (Internet Control Message Protocol),
  74, 79
ICS (Internet Connection Sharing), **85**

IEEE 1394 (FireWire) connector, *19*, 19–20, 21
IEEE (Institute of Electrical and Electronics Engineers), 8
ifconfig utility, **165–167**, 169
IGMP (Internet Group Multicast Protocol), 76, 80
IMAP4 (Internet Message Access Protocol version 4), 73, 78
port for, 83
incremental backup, **145–146**, 147
infrared communication, **31–32**
Infrared Data Association (IrDA), 31–32
Institute of Electrical and Electronics Engineers (IEEE), 8
Integrated Services Digital Network (ISDN), 88, 89
adapters, 28, 30
Internet
Ethernet and, 9
technologies, **90–92**
Internet Assigned Numbers Authority (IANA), 64
Internet Connection Firewall (ICF), 128–129, *129*
Internet Connection Sharing (ICS), 85
Internet Control Message Protocol (ICMP), 74, 79
Internet Explorer Administration Kit, 132
Internet Group Multicast Protocol (IGMP), 76, 80
Internet Message Access Protocol version 4 (IMAP4), 73, 78
port for, 83
Internet Protocol (IP), **69–70**, 76
version 4, 57–58
version 6, 58–59
Internet Protocol (TCP/IP) Properties dialog box
for Windows Server 2003, 66
for Windows XP client, 67
Alternate Configuration tab, 68
Internet Security Protocol (IPSec), 97, 99
Internetwork Packet Exchange (IPX), 53

Internetwork Packet Exchange/Sequenced Packet Exchange (IPX/SPX), **52–53**
intranets, 137, **138**, 139
IP. *See* Internet Protocol (IP)
IP addresses, 55, **57–59**
classful ranges and subnet masks, **59–60**
configuration, **65–69**
dynamic, **66–67**
self-assigned, **67–68**
static, **65–66**
public and private, **62–64**
troubleshooting, 182
ipconfig /all command, for MAC address display, 46, *46*
ipconfig command, output for computer with APIPA address, *68*
ipconfig/ifconfig utility, **165–167**, 169, *173*, *174*
IPSec (Internet Security Protocol), 97, 99
IPv4, **57–58**
IPv6, **58–59**
IPX/SPX (Internetwork Packet Exchange/ Sequenced Packet Exchange), **52–53**
IrDA (Infrared Data Association), 31–32
ISDN (Integrated Services Digital Network), 88, 89
adapters, **28**, 30

K

Kerberos authentication, **102**, 103

L

LAN switch, 26. *See also* switches
Layer 2 Tunneling Protocol (L2TP), 97, 99
LC (local connector) connector, **20**, *20*, 21
LCC (Logical Link Control), **10**, 12
lease in DHCP, 190
light-emitting diodes (LEDs), **176–177**
Lightweight Directory Access Protocol (LDAP), 76, 80

Line Printer Daemon/Line Printer Remote (LPD/LPR), 76, 80
Line Printer Daemon (LPD), **86**
Line Printer Requester (LPR) protocol, 114
link LEDs, **176–177**
link-state protocols, 56
Linux, **114–115**, 117, 189
    problem identification, **185–186**
    remote connection, **125–126**
Local Area Network (LAN) Settings dialog box, *132*
Logical Link Control (LLC), **10**, 12
logical network topologies, **4–8**
loopback address, 60

M

MAC. *See* Media Access Control (MAC) address
Mac OS X server, **114–115**, 117–118, 189
    problem identification, **186**
    remote connection, **125–126**
Macintosh computers, AppleTalk for, **54–55**
man-in-the-middle attack, 97
Manage Documents permission, 180
Manage Printer permission, 180
management information base (MIB), 85
mapped network drives, 116, *117*
McAfee Antivirus, 139
Media Access Control (MAC) address, **45–47**
    static arp cache entry for, 163
    VLANs based on, 136
media connectors, **16–21**
    exam essentials, 20–21
    F-type, **17–18**, *18*
    IEEE 1394 (FireWire), *19*, **19–20**
    LC (local connector), **20**, *20*
    MTRJ, **20**, *20*
    RJ-11, **16–17**, *17*
    RJ-45, **17**, *17*
    SC (standard connector), **19**, *19*
    ST (straight tip), **18**, *18*

media tester, **122**, *122*, 124
media types, **21–25**
    coaxial cable, *23*, **23**
    exam essentials, 24–25
    multimode fiber-optic (MMF), **23–24**, *24*
    shielded twisted-pair (UTP) cable, **22**, *22*
    single-mode fiber-optic, **23**, *24*
    twisted-pair cable categories, **21–22**
    unshielded twisted-pair (UTP) cable, 22
mesh topology, **6–7**, *7*, *8*
    troubleshooting, **194**, *195*
Microsoft Challenge Handshake Protocol (MS-CHAP), **101**, 102, 134
Microsoft Challenge Handshake Protocol version 2 (MS-CHAP v2), **101**, 102, 133–134
Microsoft Client, 115, 118
Microsoft Hotmail, 73
Microsoft Services for Unix, 114
modems, **28**, 30
modulation, 28
MTRJ connector, **20**, *20*, 21
multifactor authentication, 100
multimode fiber-optic (MMF) cable, **23–24**, *24*, 25
multiple-station access units (MSAUs), 9
My Network Places (Windows), 115, *116*

N

Name Binding Protocol (NBP), 54
name resolution
    DNS for, **84–85**
    ping utility to test, 158–159
    in TCP/IP, 56
NAT (Network Address Translation), 85
natural disaster, recovery after, **146–148**
nbtstat utility, **165**, 169, **173**, *173*
NCP (NetWare Core Protocol), 54
NetBEUI (NeBIOS with Extended User Interface), 54
NetBIOS over TCP/IP, 165

netstat utility, 163–164, *164*, 169, 172
NetWare, **115**, 118, 189
    file services, 179
    problem identification, **186–187**
    remote connection, **126**, 127
NetWare Core Protocol (NCP), 54
NetWare Link State Protocol (NLSP), **53**
NetWare Loadable Module (NLM), 126
NetWare servers, IPX/SPX for, 52
Network Address Translation (NAT), **85**
Network+ certification, xvi
network components, **25–30**
    bridges, **26–27**, 29, 51
    CSU/DSU (Channel Service Unit/Data Service Unit), **27**, 30
    exam essentials, 29–30
    fault tolerance, **141–144**
    firewalls, 29, 30, **128–130**
    gateways, **27**, 30
    hubs, **26**, 29
        in star topology, *5*, *5*
    ISDN adapters, **28**, 30
    modems, **28**, 30
    network interface cards (NICs), **27–28**
    routers, **27**, 29
        on Network layer, 51
        static IP address configuration, 66
    switches, **26**, 29
        on Data Link layer, 51
    transceivers, **28–29**, 30
    visual indicators, **176–177**
    wireless access point, **28**, 30, 51
Network File Systems (NFS), 85
network interface cards (NICs), **27–28**, 30
    on Data Link and Physical layers, 51
    MAC address, 45
    RJ-45 connector for, *17*, *17*
Network layer in OSI model, 49
    routers on, 51
Network Neighborhood (Windows), 115
Network News Transport Protocol (NNTP), **76**, 79
    port for, 83

network resources
    client capabilities for using, **118–120**
    server operating system access to, **113–118**
network services, impact of changes, **190–192**
Network Time Protocol (NTP), **75**, 79
networks, 4
    exam objectives, xxiii–xxiv
    fault tolerance, **143**
    impact of configuration, **133–135**
    implementation, exam objectives, xxii–xxiii
    infrastructure, **195–196**
    main technology features, **8–13**
        Ethernet, **9**
        exam essentials, 12–13
        FDDI, **11**, *12*
        Logical Link Control (LLC), **10**
        Token Ring, **10**
        wireless, **10–11**
    media, 118–119
    problem identification, **184–189**
New Connection Wizard (Windows XP), *126*
NFS (Network File Systems), 85
NFS/Samba, 179
NICs. *See* network interface cards (NICs)
NLM (NetWare Loadable Module), 126
NLSP (NetWare Link State Protocol), **53**
NNTP (Network News Transport Protocol), **76**, 79
    port for, 83
Novell, 52. *See also* NetWare
nslookup utility, *168*, **168**, 169, **174**, *175*
NTP (Network Time Protocol), **75**, 79
NWLink, 52

O

octets, 57
offsite storage, **146**
Open Shortest Path First (OSPF), 56
open source architecture, 114

Open system Interconnection (OSI) model, 47–50, *48*
    layer identification for component operation, 50–52
Optical Carrier (OCx), **88–89**
orthogonal frequency division multiplexing, 31

P

packet switching, **87**, 89
Palo Alto Research Center (PARC), 9
parity data, 142
passive hub, 26
Password Authentication Protocol (PAP), **100**, 102
patch panels, 122
PEAP (Protected EAP), 99
performance
    antivirus software and, 140
    VLANs and, 136
permissions, printer, 180
physical address of network component, 46
Physical layer in OSI model, 49
    hubs on, 50
    network interface cards (NICs) on, 51
    wireless access point on, 51
physical network topologies, **4–8**
ping utility, 74, **157–159**, *158*, 169, *170*, 170–171
plain old telephone service (POTS), **91**, 92
Point-to-Point Protocol over Ethernet (PPPoE), **94**, 96
Point-to-Point Protocol (PPP), **94**, 96
Point-to-Point Tunneling Protocol (PPTP), **94–95**, 96
port-based VLANs, 136
ports
    blocking, **133**, 134
    netstat to test, 163–164
    TCP/UDP, **81–82**
        association with services, 83–84

Post Office Protocol Version 3 (POP3), **73**, 78
    port for, 83
POTS (plain old telephone service), **91**, 92
power conditioner, 141
PPP (Point-to-Point Protocol), **94**, 96
PPPoE (Point-to-Point Protocol over Ethernet), **94**, 96
PPTP (Point-to-Point Tunneling Protocol), **94–95**, 96
Presentation layer in OSI model, 48
Primary Domain Controller (PDC), 188
Primary Rate Interface (PRI), 88
print devices, 179
Print permission, 180
Print Services, troubleshooting, **179–181**, 183–184
printer pools, 180–181, *181*
printers, 179
    Line Printer Daemon/Line Printer Remote (LPD/LPR), **76**
    static IP address configuration, 66
priorities for printers, 180
private IP addresses, **63**, 64
private ports, 82
private transactions, IPSec for, 97
Prometric, xvi
Protected EAP (PEAP), 99
protocols, 45
    differentiation, 52–56
    exam essentials, 56
    exam objectives, xix–xxii
    netstat to test, 163–164
    for network connections, **119**, 120
    purpose of, **84–87**
    troubleshooting, **182**, 184
    well-known ports associated with, **82–84**
proxy service, **130–132**
public IP addresses, **62**, 64
public key encryption, 98
public switched telephone network (PSTN), **91**, 92
punch-down tool, **122–123**, *123*, 124

R

radio interference, and wireless technology, 33
RADIUS (Remote Authentication Dial-In User Services), 99
   authentication, **101**, 103
RARP (Reverse Address Resolution Protocol), **75**, 79
RDP (Remote Desktop Protocol), **95**, *95*, 96
recovery of backup data, **145–146**
Red Hat, 114
redundant arrays of inexpensive disks (RAID), **142–143**, 144
registered IP addresses, 62
registered jack, 16. *See also* RJ-11 connector
registered ports, 82
remote access protocols, **92–96**
Remote Access Service (RAS), **92–93**, *93*, 96, 126
Remote Authentication Dial-In User Services (RADIUS), 99
   authentication, **101**, 103
remote connection
   configuration, **125–127**
   troubleshooting, **182**
Remote Desktop Connection, 116
Remote Desktop Protocol (RDP), **95**, *95*, 96
remote services, troubleshooting client access, **178–184**
replication, 192
reports, from proxy server, 131
Request for Comments (RFCs)
   1542 on DHCP, 190
   1918 on private IP addresses, 63
"Request timed out" message, 158, 171
Reseaux Ip Europeans Network Coordination Centre (RIP NCCC), 64
Reverse Address Resolution Protocol (RARP), **75**, 79
reverse lookup queries, 191
ring topology, 7, 7, 8
   troubleshooting, **194**, 195
RIP (Routing Information Protocol), **53**, 56

RJ-11 connector, **16–17**, *17*, 20
RJ-45 connector, *17*, 17, 20
   connecting to cable, 120
rollover cable, wire colors, 121
routers, **27**, 29
   on Network layer, 51
   static IP address configuration, 66
Routing and Remote Access Server (RRAS), **93**, *93*, 126
Routing Information Protocol (RIP), **53**, 56
Routing Table Maintenance Protocol (RMTP), **55**

S

Samba, 114, 179
SAP (Service Advertising Protocol), **53**
satellite Internet connection, **91**, 92
SC (standard connector) connector, *19*, **19**, 21
scope in DHCP, 190
SDSL (Symmetric Digital Subscriber Line), **90**, 91
Secure Copy Protocol (SCP), **76**, 80
Secure Shell (SSH), **74**, 78
   port for, 83
   for Unix server connection, 114, 125
Secure Sockets Layer (SSL), **98**, 99
security
   Hypertext Transfer Protocol Secure (HTTPS) for, 73
   VLANs and, 135
security protocols, **96–100**
Sequenced Packet Exchange (SPX), **53**
Serial Line Interface Protocol (SLIP), **93–94**, 96
Server Message Block (SMB), **86**, 114, **178–179**
server operating system, access to network resources, **113–118**
Service Advertising Protocol (SAP), **53**
services
   purpose of, **84–87**
   well-known ports associated with, **82–84**

Services for Unix (Microsoft), 114
Session layer in OSI model, 49
share level in SMB, 179
shielded twisted-pair (UTP) cable, 22, *22*, 25
Simple Mail Transfer Protocol (SMTP), **72**, 77
    port for, 83
Simple Network Management Protocol (SNMP), **85**, 87
single master replication, 188
single-mode fiber-optic cable, 23, *24*, 25
SLIP. *See* Serial Line Interface Protocol (SLIP)
Small Office/Home Office (SOHO) routers, troubleshooting, **183**, 184
SmartFTP, 71
SMB (Server Message Block), **86**, 114, **178–179**
SMTP. *See* Simple Mail Transfer Protocol (SMTP)
sniffing, 100
SNMP (Simple Network Management Protocol), **85**, 87
SONET (Synchronous Optical Network), 88
SPX (Sequenced Packet Exchange), 53
SSH (Secure Shell), **74**, 78
    port for, 83
    for Unix server connection, 114, 125
SSL (Secure Sockets Layer), **98**, 99
ST (straight tip) connector, **18**, *18*, 21
standardization, and Linux, 114
star topology, **5**, *5*, 8
    for Token Ring, 9
    troubleshooting, **193**, 194
static entries in arp cache, 162–163
static IP address configuration, **65–66**, 69
straight-through cable, wire colors, 121
subnet mask, 58, 59–60, **61–62**
    troubleshooting, 182
SUSE, 114
switches, **26**, 29
    on Data Link layer, 51
Symantec, Norton AntiVirus, 139
Symmetric Digital Subscriber Line (SDSL), 90, 91
SYN ACK message, 70
SYN message, 70
Synchronous Optical Network (SONET), 88

T

T Carrier level 1 (T1), **88**, 89
T Carrier level 3 (T3), **88**, 89
T connector, **5**, 6
TCP/IP. *See* Transmission Control Protocol/Internet Protocol (TCP/IP)
TCP (Transmission Control Protocol), **70**, 77
    ports, **81–82**
technology, vs. topologies, 12
Telnet, **73–74**, 78
    port for, 83
    for Unix server connection, 114, 125
Terminal Services, 95
TFTP. *See* Trivial File Transfer Protocol (TFTP)
three-way handshake, 70, 101
"Time Exceeded" message, 74
time, synchronization between computers, 75
time to live (TTL), 160
Token Ring technology, 7, **10**, 12
TokenTalk Link Access Protocol (TLAP), 54
tone generator, **123**, *124*
topologies
    exam essentials, 8
    exam objectives, xviii–xix
    logical and physical, **4–8**
    vs. technology, 12
    troubleshooting, **193–195**
Torvalds, Linus, 114
tracert/traceroute utility, **159–161**, *160*, 169, *171*, 171
transceivers, **28–29**, 30
translational bridge, 27
Transmission Control Protocol/Internet Protocol (TCP/IP), **55–56**
    Address Resolution Protocol (ARP), **74–75**, 79
    exam essentials, 81
    File Transfer Protocol (FTP), **71**, 72, 77

Hypertext Transfer Protocol (HTTP), 72, 77
Hypertext Transfer Protocol Secure (HTTPS), 73, 78
Internet Control Message Protocol (ICMP), 74, 79
Internet Group Multicast Protocol (IGMP), 76, 80
Internet Message Access Protocol version 4 (IMAP4), 73, 78
Internet Protocol (IP), **69–70**, 76
Lightweight Directory Access Protocol (LDAP), 76, 80
Line Printer Daemon/Line Printer Remote (LPD/LPR), 76, 80
Network News Transport Protocol (NNTP), **76**, 79
Network Time Protocol (NTP), **75**, 79
ports, 83
Post Office Protocol Version 3 (POP3), 73, 78
Reverse Address Resolution Protocol (RARP), **75**, 79
Secure Copy Protocol (SCP), 76, 80
Secure Shell (SSH), **74**, 78
Simple Mail Transfer Protocol (SMTP), 72, 77
Telnet, **73–74**, 78
Transmission Control Protocol (TCP), 70, 77
Trivial File Transfer Protocol (TFTP), **71–72**, 77
User Datagram Protocol (UDP), **70–71**, 77
Transmission Control Protocol (TCP), **70**, 77
ports, **81–82**
transparent bridge, 26
Transport layer in OSI model, 49
transport mode for IPSec, 97
Trivial File Transfer Protocol (TFTP), **71–72**, 77
port for, 83

troubleshooting
client access to remote services, **178–184**
authentication, **181**
file services, **178–179**
physical connectivity, **183**
print services, **179–181**
protocol configuration, **182**
SOHO routers, **183**
infrastructure, **195–196**
strategy for, **197–198**
topologies, **193–195**
utilities, **157–169**
arp, **161–163**, *162*, 169, *172*
ipconfig/ifconfig, **165–167**, 169, 173, *174*
nbtstat, **165**, 169, **173**, *173*
netstat, **163–164**, *164*, 169, **172**, *172*
nslookup, *168*, **168**, 169, **174**, *175*
ping utility, 74, **157–159**, *158*, 169, **170**, *170–171*
tracert/traceroute, **159–161**, *160*, 169, *171*, **171**
winipcfg, *167*, **167**, 169
trunks, 135
tunnel mode for IPSec, 97
twisted-pair cable, categories, **21–22**, 24–25
two-way handshake, 100

U

uniform resource locator (URL), 72
uninterrupted power supply (UPS), **141**
Universal Naming Convention (UNC) command, 116
Unix, **114–115**, 117, 189
problem identification, **185**
remote connection, **125–126**, 127
unshielded twisted-pair (UTP) cable, 22, 25
for Ethernet, 9
User Datagram Protocol (UDP), **70–71**, 77
ports, **81–82**
user level in SMB, 179

V

Virtual File Systems (VFS), 85
virtual local area networks (VLANs), 135–137
    switches for, 26
Virtual Private Network (VPN), 95, 96
viruses. *See also* antivirus software
VLAN membership, 136

W

WAP. *See* wireless access point
warm sites, 148
web resources
    for firewall software, 129
    on port numbers, 133
    for SSH, 125
well-known ports, 82
    identifying association with services and protocols, 82–84
WEP (Wired Equivalent Privacy), 98, 99
Wi-Fi Protected Access (WPA), 98, 100
wide area networks (WANs), 87–89
Windows Internet Name Services (WINS), 85
    impact of changes, 191–192
Windows operating system, 115–116, 118, 189
    Internet Connection Firewall (ICF), 128–129, *129*
    remote connection, 126, 127
    versions, 187–188
Windows Server 2003, 188
    static IP address configuration, 66
winipcfg utility, *167*, 167, 169
WINS address, troubleshooting, 182
Wired Equivalent Privacy (WEP), 98, 99
wired infrastructure, 195–196
wireless access point, 28, 30
    on Physical layer, 51
wireless technology, 10–11, 12, 31–32
    exam essentials, 32
    for Internet connection, 91, 92
    performance factors, 33–34
    troubleshooting, 196
wiring tools, 120–124
WPA (Wi-Fi Protected Access), 98, 100

X

X.25 technology, 87, 89
xDSL (Digital Subscriber Line), 90, 91
Xerox, 9

Z

Zero Configuration (Zeroconf), 86, 87
zone database files, 191
Zone Information Protocol (ZIP), 54
zone transfer, 191

Sybex Covers CompTIA® CERTIFICATION PROGRAMS

Sybex publishes self-study materials for the following CompTIA certifications:

- A+
- i-Net+
- Project+
- Linux+
- Network+
- Security+
- Server+

STUDY GUIDES

- Practical, in-depth coverage of all exam objectives
- Includes hands-on exercises and hundreds of review questions
- CD includes a test engine, electronic flashcards for PCs, Pocket PCs, and Palm devices and a PDF version of the entire book

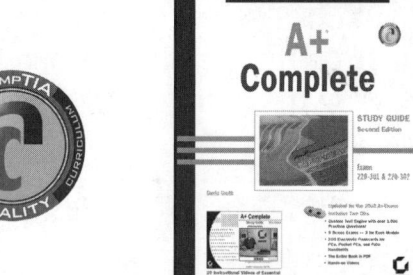

VIRTUAL LABS™

- Realistic, interactive simulations of key network features, such as router and switch functionality
- Step-by-step labs covering critical certification skills
- Customizable labs to meet your needs

In addition to being CAQC approved, Sybex is a cornerstone member of the Security+, Linux+, and Server+ Cornerstone Committees.

Go to **certification.sybex.com** for a complete listing of certification products

ISBN 0-7821-4244-3

ISBN 0-7821-4350-4

ISBN 0-7821-3026-7

CompTIA. One Industry. One Voice.

Sybex—The Leader in Certification

SYBEX®
www.sybex.com

You Can Never be TOO Prepared

Extremely Affordable!

Downloadable Practice Tests from SYBEX

Sybex practice tests are a valuable way to reinforce your knowledge while preparing for your certification exam. This cutting edge testing software challenges you with questions similar to the format you will encounter on the real exams. Written by experts in the field, each practice test offers easy navigation, explanations for correct answers, and scoring by exam objective/topic area.

Sybex Practice Tests are available for the following:

- CCNA™ (640-801)
- A+® Core Hardware (220-301)
- A+® Operating Systems Technologies (220-302)
- Network+® (N10-002)
- MCSA/MCSE Windows® XP Pro (70-270)

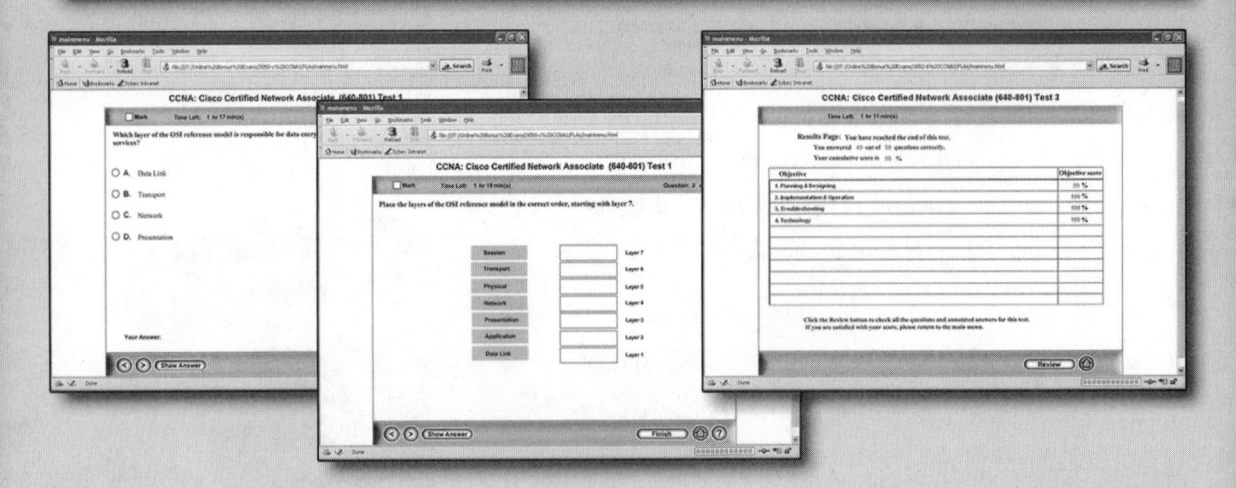

■ Detailed score reporting
■ Question formats similar to those on actual exams, including drag and drop
■ Multiple exams available for each certification

For pricing, online demos, and to purchase tests, visit www.sybex.com/practicetests

SYBEX®
www.sybex.com